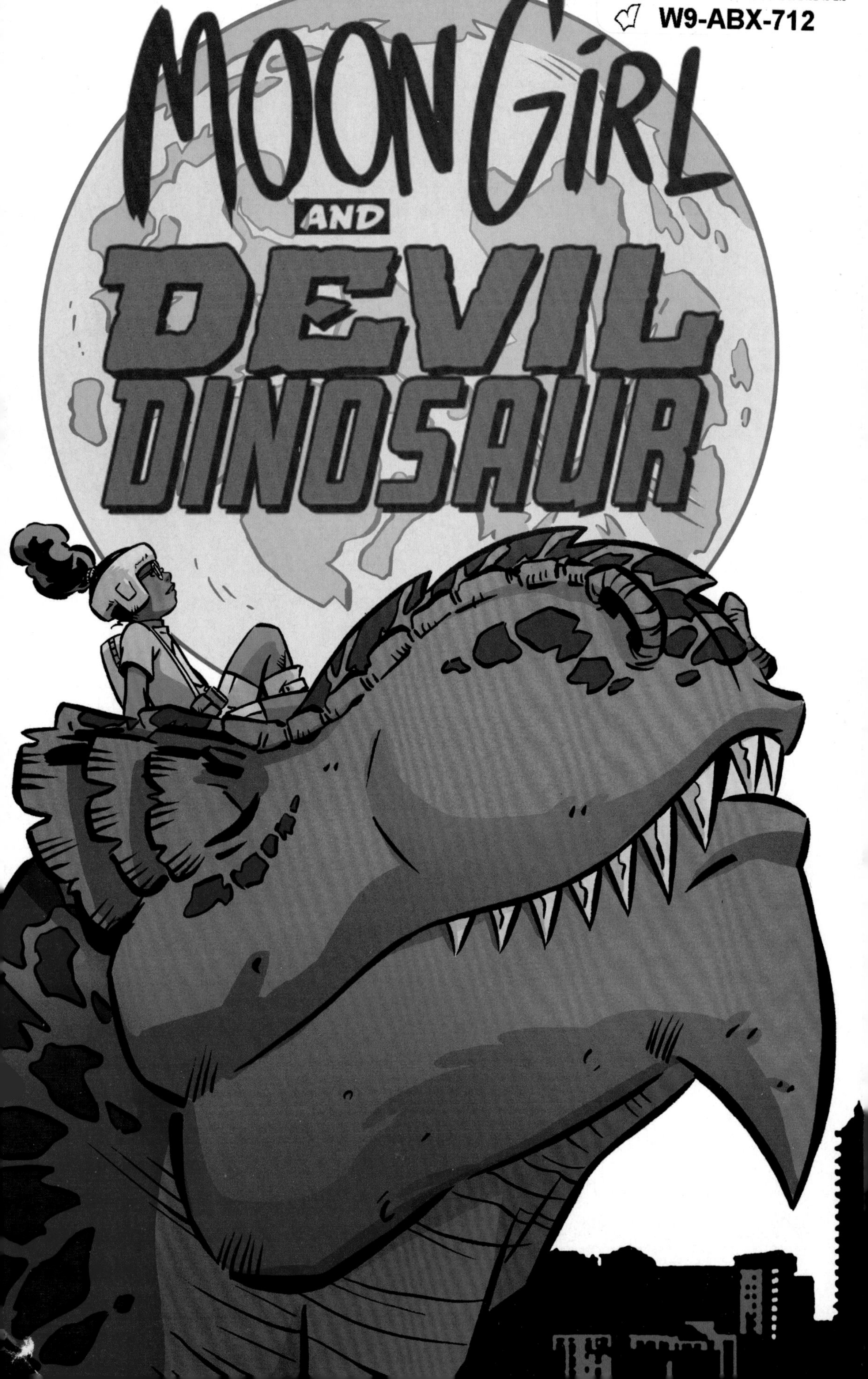
MOON GIRL
AND
DEVIL DINOSAUR

LUNELLA LAFAYETTE is a 9-YEAR-OLD PRODIGY LIVING WITH HER MOM AND DAD IN MANHATTAN'S LOWER EAST SIDE. DEVIL DINOSAUR is a BRIGHT RED TIME-DISPLACED *TYRANNOSAURUS REX*. THEY ARE SHUNNED AND IGNORED BY MOST, BUT FOR BETTER OR WORSE, THEY HAVE EACH OTHER! AFTER GOING THROUGH TERRIGENESIS, LUNELLA DISCOVERED THAT DURING THE FULL MOON LUNAR PHASE, SHE AND DEVIL WILL SPONTANEOUSLY SWITCH BRAINS.

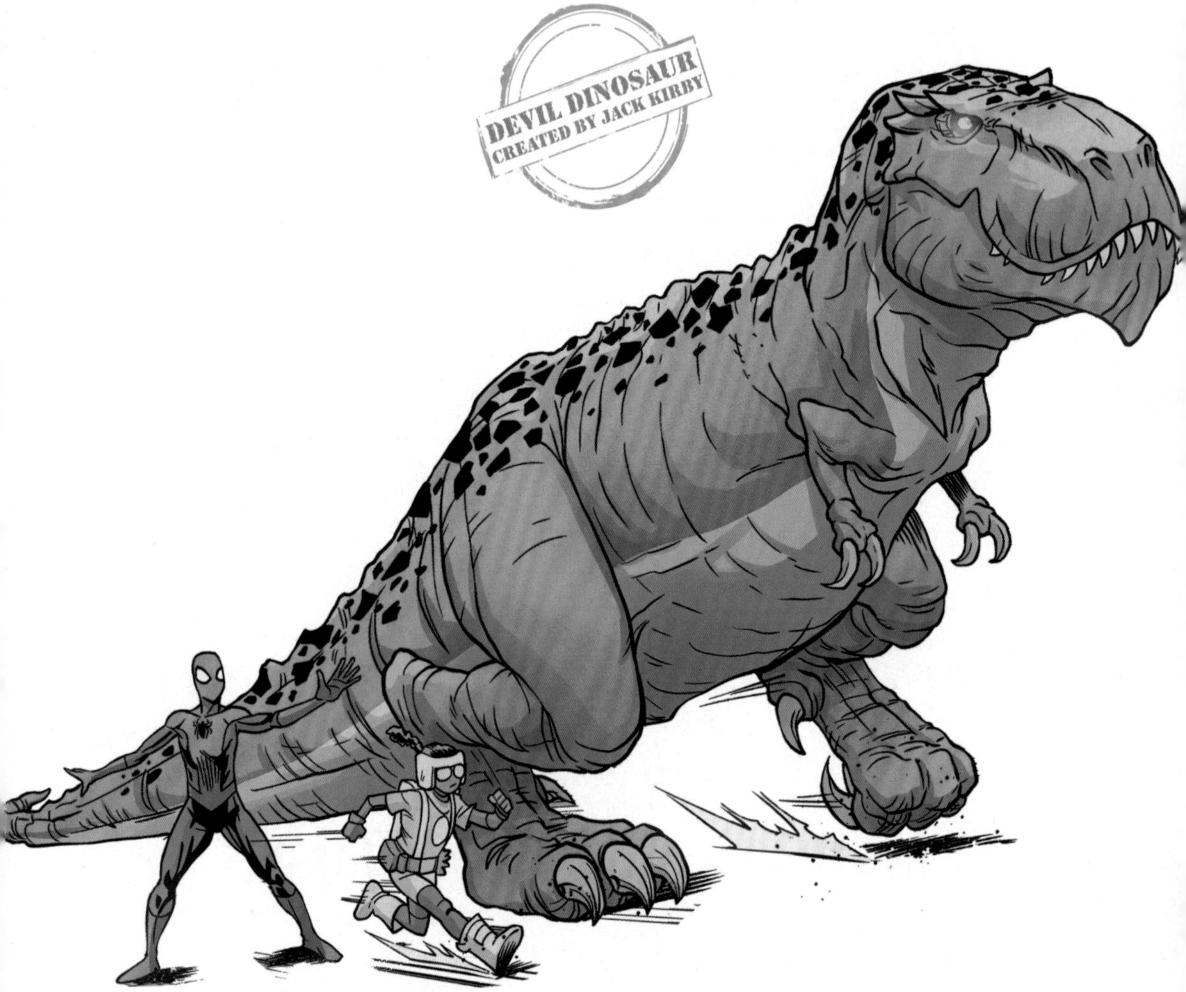
DEVIL DINOSAUR
CREATED BY JACK KIRBY

COLLECTION EDITOR: Jennifer Grünwald
ASSISTANT EDITOR: Caitlin O'Connell
ASSOCIATE MANAGING EDITOR: Kateri Woody
EDITOR, SPECIAL PROJECTS: Mark D. Beazley
VP, PRODUCTION & SPECIAL PROJECTS: Jeff Youngquist
BOOK DESIGNERS: Salena Mahina & Jay Bowen

SVP PRINT, SALES & MARKETING: David Gabriel
DIRECTOR, LICENSED PUBLISHING: Sven Larsen
EDITOR IN CHIEF: C.B. Cebulski
CHIEF CREATIVE OFFICER: Joe Quesada
PRESIDENT: Dan Buckley
EXECUTIVE PRODUCER: Alan Fine

MOON GIRL AND DEVIL DINOSAUR VOL. 8: YANCY STREET LEGENDS. Contains material originally published in magazine form as MOON GIRL AND DEVIL DINOSAUR (2015) #42-47. First printing 2019. ISBN 978-1-302-91437-0. Published by MARVEL WORLDWIDE, INC., a subsidiary of MARVEL ENTERTAINMENT, LLC. OFFICE OF PUBLICATION: 135 West 50th Street, New York, NY 10020. **Printed in Canada.** DAN BUCKLEY, President, Marvel Entertainment; JOHN NEE, Publisher; JOE QUESADA, Chief Creative Officer; TOM BREVOORT, SVP of Publishing; DAVID BOGART, Associate Publisher & SVP of Talent Affairs; DAVID GABRIEL, VP of Print & Digital Publishing; JEFF YOUNGQUIST, VP of Production & Special Projects; DAN CARR, Executive Director of Publishing Technology; ALEX MORALES, Director of Publishing Operations; DAN EDINGTON, Managing Editor; SUSAN CRESPI, Production Manager; STAN LEE, Chairman Emeritus. For information regarding advertising in Marvel Comics or on Marvel.com, please contact Vit DeBellis, Custom Solutions & Integrated Advertising Manager, at vdebellis@marvel.com. For Marvel subscription inquiries, please call 888-511-5480. **Manufactured between 10/25/2019 and 11/26/2019 by SOLISCO PRINTERS, SCOTT, QC, CANADA.**

10 9 8 7 6 5 4 3 2 1

MOON GIRL AND DEVIL DINOSAUR

YANCY STREET LEGENDS

Brandon Montclare
WRITER

ISSUE #42
Ray-Anthony Height
PENCILER

Le Beau Underwood, Ray-Anthony Height & Nate Lovett
INKERS

ISSUE #43
Gustavo Duarte WITH Ray-Anthony Height
ARTISTS

ISSUES #44-47
Alitha E. Martinez
ARTIST

VC's Travis Lanham
LETTERER

Tamra Bonvillain
COLOR ARTIST

Natacha Bustos (#42-43) & **Rahzzah** (#44-47)
COVER ART

Chris Robinson
EDITOR

Jordan D. White
CONSULTING EDITOR

SPECIAL THANKS TO MARK PANICCIA, WIL MOSS & SARAH BRUNSTAD

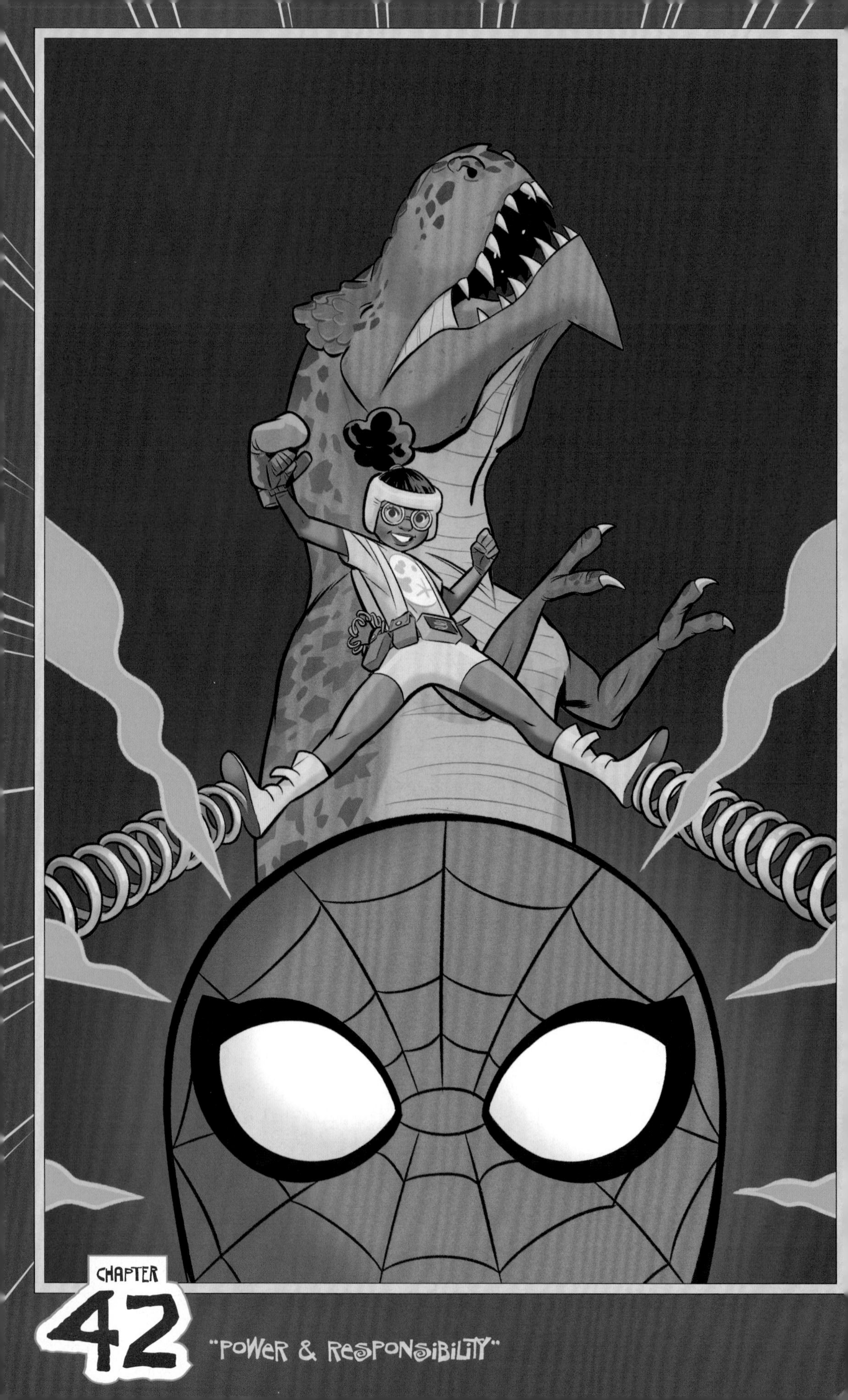
CHAPTER
42
"POWER & RESPONSIBILITY"

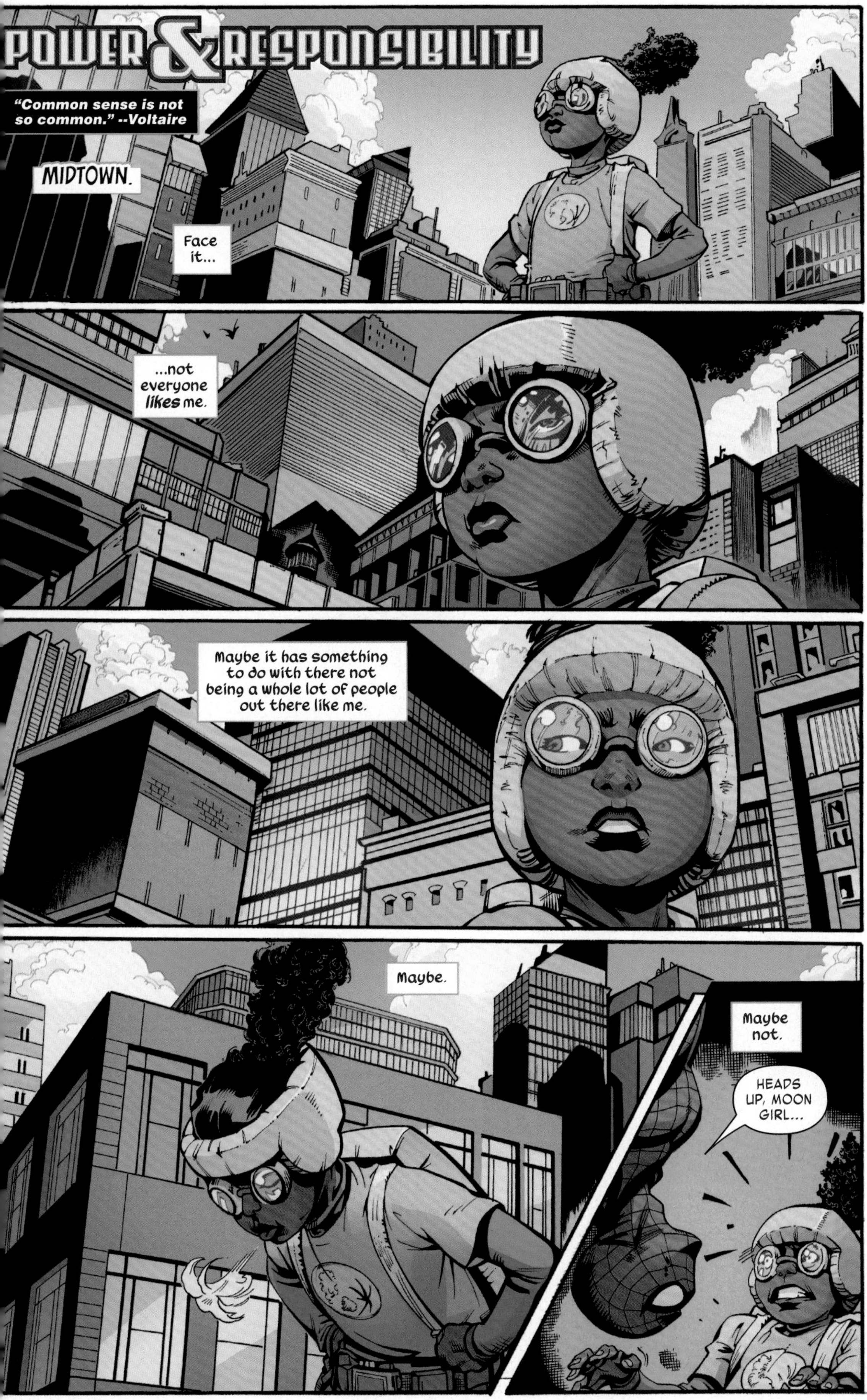
POWER & RESPONSIBILITY
"Common sense is not so common." --Voltaire
MIDTOWN.
Face it...
...not everyone likes me.
Maybe it has something to do with there not being a whole lot of people out there like me.
Maybe.
Maybe not.
HEADS UP, MOON GIRL...

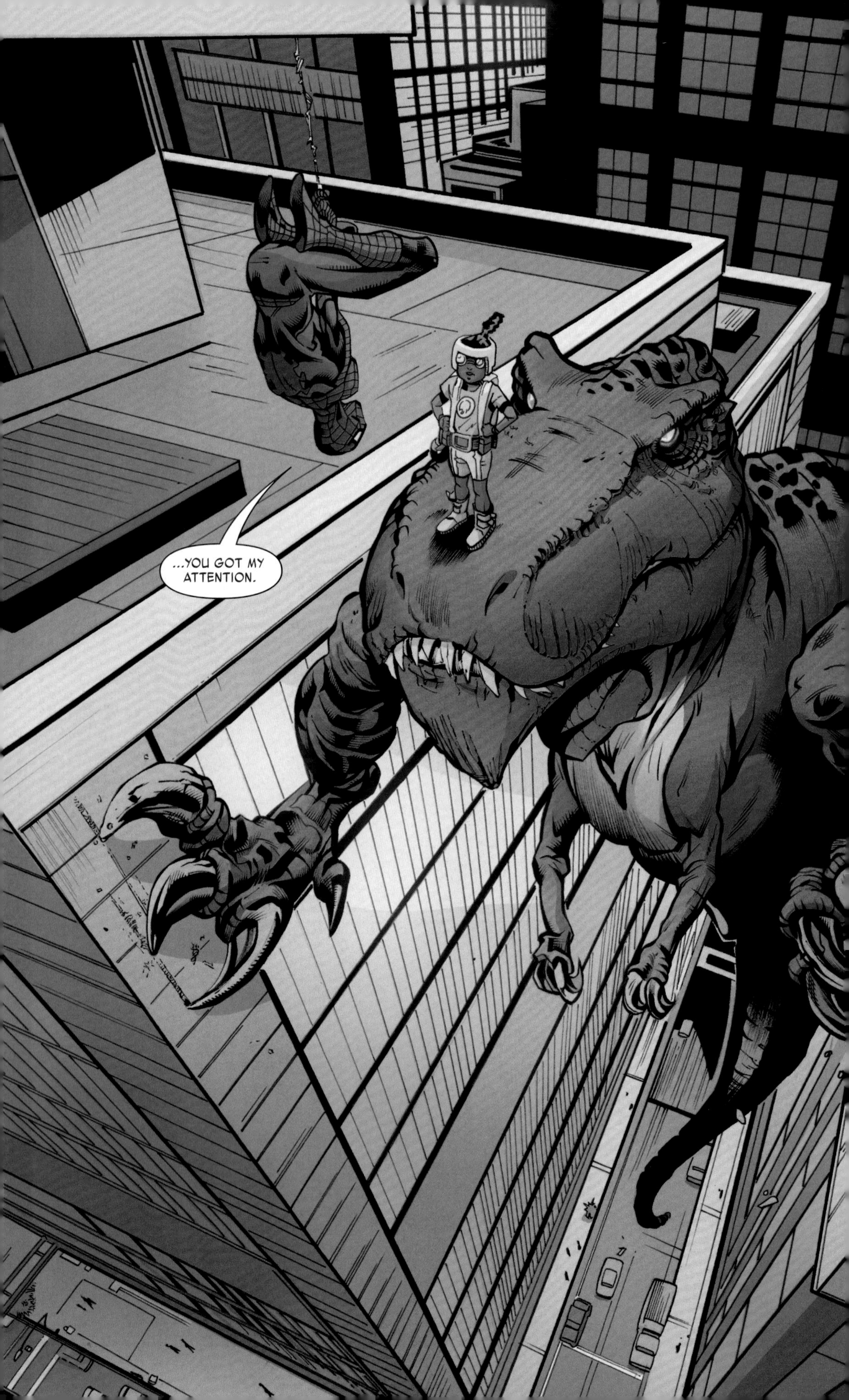
...YOU GOT MY ATTENTION.

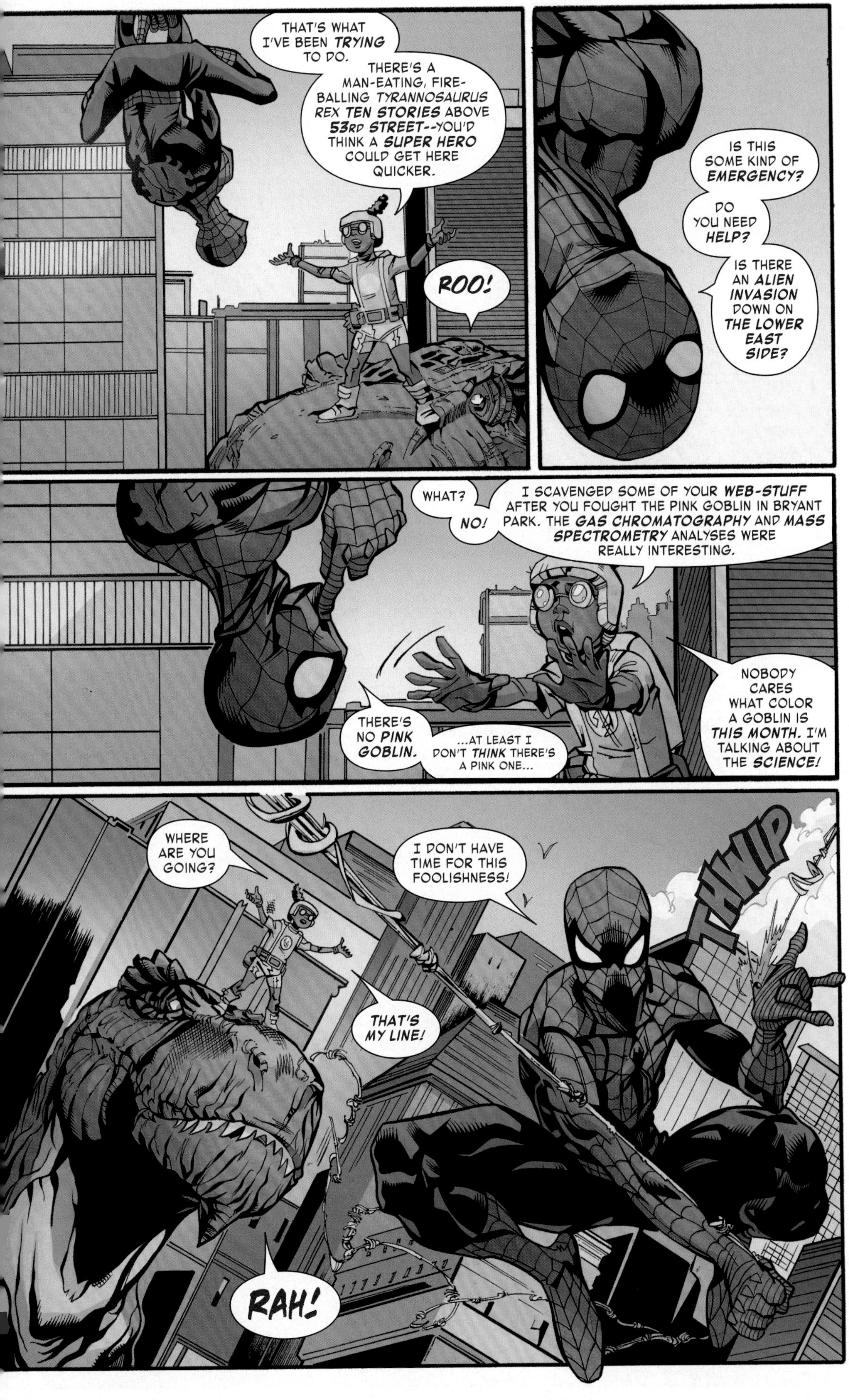
THAT'S WHAT I'VE BEEN TRYING TO DO.
THERE'S A MAN-EATING, FIRE-BALLING TYRANNOSAURUS REX TEN STORIES ABOVE 53RD STREET--YOU'D THINK A SUPER HERO COULD GET HERE QUICKER.
ROO!
IS THIS SOME KIND OF EMERGENCY?
DO YOU NEED HELP?
IS THERE AN ALIEN INVASION DOWN ON THE LOWER EAST SIDE?
WHAT?
NO!
I SCAVENGED SOME OF YOUR WEB-STUFF AFTER YOU FOUGHT THE PINK GOBLIN IN BRYANT PARK. THE GAS CHROMATOGRAPHY AND MASS SPECTROMETRY ANALYSES WERE REALLY INTERESTING.
THERE'S NO PINK GOBLIN.
...AT LEAST I DON'T THINK THERE'S A PINK ONE...
NOBODY CARES WHAT COLOR A GOBLIN IS THIS MONTH. I'M TALKING ABOUT THE SCIENCE!
WHERE ARE YOU GOING?
I DON'T HAVE TIME FOR THIS FOOLISHNESS!
THWIP
THAT'S MY LINE!
RAH!

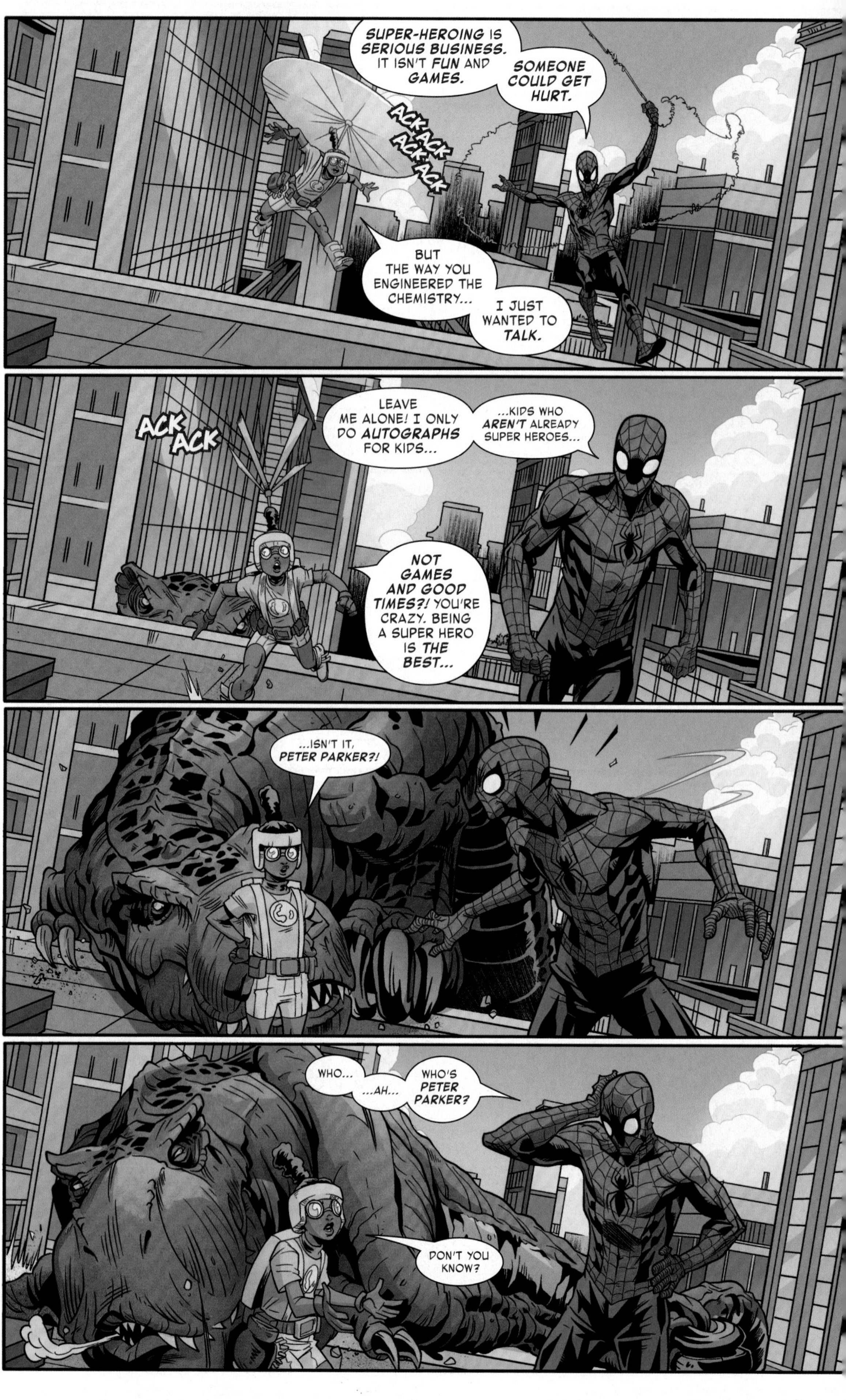
SUPER-HEROING IS SERIOUS BUSINESS. IT ISN'T FUN AND GAMES.
SOMEONE COULD GET HURT.
ACK ACK ACK ACK
BUT THE WAY YOU ENGINEERED THE CHEMISTRY...
I JUST WANTED TO TALK.
ACK ACK
LEAVE ME ALONE! I ONLY DO AUTOGRAPHS FOR KIDS...
...KIDS WHO AREN'T ALREADY SUPER HEROES...
NOT GAMES AND GOOD TIMES?! YOU'RE CRAZY. BEING A SUPER HERO IS THE BEST...
...ISN'T IT, PETER PARKER?!
WHO...
...AH...
WHO'S PETER PARKER?
DON'T YOU KNOW?

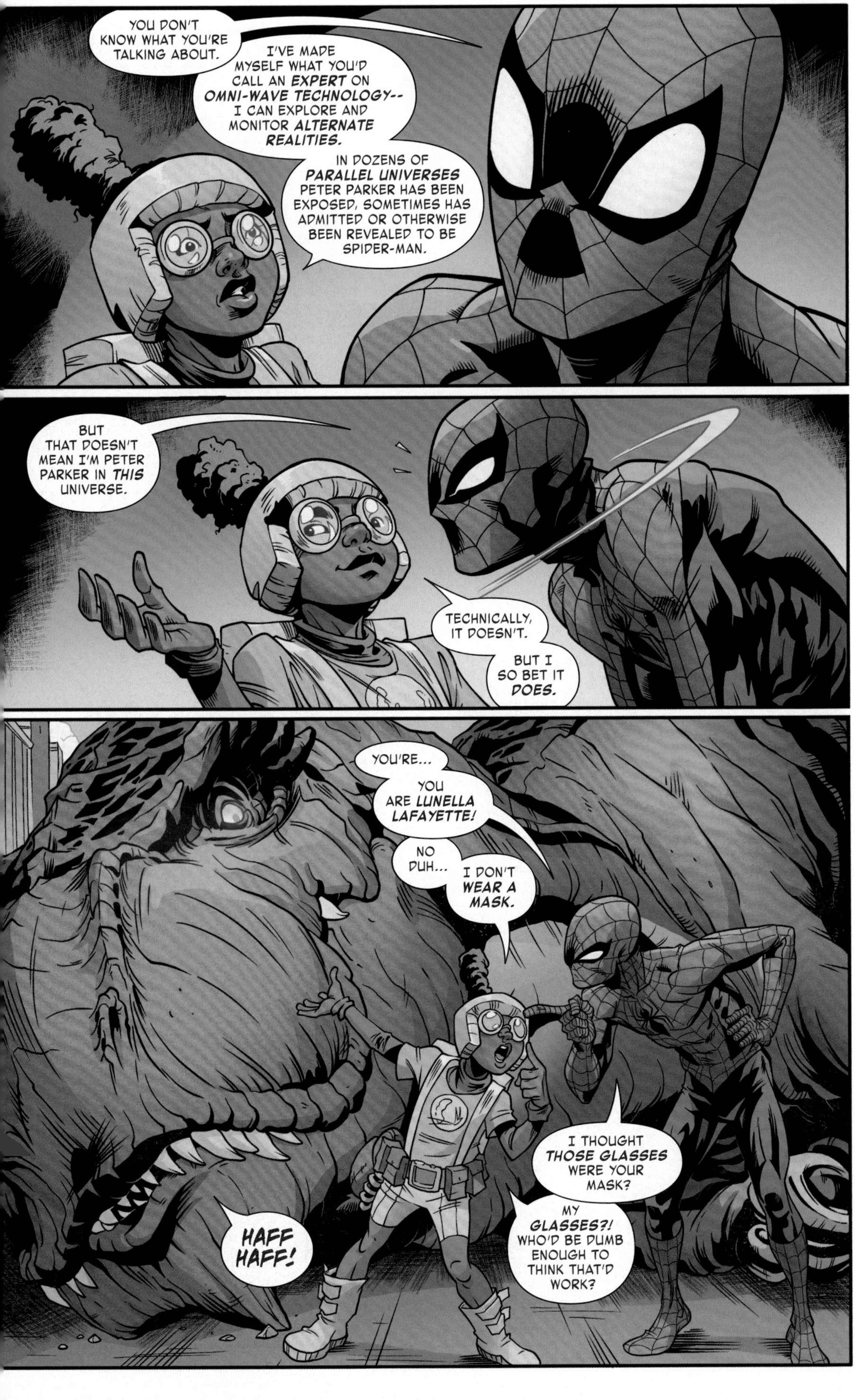
YOU DON'T KNOW WHAT YOU'RE TALKING ABOUT.
I'VE MADE MYSELF WHAT YOU'D CALL AN EXPERT ON OMNI-WAVE TECHNOLOGY-- I CAN EXPLORE AND MONITOR ALTERNATE REALITIES.
IN DOZENS OF PARALLEL UNIVERSES PETER PARKER HAS BEEN EXPOSED, SOMETIMES HAS ADMITTED OR OTHERWISE BEEN REVEALED TO BE SPIDER-MAN.
BUT THAT DOESN'T MEAN I'M PETER PARKER IN THIS UNIVERSE.
TECHNICALLY, IT DOESN'T.
BUT I SO BET IT DOES.
YOU'RE...
YOU ARE LUNELLA LAFAYETTE!
NO DUH...
I DON'T WEAR A MASK.
I THOUGHT THOSE GLASSES WERE YOUR MASK?
MY GLASSES?! WHO'D BE DUMB ENOUGH TO THINK THAT'D WORK?
HAFF HAFF!

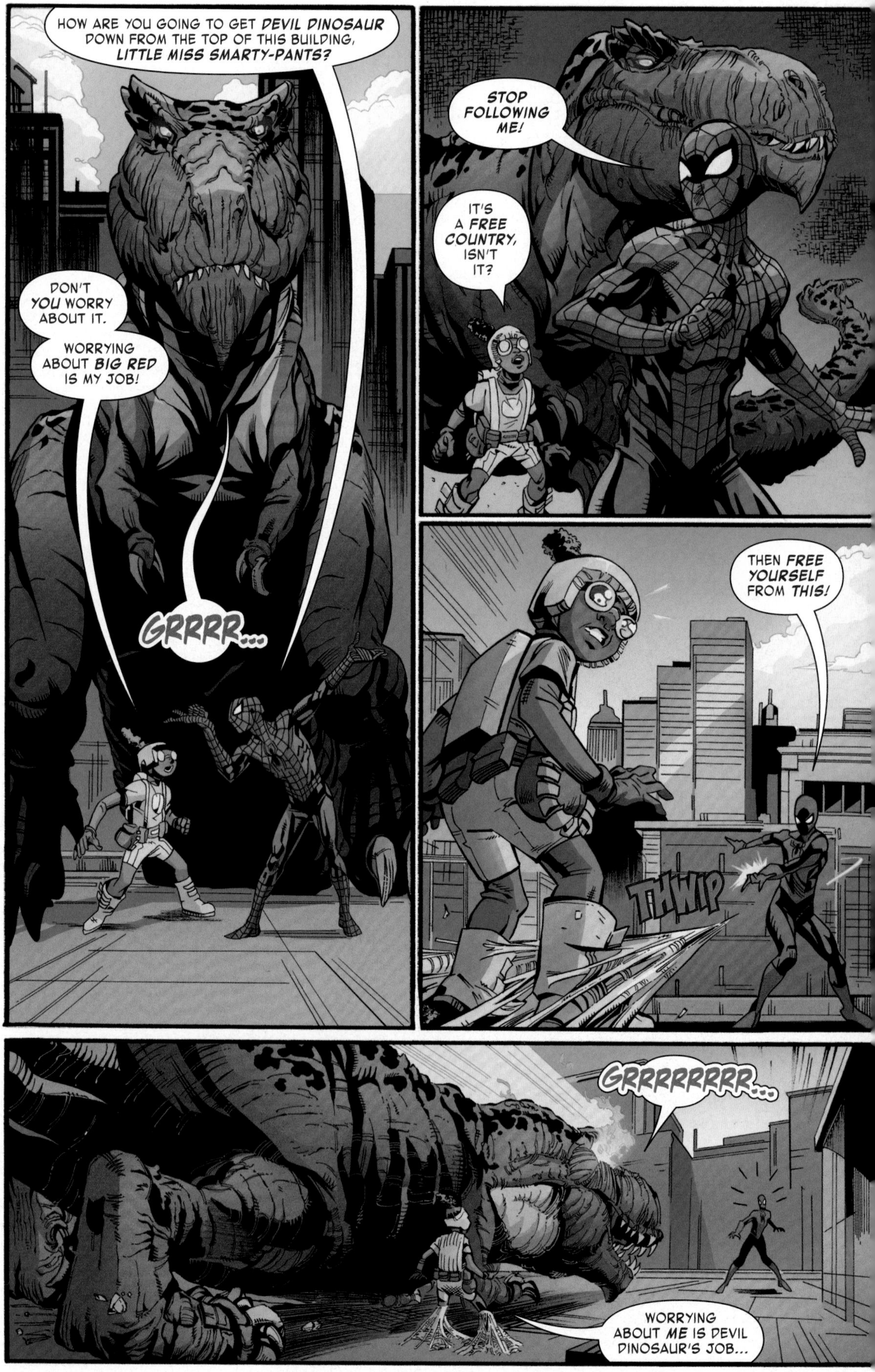
HOW ARE YOU GOING TO GET DEVIL DINOSAUR DOWN FROM THE TOP OF THIS BUILDING, LITTLE MISS SMARTY-PANTS?
DON'T YOU WORRY ABOUT IT.
WORRYING ABOUT BIG RED IS MY JOB!
GRRRR...
STOP FOLLOWING ME!
IT'S A FREE COUNTRY, ISN'T IT?
THEN FREE YOURSELF FROM THIS!
THWIP
GRRRRRRRR...
WORRYING ABOUT ME IS DEVIL DINOSAUR'S JOB...

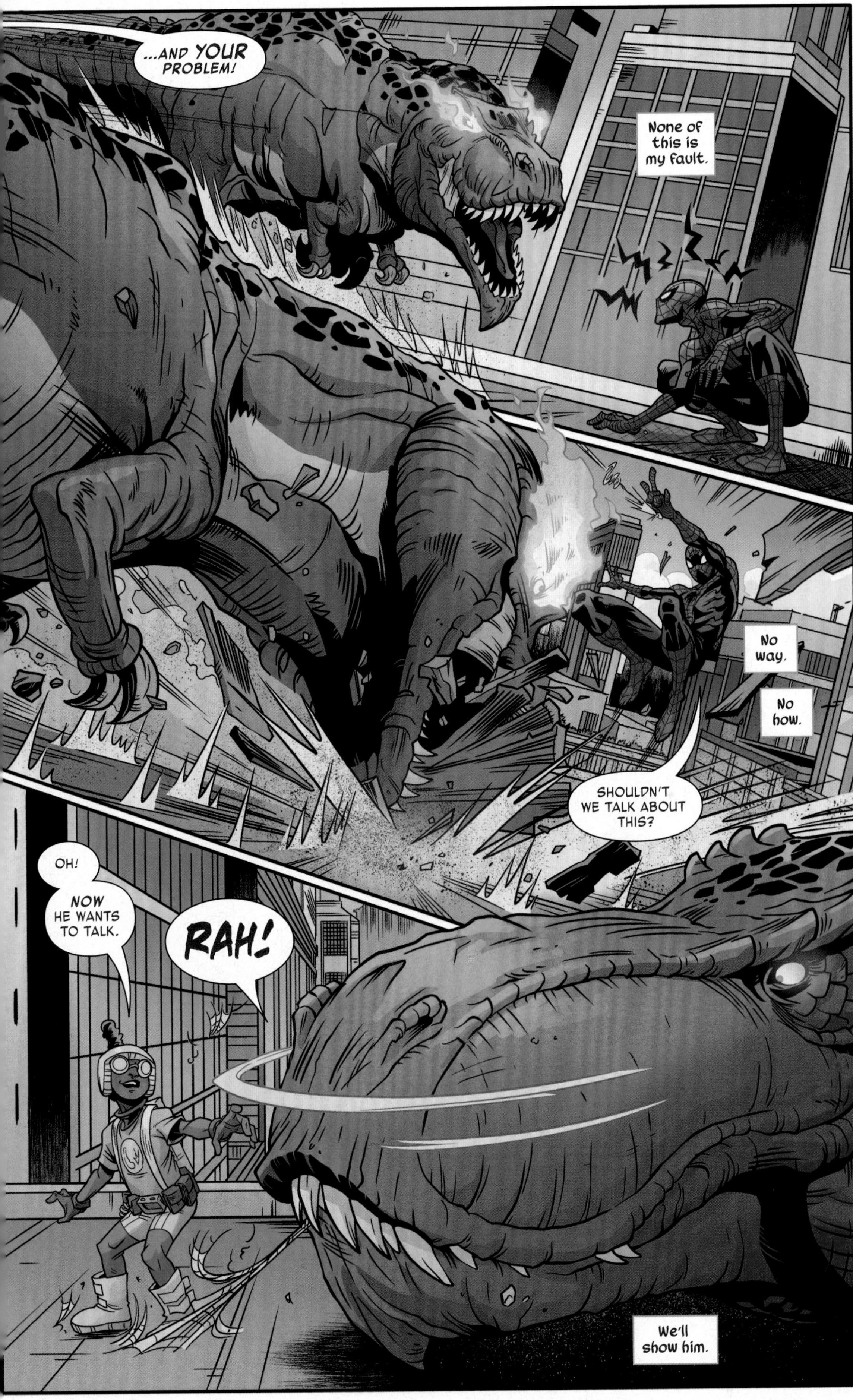
...AND YOUR PROBLEM!
None of this is my fault.
No way.
No how.
SHOULDN'T WE TALK ABOUT THIS?
OH!
NOW HE WANTS TO TALK.
RAH!
We'll show him.

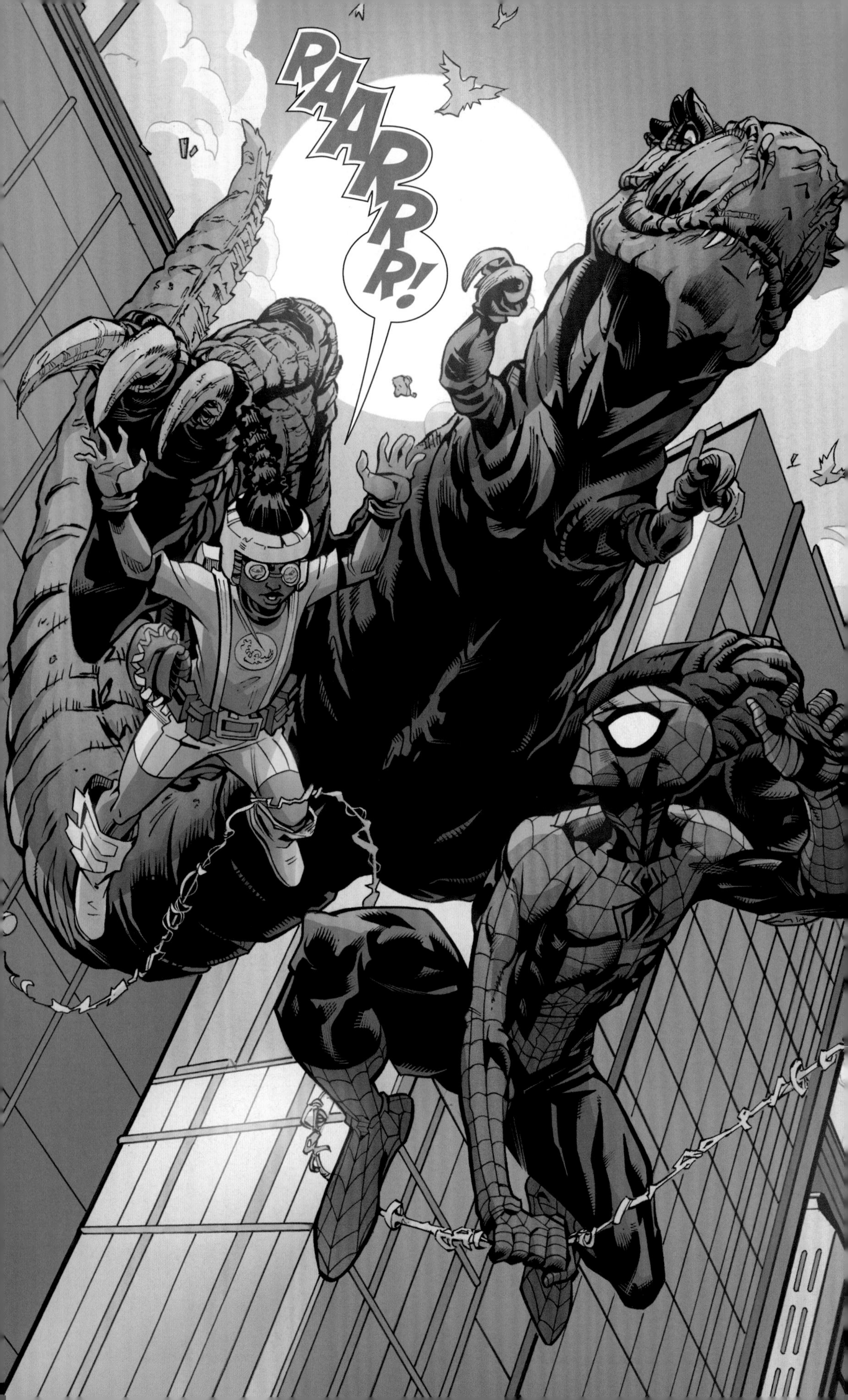
RAARRR!

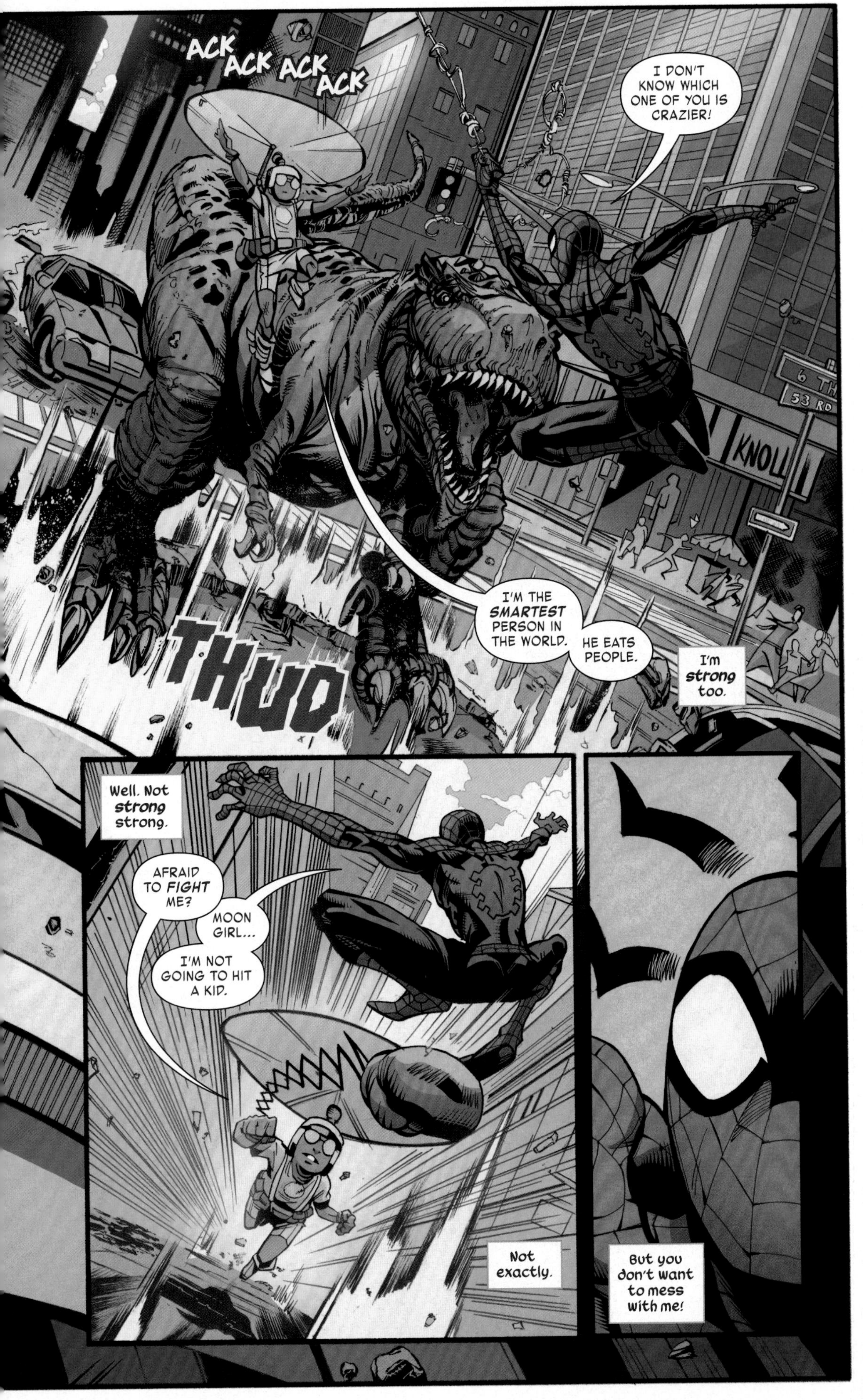
ACK ACK ACK ACK
I DON'T KNOW WHICH ONE OF YOU IS CRAZIER!
I'M THE SMARTEST PERSON IN THE WORLD.
HE EATS PEOPLE.
THUD
I'm strong too.
Well. Not strong strong.
AFRAID TO FIGHT ME?
MOON GIRL...
I'M NOT GOING TO HIT A KID.
Not exactly.
But you don't want to mess with me!

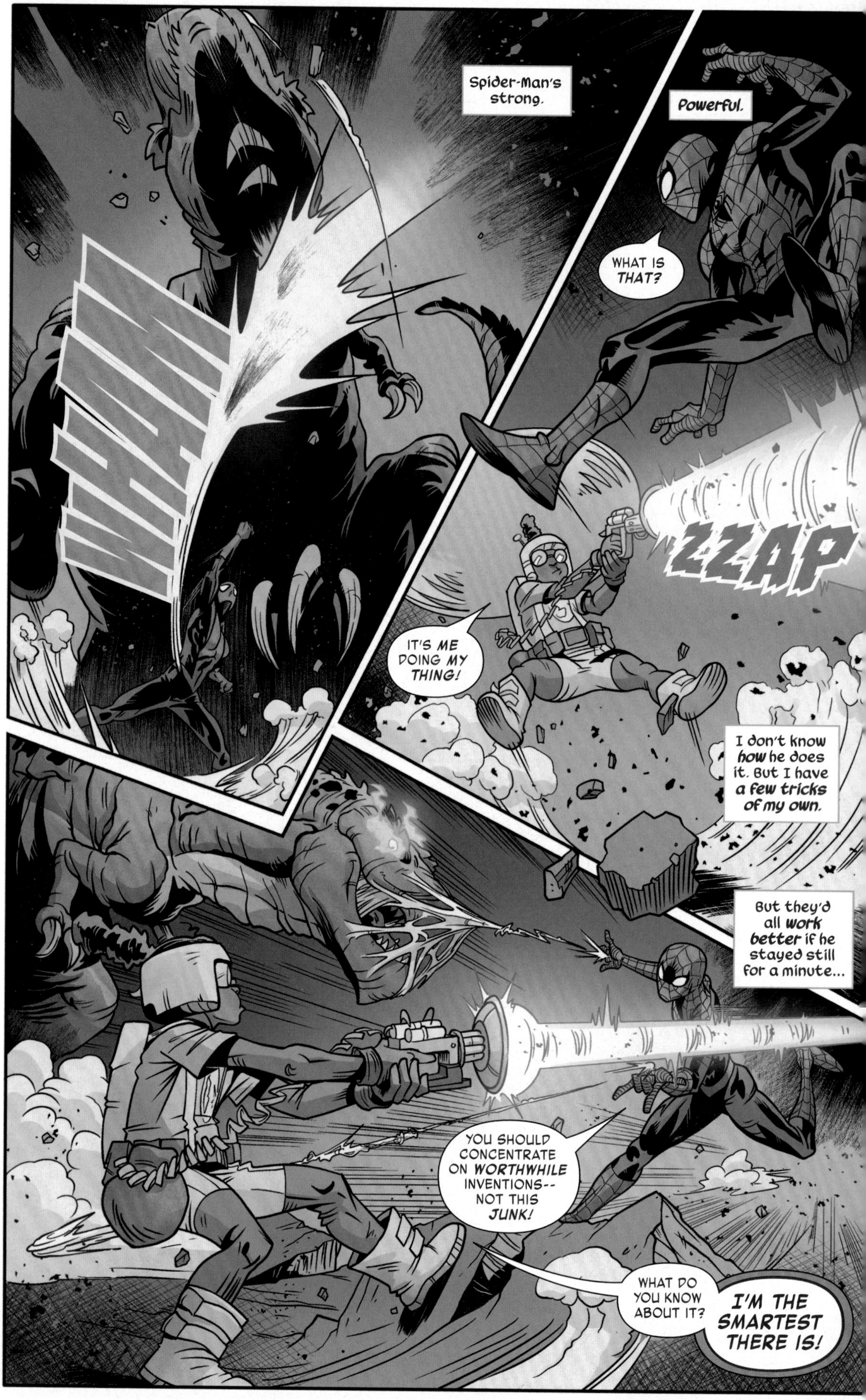
Spider-Man's strong.
Powerful.
WHAT IS THAT?
ZZAP
IT'S ME DOING MY THING!
I don't know how he does it. But I have a few tricks of my own.
But they'd all work better if he stayed still for a minute...
YOU SHOULD CONCENTRATE ON WORTHWHILE INVENTIONS-- NOT THIS JUNK!
WHAT DO YOU KNOW ABOUT IT?
I'M THE SMARTEST THERE IS!

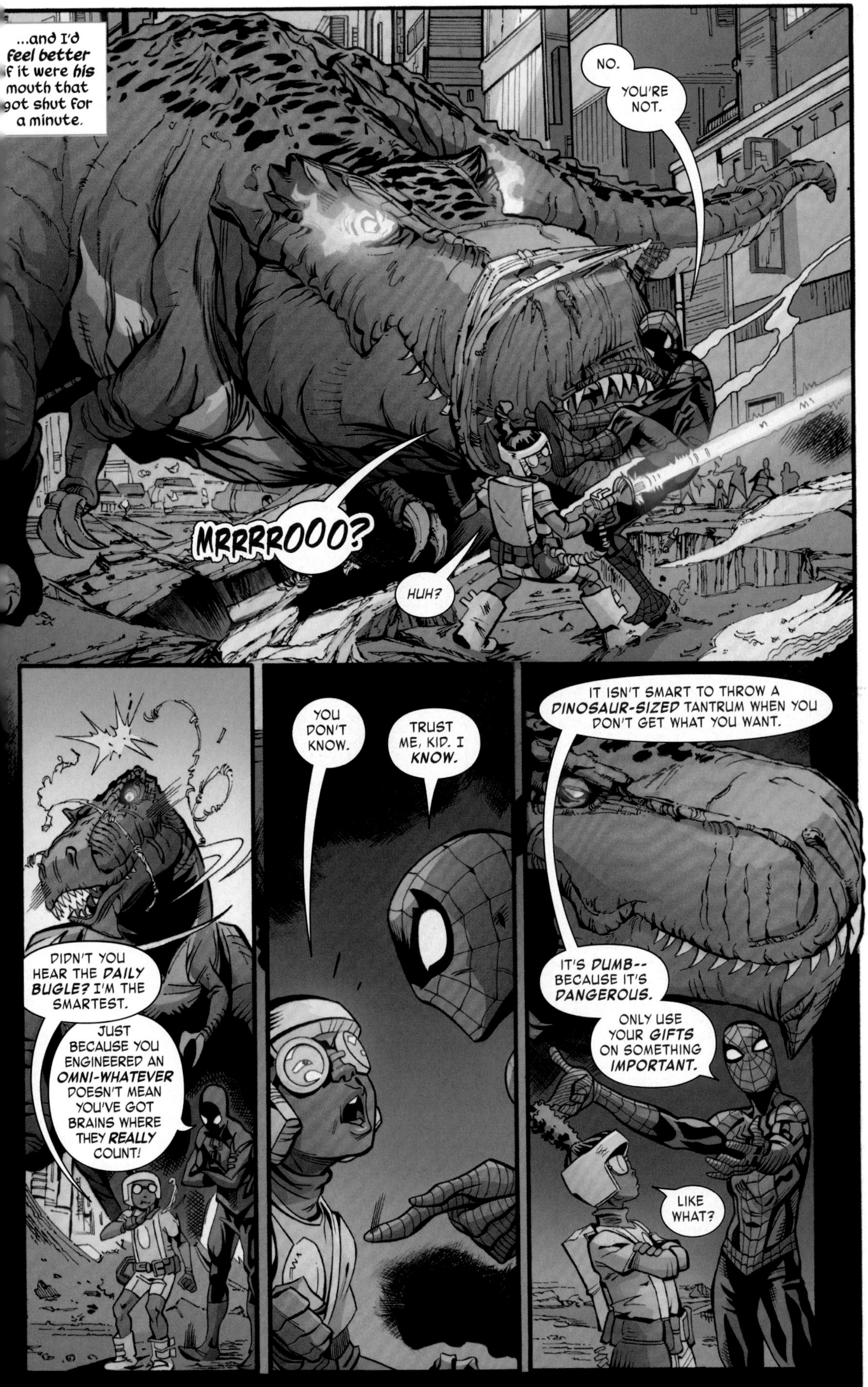
...and I'd feel better if it were his mouth that got shut for a minute.
NO.
YOU'RE NOT.
MRRRROOO?
HUH?
DIDN'T YOU HEAR THE DAILY BUGLE? I'M THE SMARTEST.
JUST BECAUSE YOU ENGINEERED AN OMNI-WHATEVER DOESN'T MEAN YOU'VE GOT BRAINS WHERE THEY REALLY COUNT!
YOU DON'T KNOW.
TRUST ME, KID. I KNOW.
IT ISN'T SMART TO THROW A DINOSAUR-SIZED TANTRUM WHEN YOU DON'T GET WHAT YOU WANT.
IT'S DUMB-- BECAUSE IT'S DANGEROUS.
ONLY USE YOUR GIFTS ON SOMETHING IMPORTANT.
LIKE WHAT?

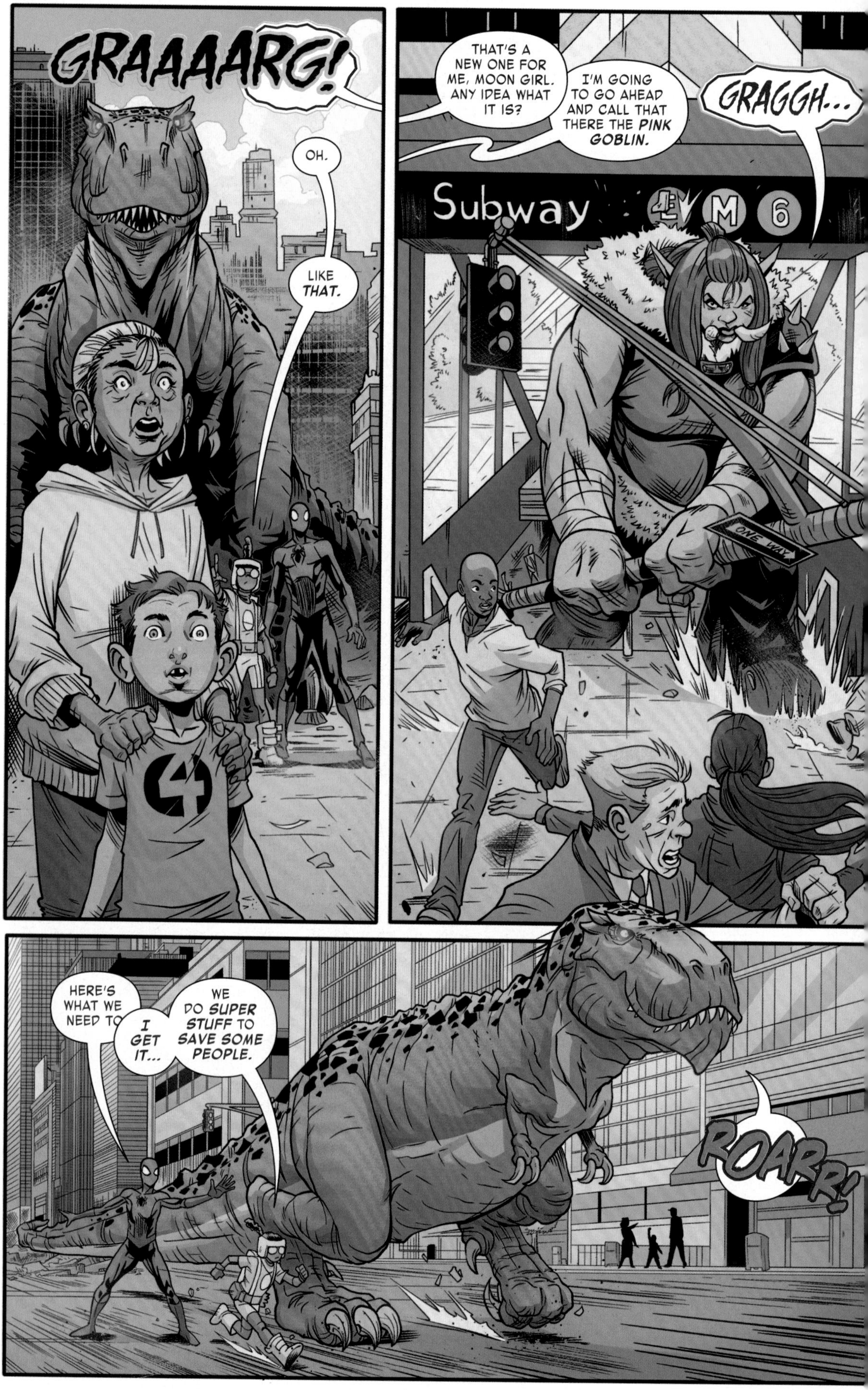
GRAAAARG!
OH.
LIKE *THAT.*
THAT'S A NEW ONE FOR ME, MOON GIRL. ANY IDEA WHAT IT IS?
I'M GOING TO GO AHEAD AND CALL THAT THERE THE *PINK GOBLIN.*
GRAGGH...
Subway
M
6
ONE WAY
HERE'S WHAT WE NEED TO
I GET IT...
WE DO *SUPER STUFF* TO *SAVE SOME PEOPLE.*
ROARR!

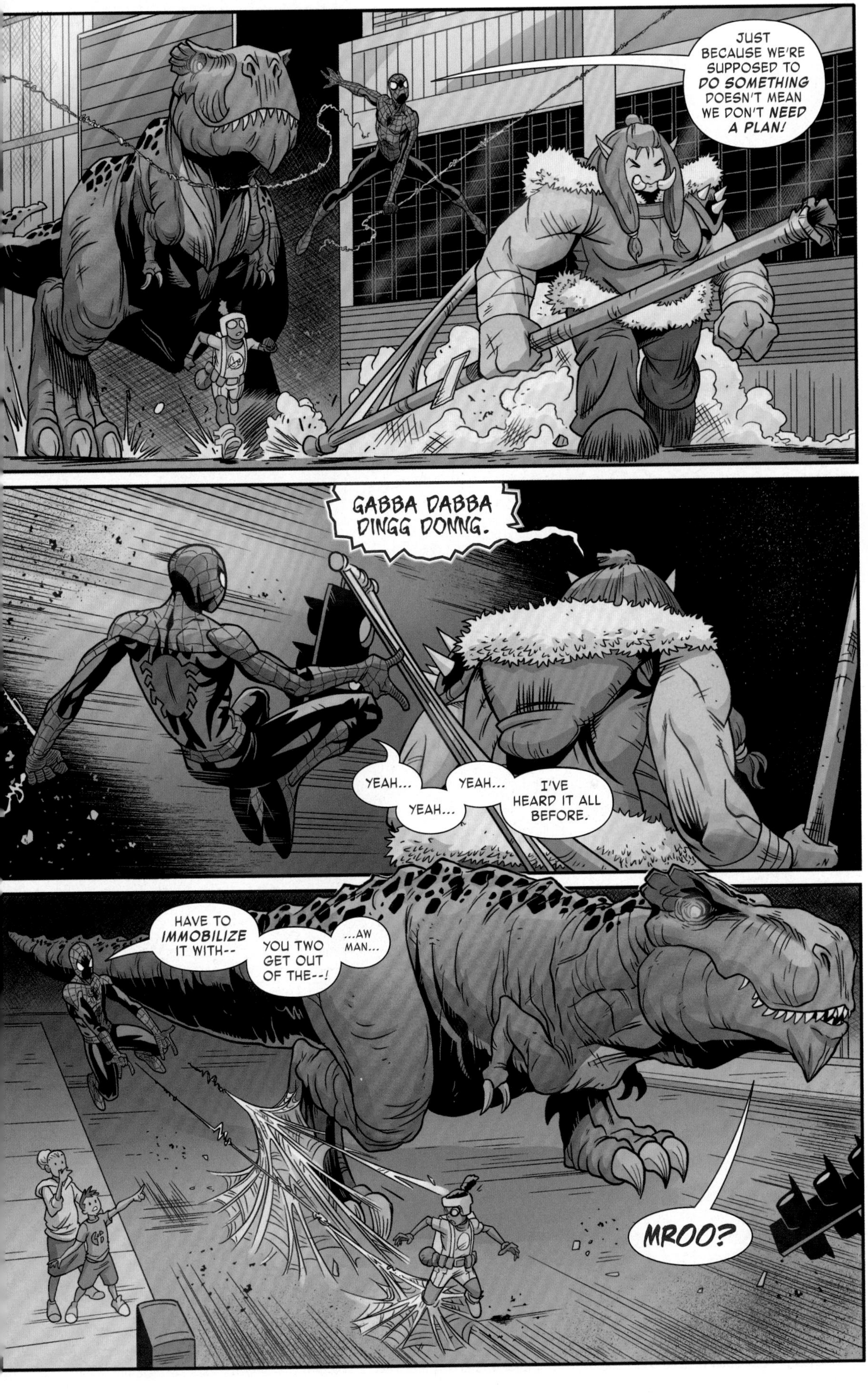
JUST BECAUSE WE'RE SUPPOSED TO DO SOMETHING DOESN'T MEAN WE DON'T NEED A PLAN!
GABBA DABBA DINGG DONNG.
YEAH...
YEAH...
YEAH...
I'VE HEARD IT ALL BEFORE.
HAVE TO IMMOBILIZE IT WITH--
YOU TWO GET OUT OF THE--!
...AW MAN...
MROO?

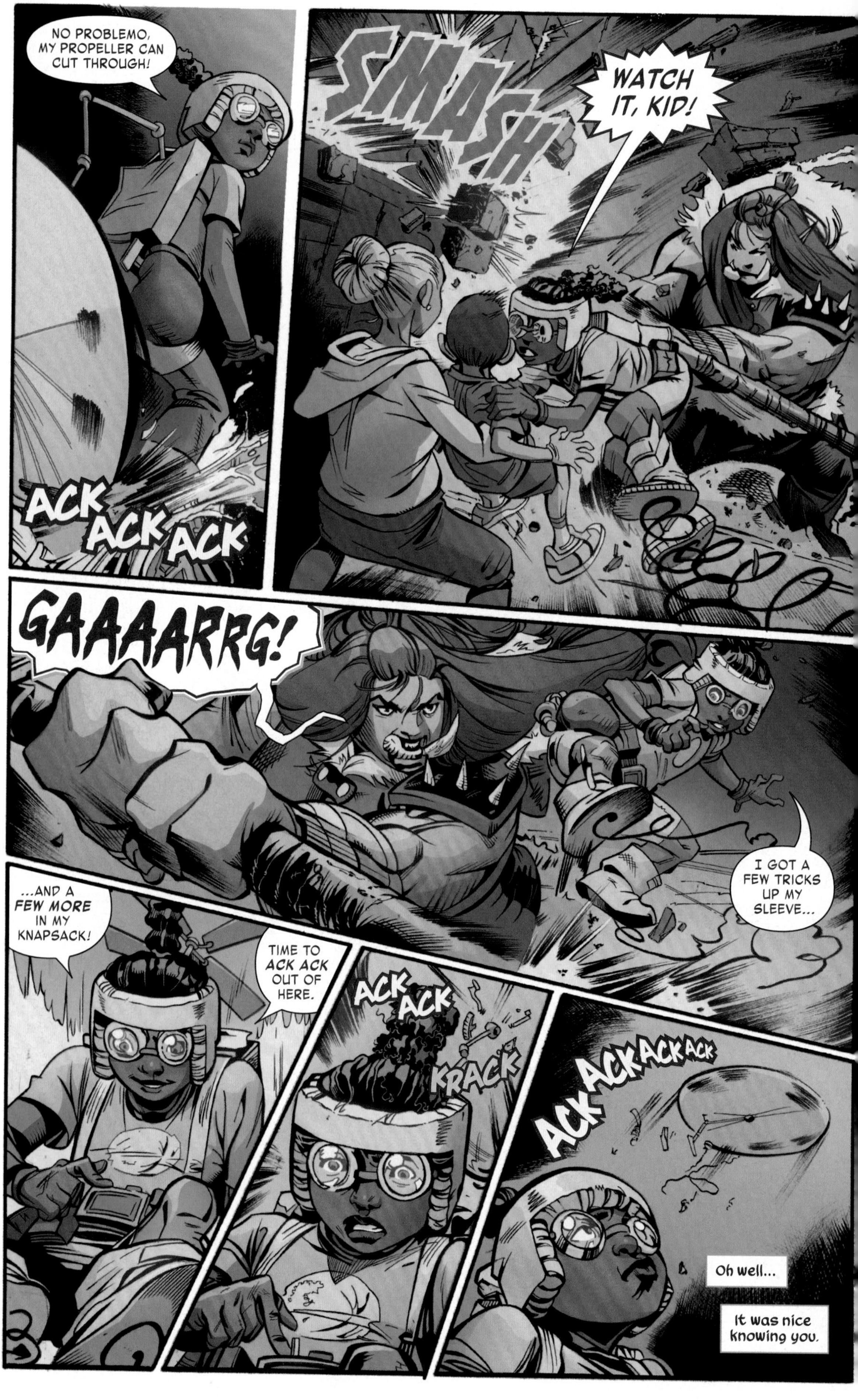
NO PROBLEMO, MY PROPELLER CAN CUT THROUGH!
ACK ACK ACK
SMASH
WATCH IT, KID!
GAAAARRG!
I GOT A FEW TRICKS UP MY SLEEVE...
...AND A FEW MORE IN MY KNAPSACK!
TIME TO ACK ACK OUT OF HERE.
ACK ACK
KRACK
ACK ACK ACK ACK
Oh well...
It was nice knowing you.

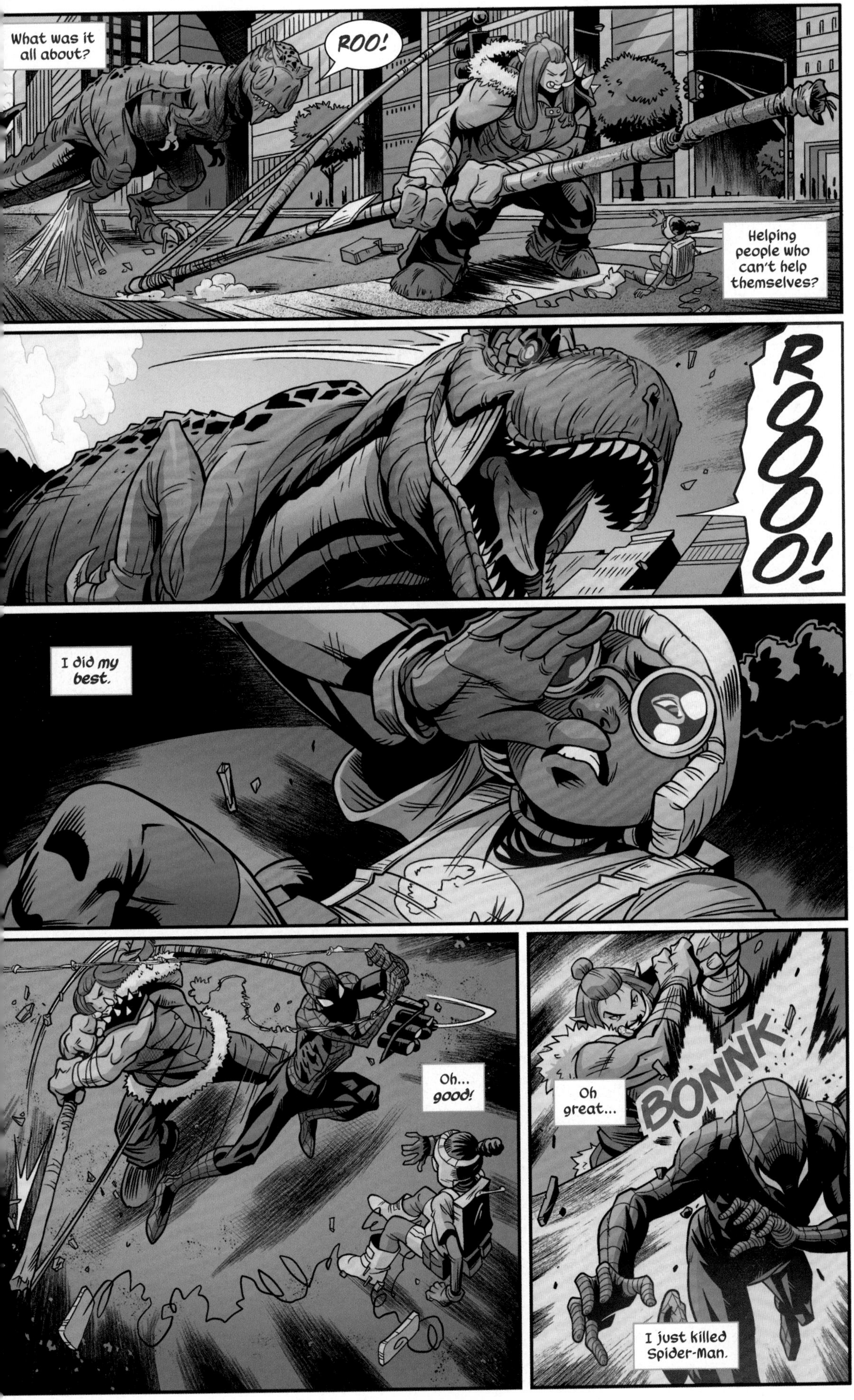
What was it all about?
ROO!
Helping people who can't help themselves?
ROOOOO!
I did my best.
Oh... good!
Oh great...
BONNK
I just killed Spider-Man.

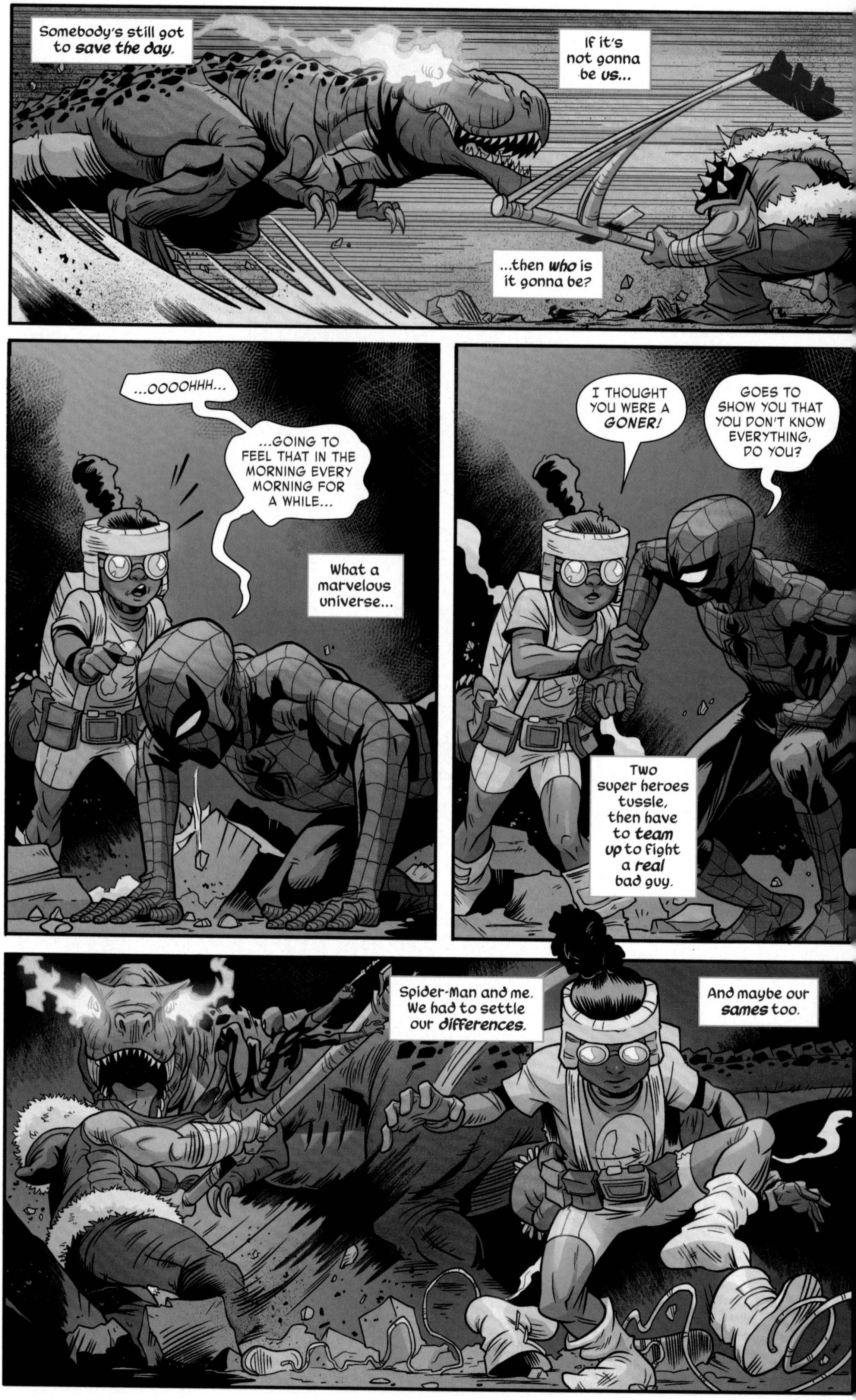
Somebody's still got to save the day.
If it's not gonna be us...
...then who is it gonna be?
...OOOOHHH...
...GOING TO FEEL THAT IN THE MORNING EVERY MORNING FOR A WHILE...
What a marvelous universe...
I THOUGHT YOU WERE A GONER!
GOES TO SHOW YOU THAT YOU DON'T KNOW EVERYTHING, DO YOU?
Two super heroes tussle, then have to team up to fight a real bad guy.
Spider-Man and me. We had to settle our differences.
And maybe our sames too.

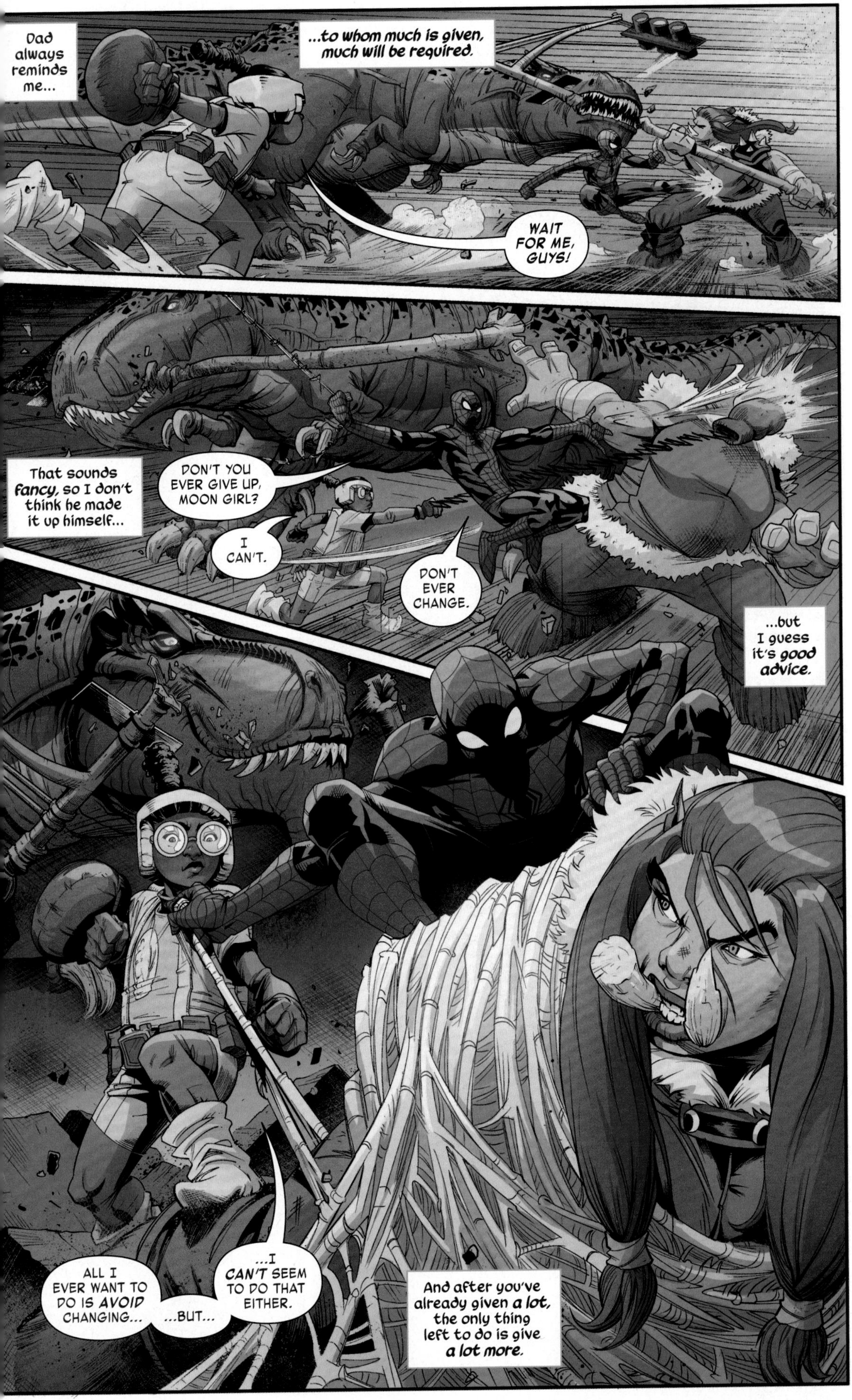

Dad always reminds me...
...to whom much is given, much will be required.
WAIT FOR ME, GUYS!
That sounds fancy, so I don't think he made it up himself...
DON'T YOU EVER GIVE UP, MOON GIRL?
I CAN'T.
DON'T EVER CHANGE.
...but I guess it's good advice.
ALL I EVER WANT TO DO IS AVOID CHANGING...
...BUT...
...I CAN'T SEEM TO DO THAT EITHER.
And after you've already given a lot, the only thing left to do is give a lot more.

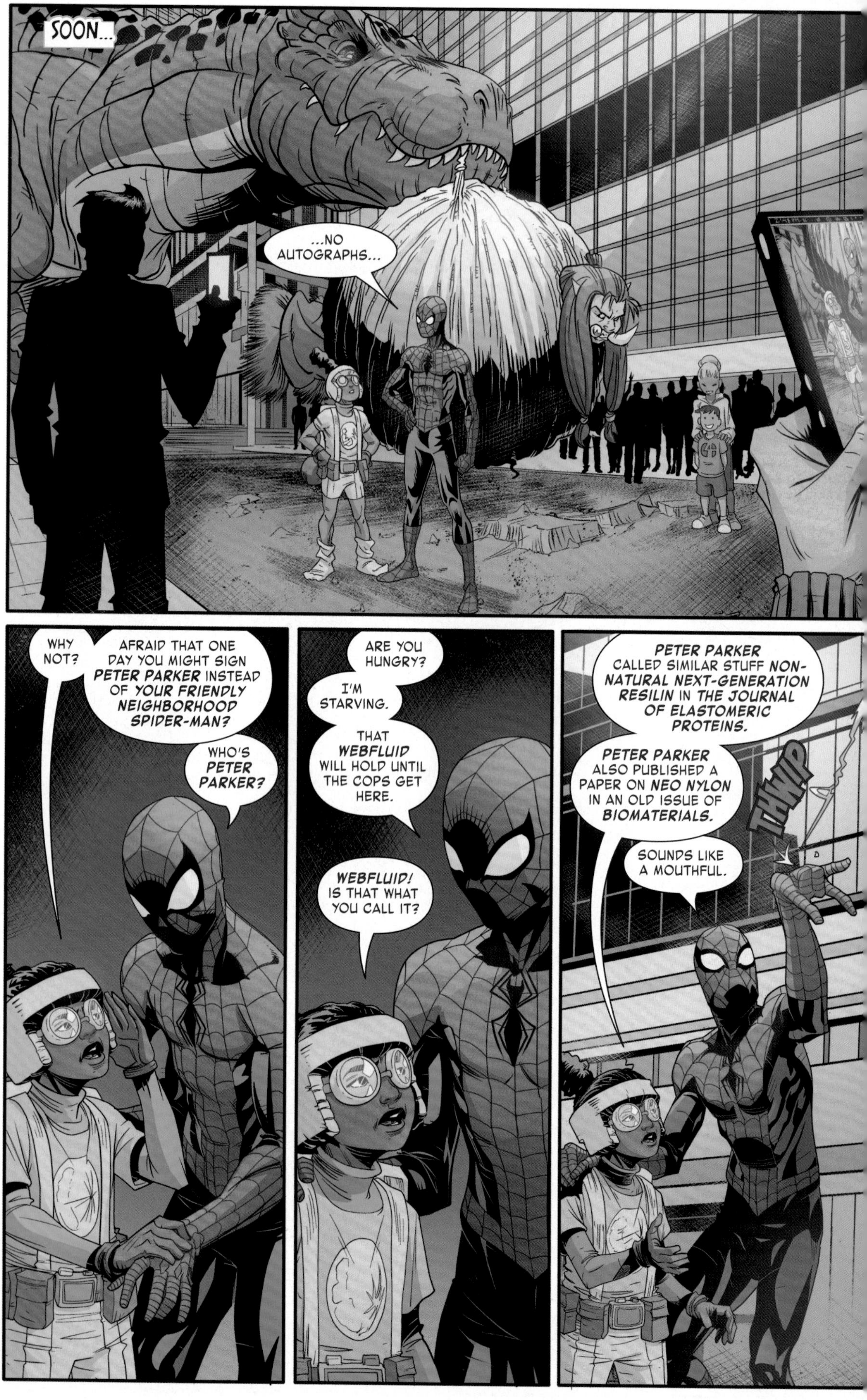
SOON...
...NO AUTOGRAPHS...
WHY NOT?
AFRAID THAT ONE DAY YOU MIGHT SIGN PETER PARKER INSTEAD OF YOUR FRIENDLY NEIGHBORHOOD SPIDER-MAN?
WHO'S PETER PARKER?
ARE YOU HUNGRY?
I'M STARVING.
THAT WEBFLUID WILL HOLD UNTIL THE COPS GET HERE.
WEBFLUID! IS THAT WHAT YOU CALL IT?
PETER PARKER CALLED SIMILAR STUFF NON-NATURAL NEXT-GENERATION RESILIN IN THE JOURNAL OF ELASTOMERIC PROTEINS.
PETER PARKER ALSO PUBLISHED A PAPER ON NEO NYLON IN AN OLD ISSUE OF BIOMATERIALS.
THWIP
SOUNDS LIKE A MOUTHFUL.

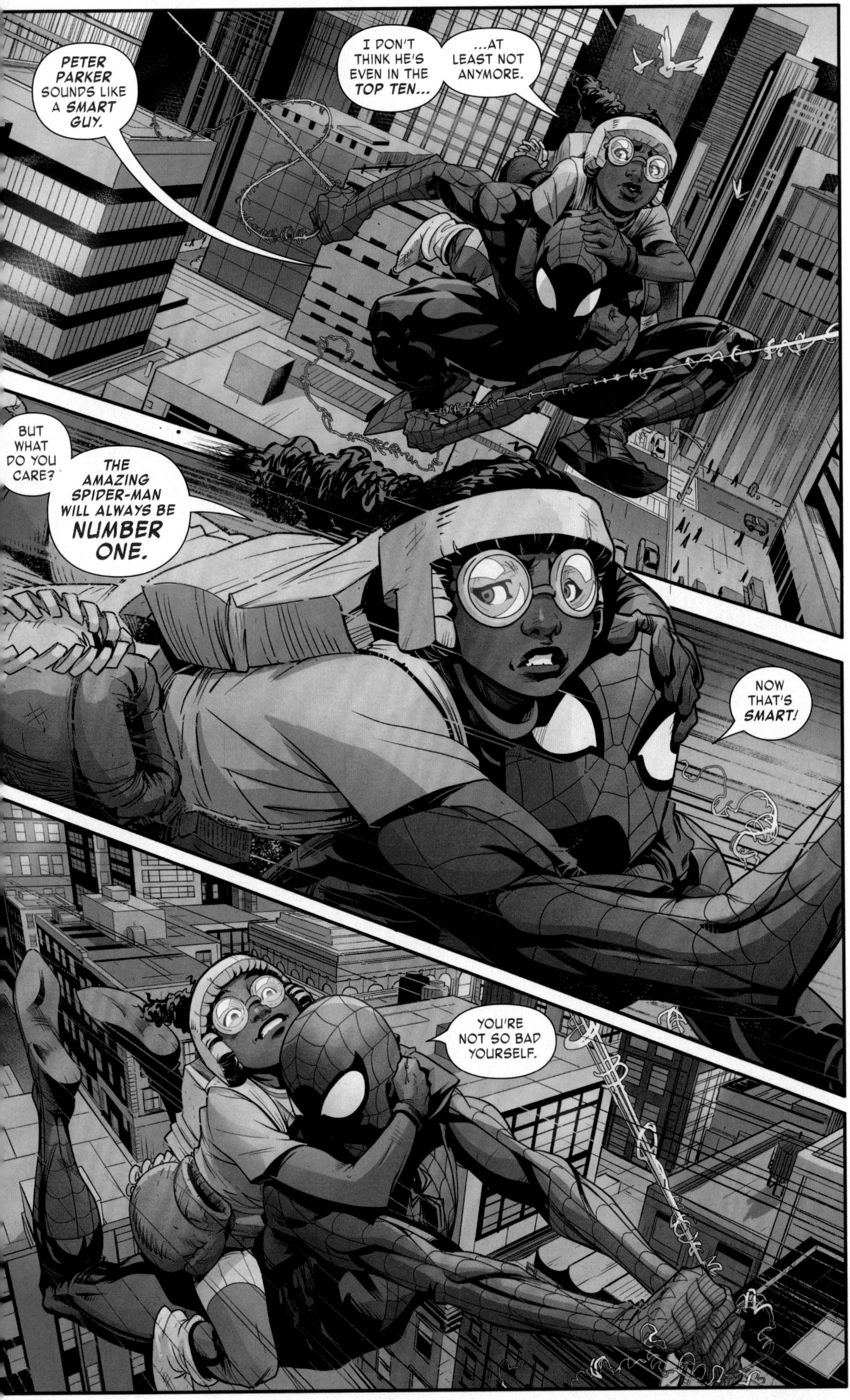
PETER PARKER SOUNDS LIKE A SMART GUY.
I DON'T THINK HE'S EVEN IN THE TOP TEN...
...AT LEAST NOT ANYMORE.
BUT WHAT DO YOU CARE?
THE AMAZING SPIDER-MAN WILL ALWAYS BE NUMBER ONE.
NOW THAT'S SMART!
YOU'RE NOT SO BAD YOURSELF.

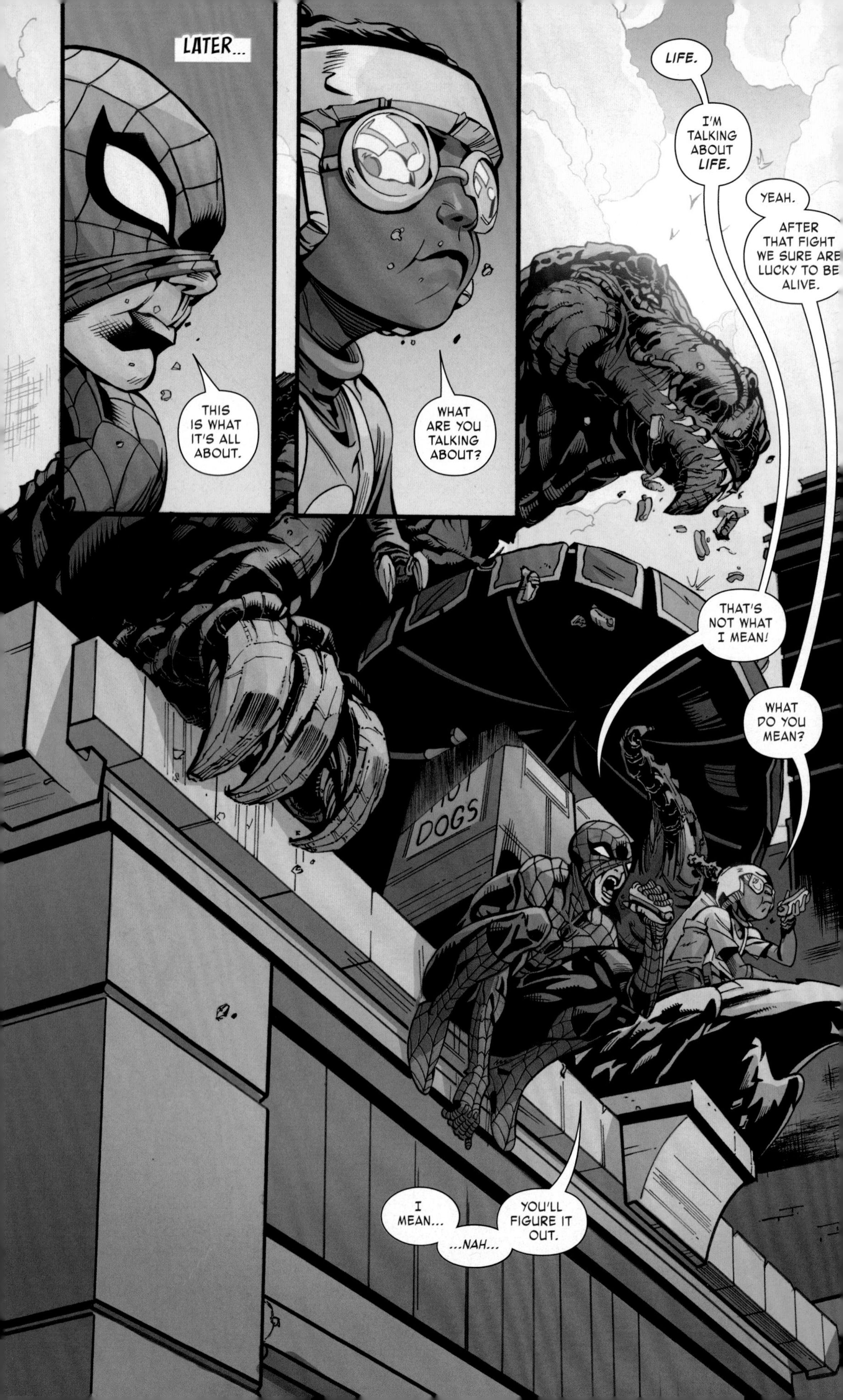
LATER...
THIS IS WHAT IT'S ALL ABOUT.
WHAT ARE YOU TALKING ABOUT?
LIFE.
I'M TALKING ABOUT LIFE.
YEAH.
AFTER THAT FIGHT WE SURE ARE LUCKY TO BE ALIVE.
THAT'S NOT WHAT I MEAN!
WHAT DO YOU MEAN?
DOGS
I MEAN...
...NAH...
YOU'LL FIGURE IT OUT.

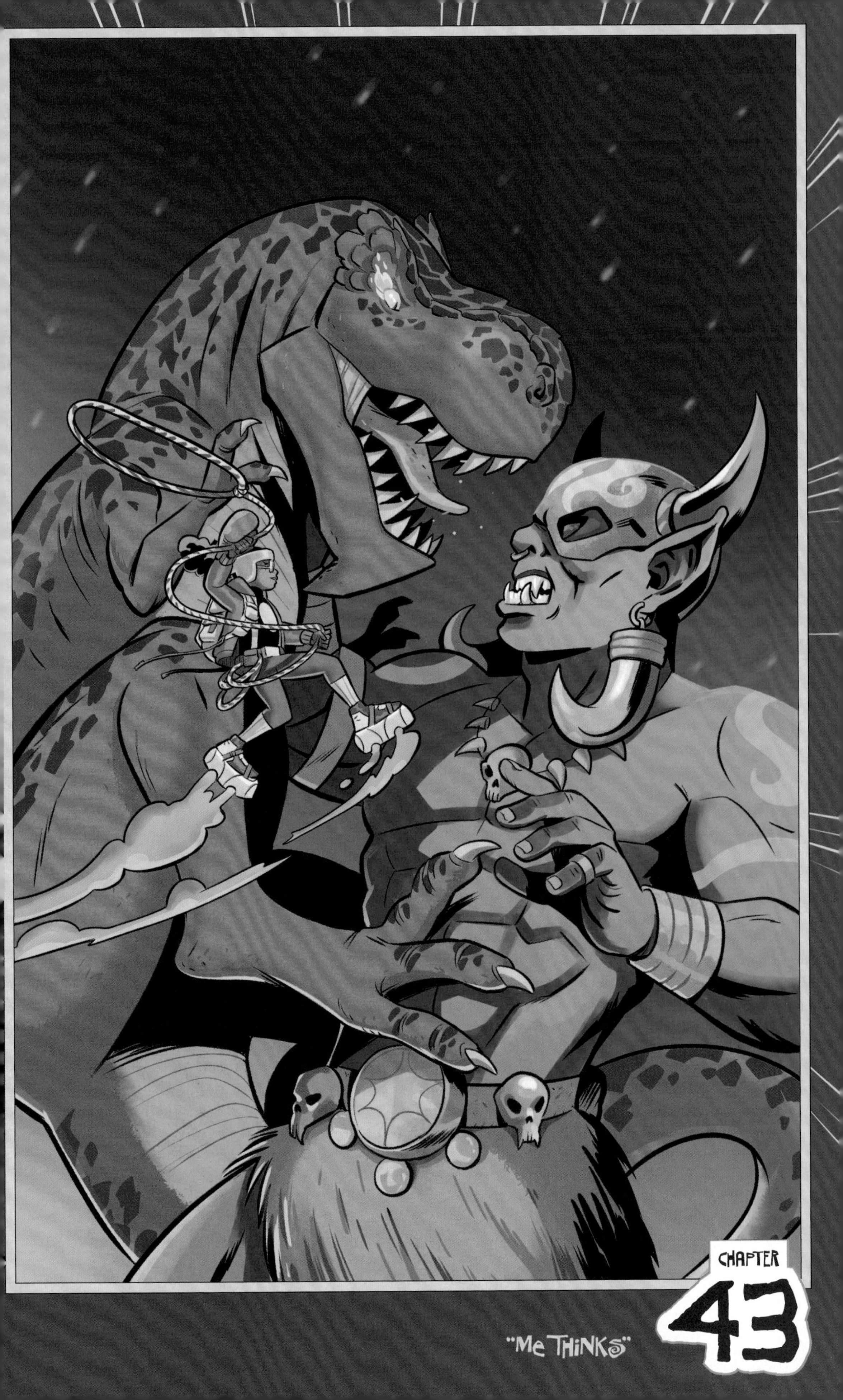
CHAPTER
43
"Me THiNKS"

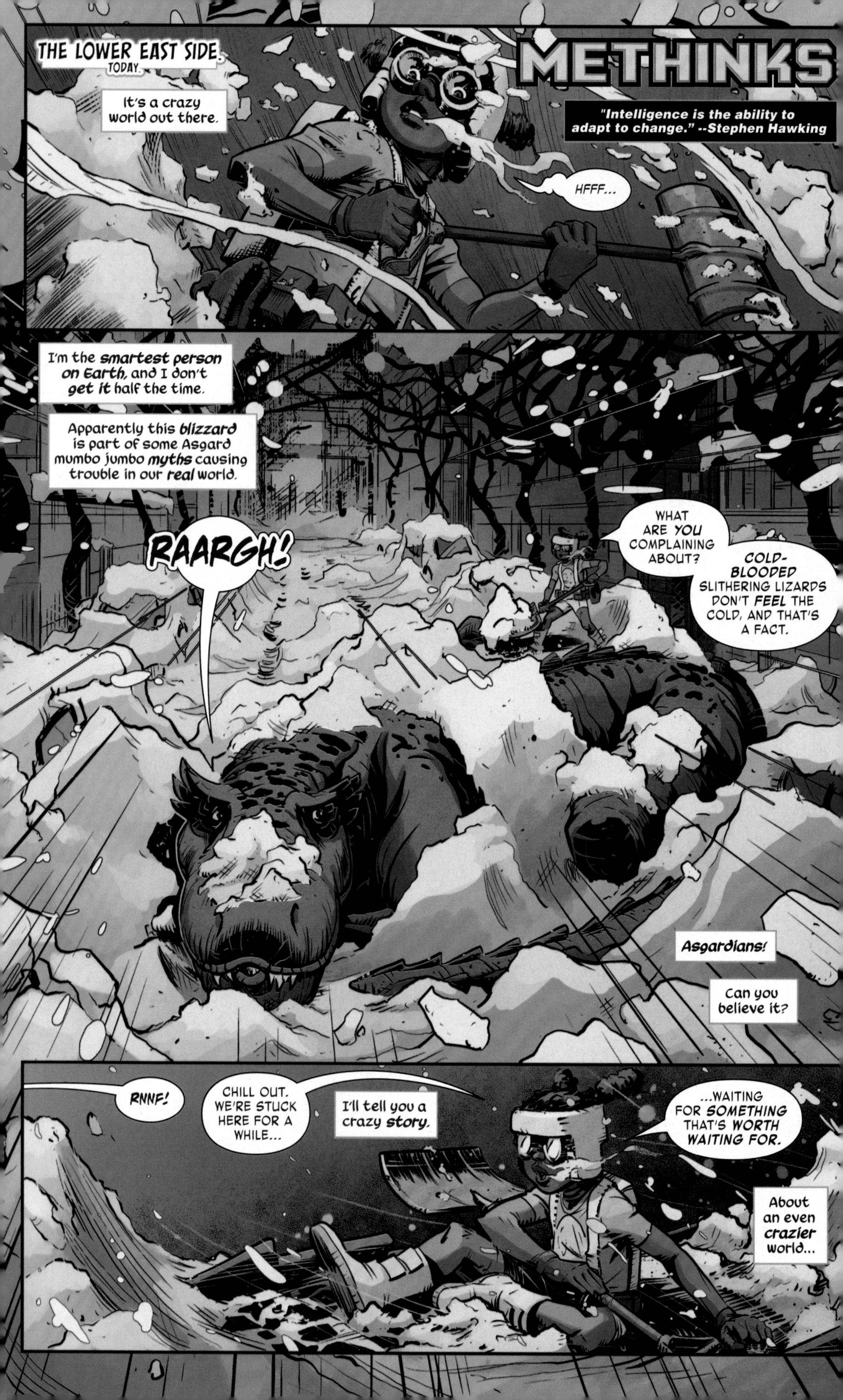
THE LOWER EAST SIDE. TODAY.
It's a crazy world out there.
METHINKS
"Intelligence is the ability to adapt to change." --Stephen Hawking
HFFF...
I'm the smartest person on Earth, and I don't get it half the time.
Apparently this blizzard is part of some Asgard mumbo jumbo myths causing trouble in our real world.
RAARGH!
WHAT ARE YOU COMPLAINING ABOUT?
COLD-BLOODED SLITHERING LIZARDS DON'T FEEL THE COLD, AND THAT'S A FACT.
Asgardians!
Can you believe it?
RNNF!
CHILL OUT. WE'RE STUCK HERE FOR A WHILE...
I'll tell you a crazy story.
...WAITING FOR SOMETHING THAT'S WORTH WAITING FOR.
About an even crazier world...

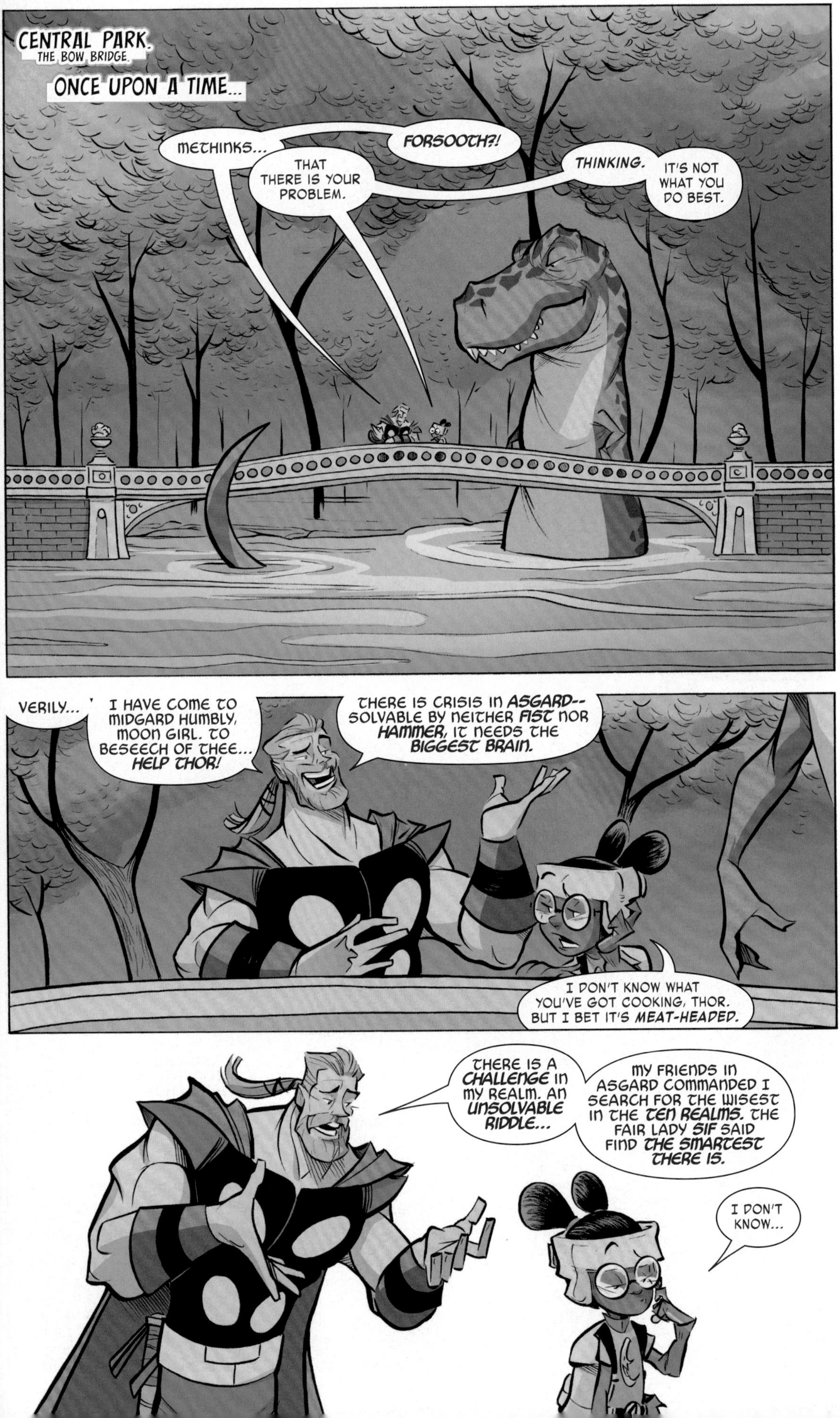
CENTRAL PARK. THE BOW BRIDGE.
ONCE UPON A TIME...
METHINKS...
FORSOOTH?!
THAT THERE IS YOUR PROBLEM.
THINKING.
IT'S NOT WHAT YOU DO BEST.
VERILY...
I HAVE COME TO MIDGARD HUMBLY, MOON GIRL. TO BESEECH OF THEE... HELP THOR!
THERE IS CRISIS IN ASGARD-- SOLVABLE BY NEITHER FIST NOR HAMMER, IT NEEDS THE BIGGEST BRAIN.
I DON'T KNOW WHAT YOU'VE GOT COOKING, THOR. BUT I BET IT'S MEAT-HEADED.
THERE IS A CHALLENGE IN MY REALM. AN UNSOLVABLE RIDDLE...
MY FRIENDS IN ASGARD COMMANDED I SEARCH FOR THE WISEST IN THE TEN REALMS. THE FAIR LADY SIF SAID FIND THE SMARTEST THERE IS.
I DON'T KNOW...

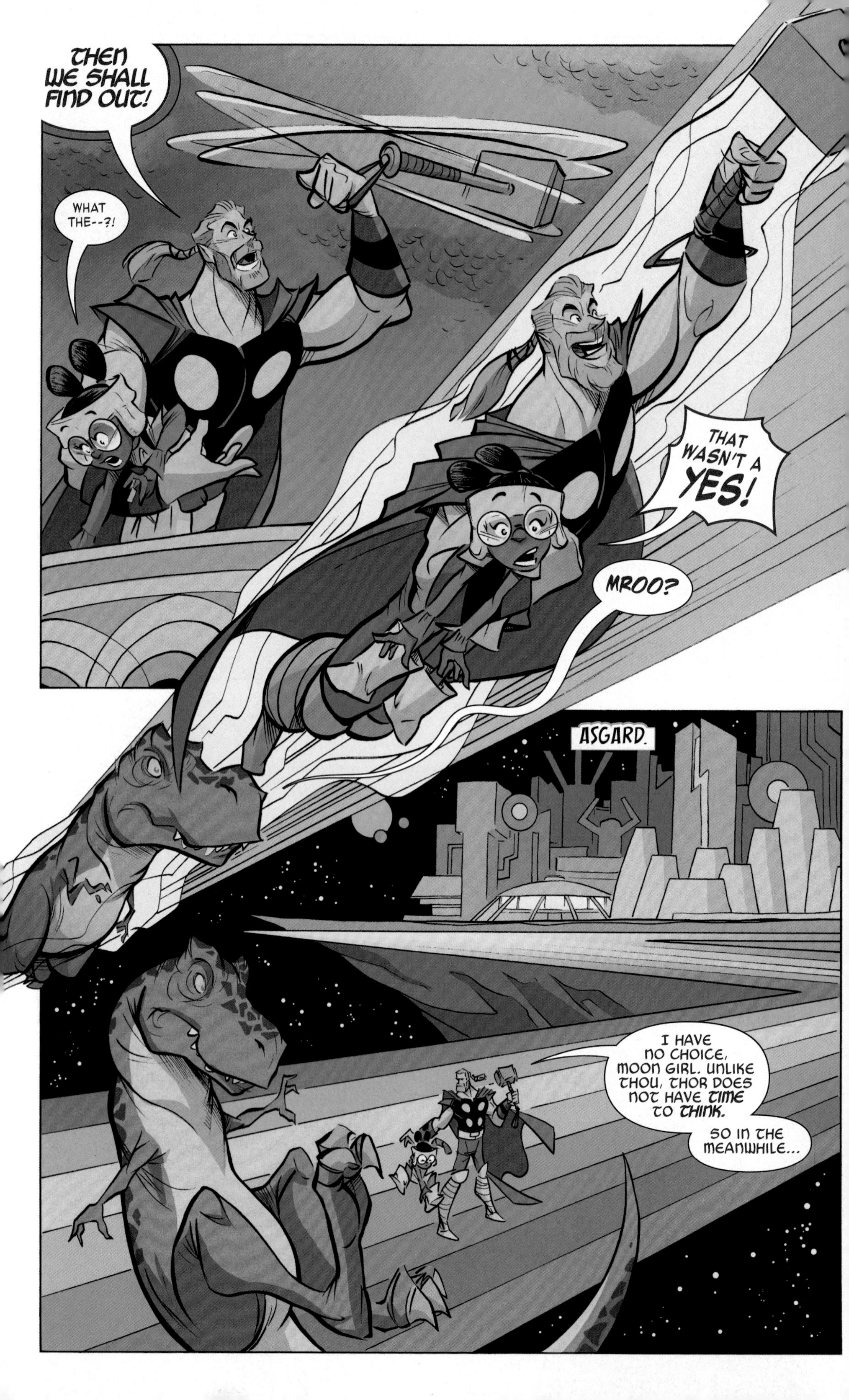
THEN WE SHALL FIND OUT!
WHAT THE--?!
THAT WASN'T A YES!
MROO?
ASGARD.
I HAVE NO CHOICE, MOON GIRL. UNLIKE THOU, THOR DOES NOT HAVE TIME TO THINK.
SO IN THE MEANWHILE...

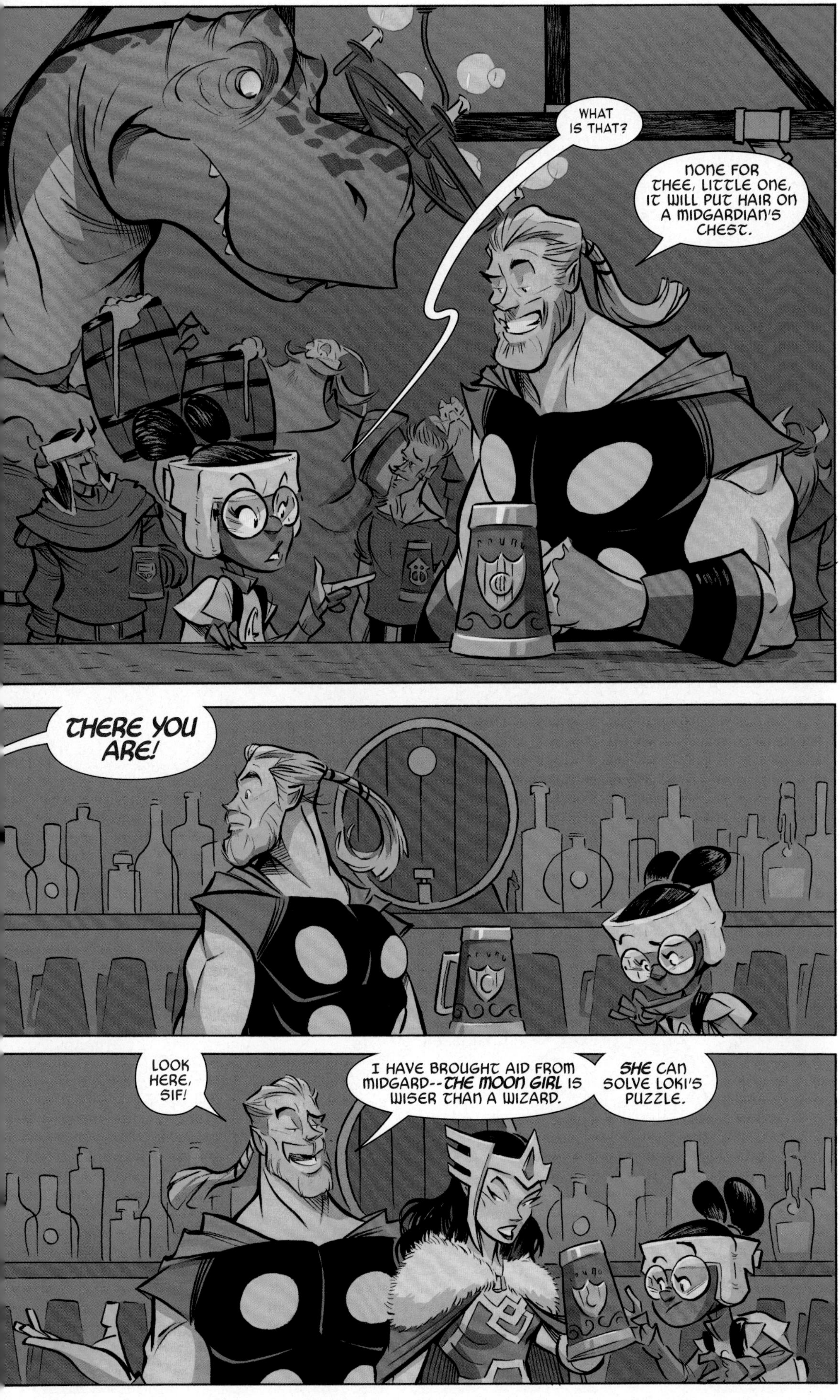
WHAT IS THAT?
NONE FOR THEE, LITTLE ONE, IT WILL PUT HAIR ON A MIDGARDIAN'S CHEST.
THERE YOU ARE!
LOOK HERE, SIF!
I HAVE BROUGHT AID FROM MIDGARD--THE MOON GIRL IS WISER THAN A WIZARD.
SHE CAN SOLVE LOKI'S PUZZLE.

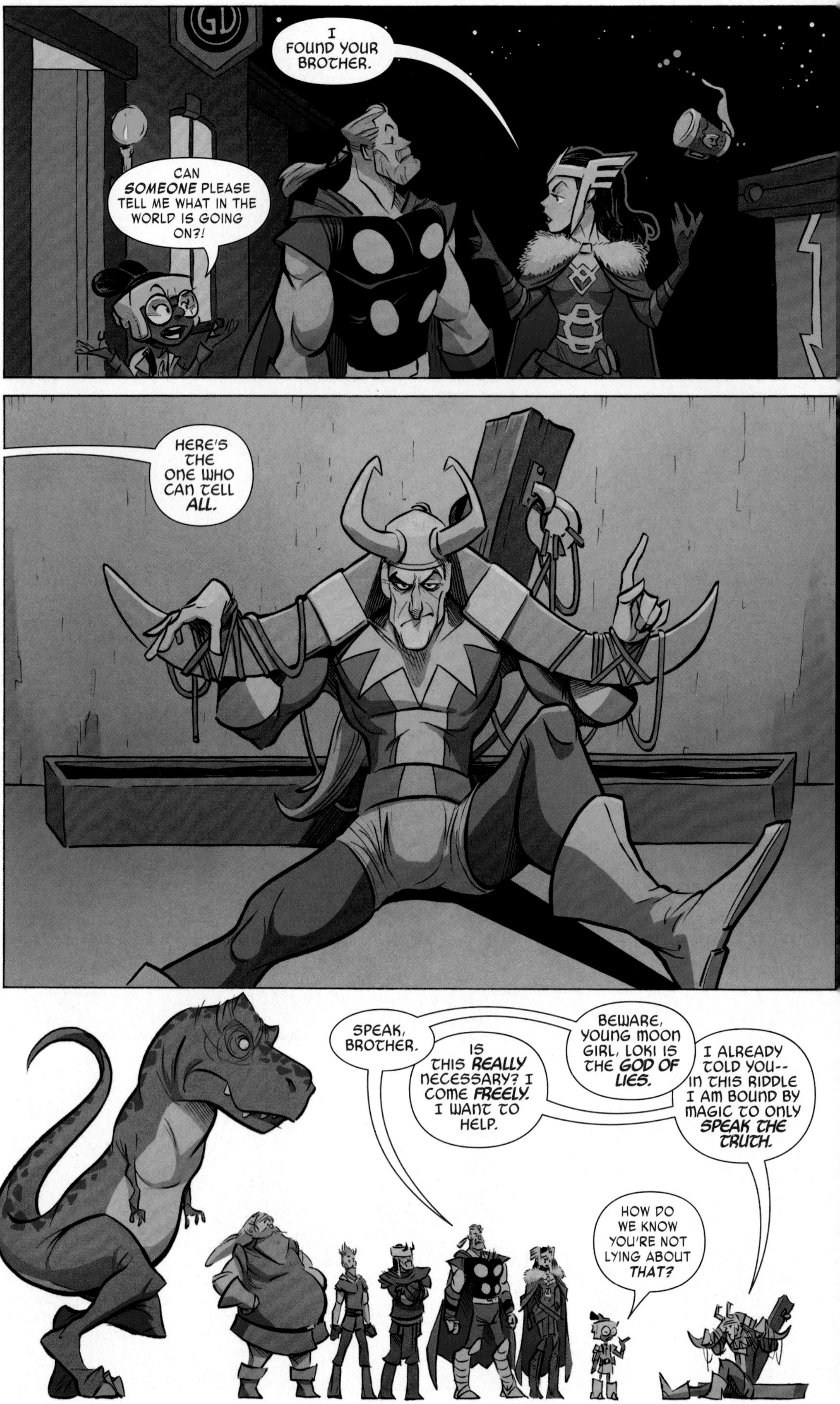
I FOUND YOUR BROTHER.
CAN *SOMEONE* PLEASE TELL ME WHAT IN THE WORLD IS GOING ON?!
HERE'S THE ONE WHO CAN TELL *ALL.*
SPEAK, BROTHER.
IS THIS *REALLY* NECESSARY? I COME *FREELY.* I WANT TO HELP.
BEWARE, YOUNG MOON GIRL, LOKI IS THE *GOD OF LIES.*
I ALREADY TOLD YOU-- IN THIS RIDDLE I AM BOUND BY MAGIC TO ONLY *SPEAK THE TRUTH.*
HOW DO WE KNOW YOU'RE NOT LYING ABOUT *THAT?*

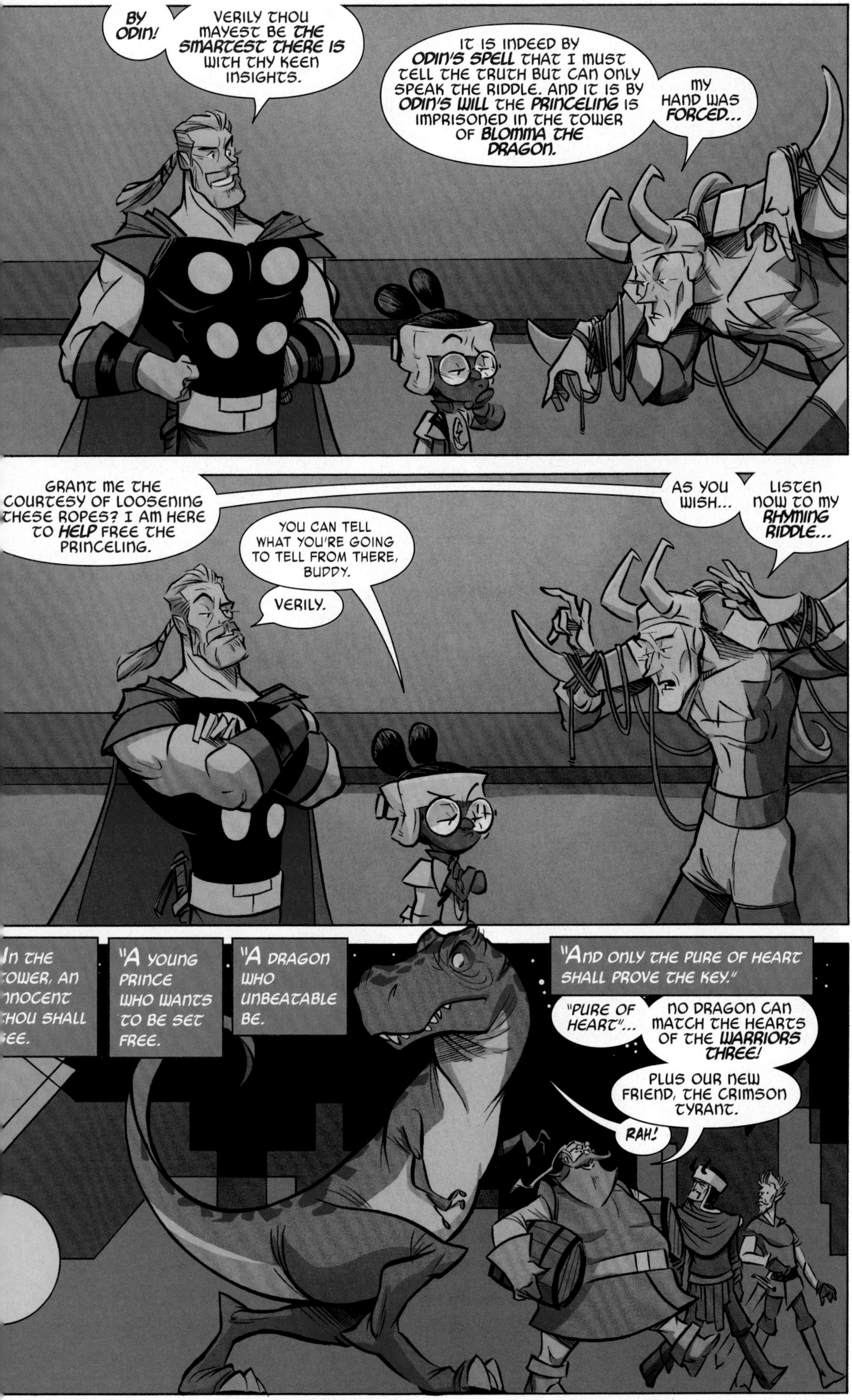
BY ODIN!
VERILY THOU MAYEST BE THE SMARTEST THERE IS WITH THY KEEN INSIGHTS.
IT IS INDEED BY ODIN'S SPELL THAT I MUST TELL THE TRUTH BUT CAN ONLY SPEAK THE RIDDLE. AND IT IS BY ODIN'S WILL THE PRINCELING IS IMPRISONED IN THE TOWER OF BLOMMA THE DRAGON.
MY HAND WAS FORCED...
GRANT ME THE COURTESY OF LOOSENING THESE ROPES? I AM HERE TO HELP FREE THE PRINCELING.
YOU CAN TELL WHAT YOU'RE GOING TO TELL FROM THERE, BUDDY.
VERILY.
AS YOU WISH...
LISTEN NOW TO MY RHYMING RIDDLE...
In THE TOWER, AN INNOCENT THOU SHALL SEE.
"A YOUNG PRINCE WHO WANTS TO BE SET FREE.
"A DRAGON WHO UNBEATABLE BE.
"AND ONLY THE PURE OF HEART SHALL PROVE THE KEY."
"PURE OF HEART"...
NO DRAGON CAN MATCH THE HEARTS OF THE WARRIORS THREE!
PLUS OUR NEW FRIEND, THE CRIMSON TYRANT.
RAH!

WELL...?

MY RIDDLE IS--
OOF!

QUIET, YOU!
I WILL KEEP THIS ONE OUT OF TROUBLE.

YANK

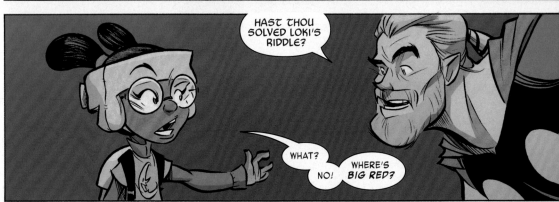

HAST THOU SOLVED LOKI'S RIDDLE?

WHAT?

NO!

WHERE'S BIG RED?

WE NEED NOT THE DEVIL DINOSAUR.

INDEED--IF STRENGTH COULD WIN THIS DAY, THOR WOULD HAVE WON IT MANY DAYS AGO.

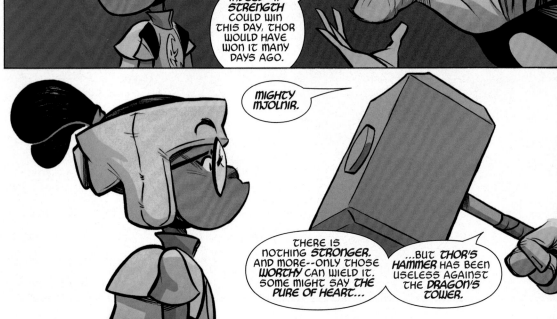

MIGHTY MJOLNIR.

THERE IS NOTHING STRONGER. AND MORE--ONLY THOSE WORTHY CAN WIELD IT. SOME MIGHT SAY THE PURE OF HEART...

...BUT THOR'S HAMMER HAS BEEN USELESS AGAINST THE DRAGON'S TOWER.

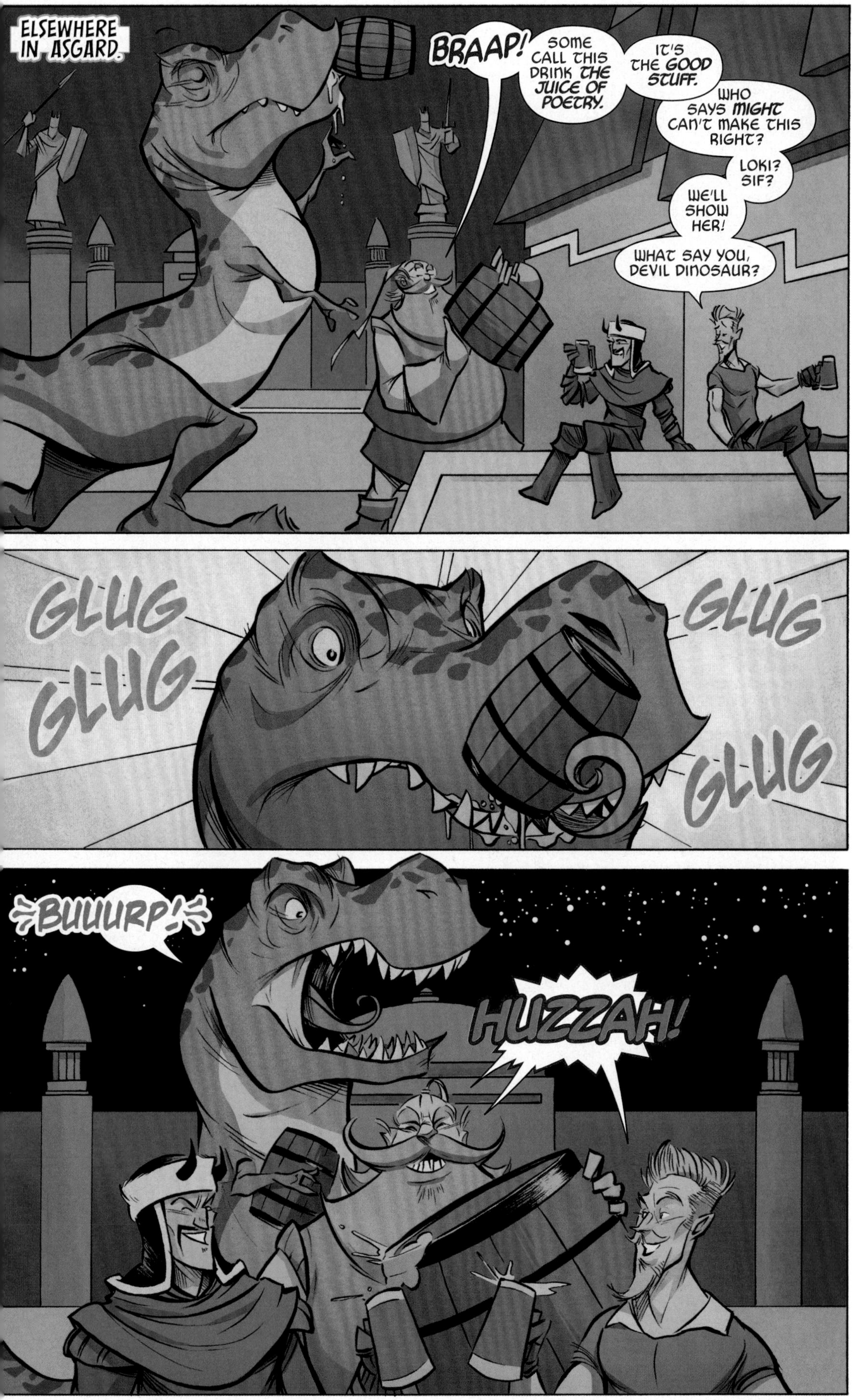

ELSEWHERE IN ASGARD.
BRAAP!
SOME CALL THIS DRINK THE JUICE OF POETRY.
IT'S THE GOOD STUFF.
WHO SAYS MIGHT CAN'T MAKE THIS RIGHT?
LOKI? SIF?
WE'LL SHOW HER!
WHAT SAY YOU, DEVIL DINOSAUR?
GLUG
GLUG
GLUG
GLUG
BUUURP!
HUZZAH!

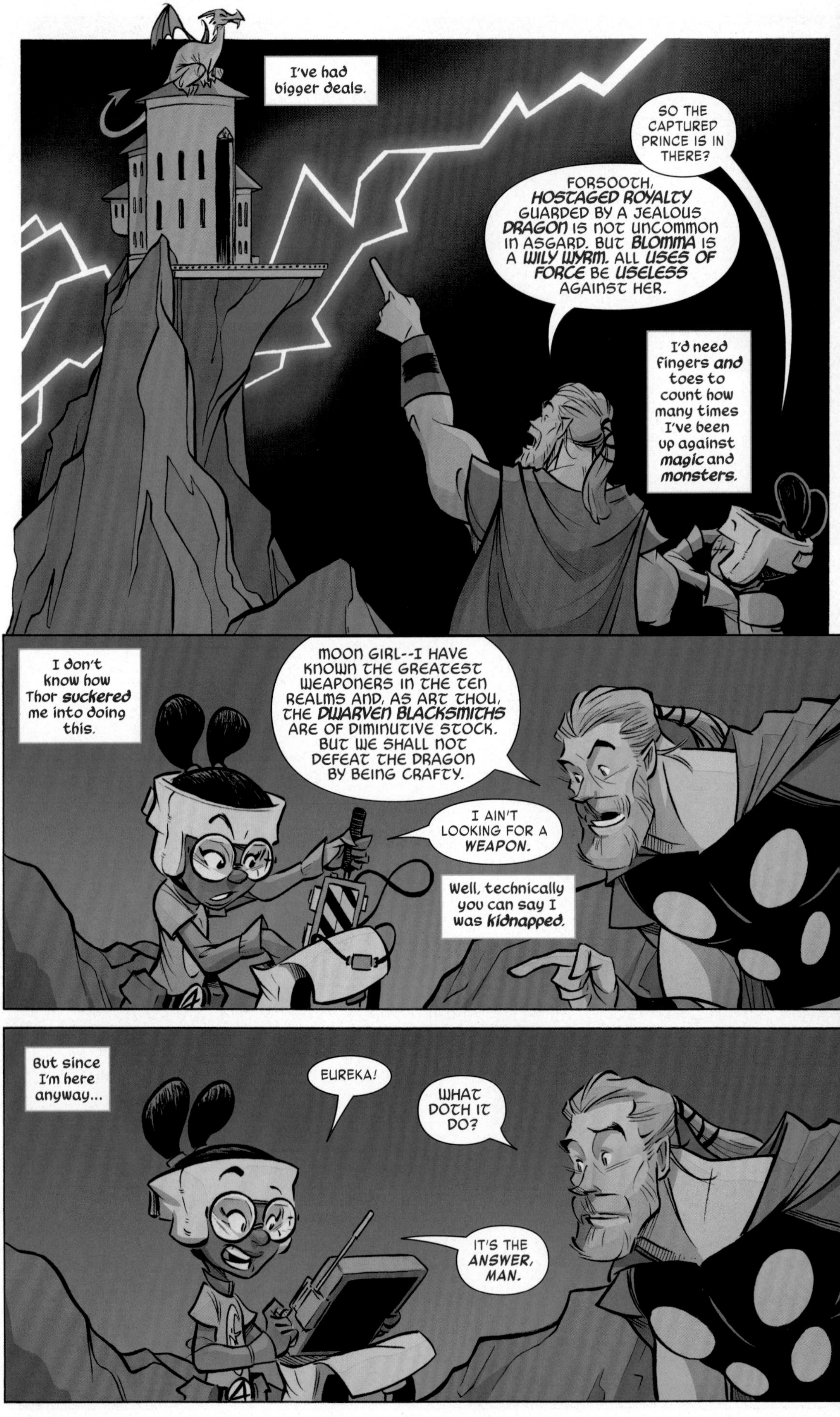
I've had bigger deals.
SO THE CAPTURED PRINCE IS IN THERE?
FORSOOTH, HOSTAGED ROYALTY GUARDED BY A JEALOUS DRAGON IS NOT UNCOMMON IN ASGARD. BUT BLOMMA IS A WILY WYRM. ALL USES OF FORCE BE USELESS AGAINST HER.
I'd need fingers and toes to count how many times I've been up against magic and monsters.
I don't know how Thor suckered me into doing this.
MOON GIRL--I HAVE KNOWN THE GREATEST WEAPONERS IN THE TEN REALMS AND, AS ART THOU, THE DWARVEN BLACKSMITHS ARE OF DIMINUTIVE STOCK. BUT WE SHALL NOT DEFEAT THE DRAGON BY BEING CRAFTY.
I AIN'T LOOKING FOR A WEAPON.
Well, technically you can say I was kidnapped.
But since I'm here anyway...
EUREKA!
WHAT DOTH IT DO?
IT'S THE ANSWER, MAN.

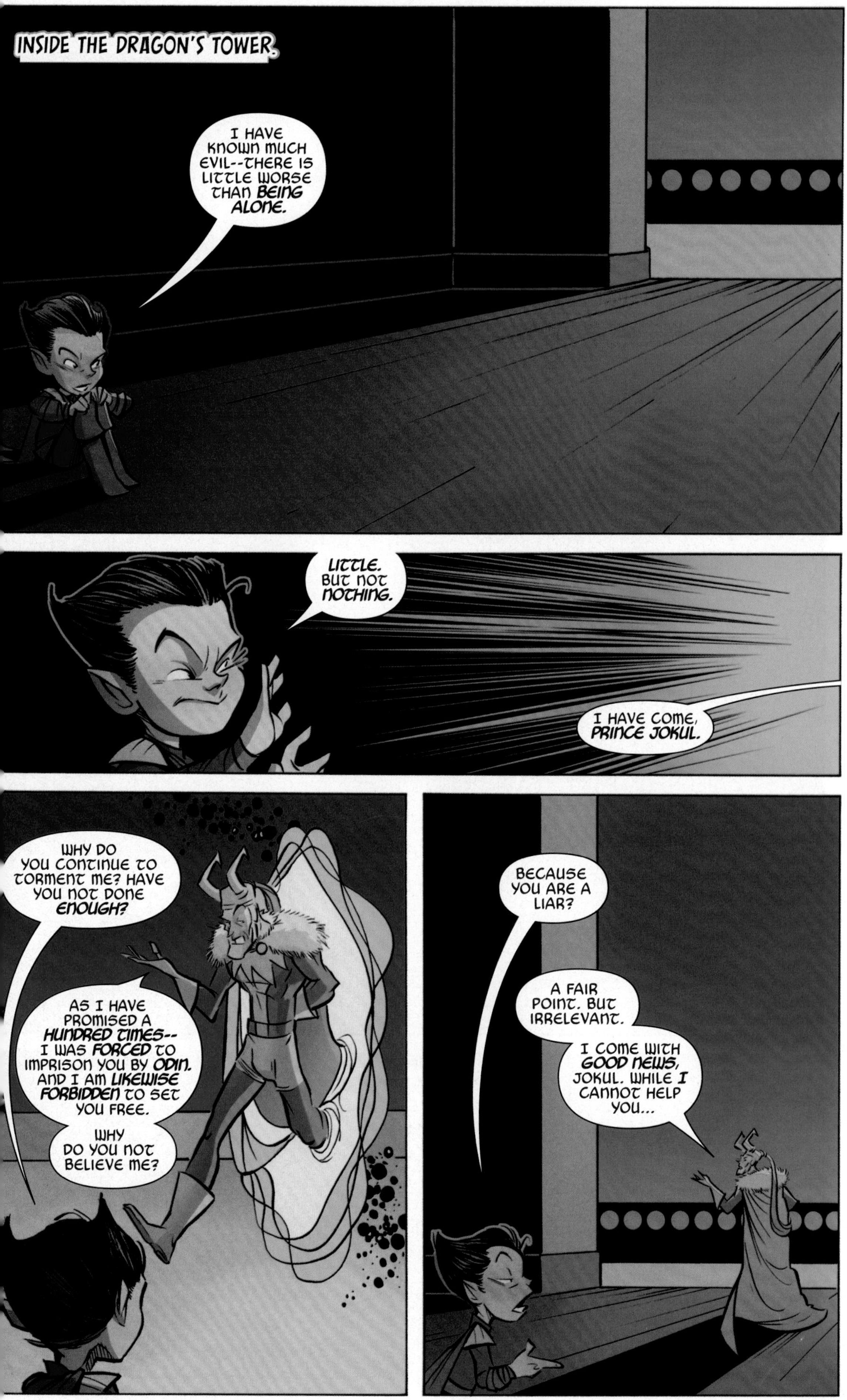
INSIDE THE DRAGON'S TOWER.
I HAVE KNOWN MUCH EVIL--THERE IS LITTLE WORSE THAN BEING ALONE.
LITTLE. BUT NOT NOTHING.
I HAVE COME, PRINCE JOKUL.
WHY DO YOU CONTINUE TO TORMENT ME? HAVE YOU NOT DONE ENOUGH?
AS I HAVE PROMISED A HUNDRED TIMES-- I WAS FORCED TO IMPRISON YOU BY ODIN. AND I AM LIKEWISE FORBIDDEN TO SET YOU FREE.
WHY DO YOU NOT BELIEVE ME?
BECAUSE YOU ARE A LIAR?
A FAIR POINT. BUT IRRELEVANT.
I COME WITH GOOD NEWS, JOKUL. WHILE I CANNOT HELP YOU...

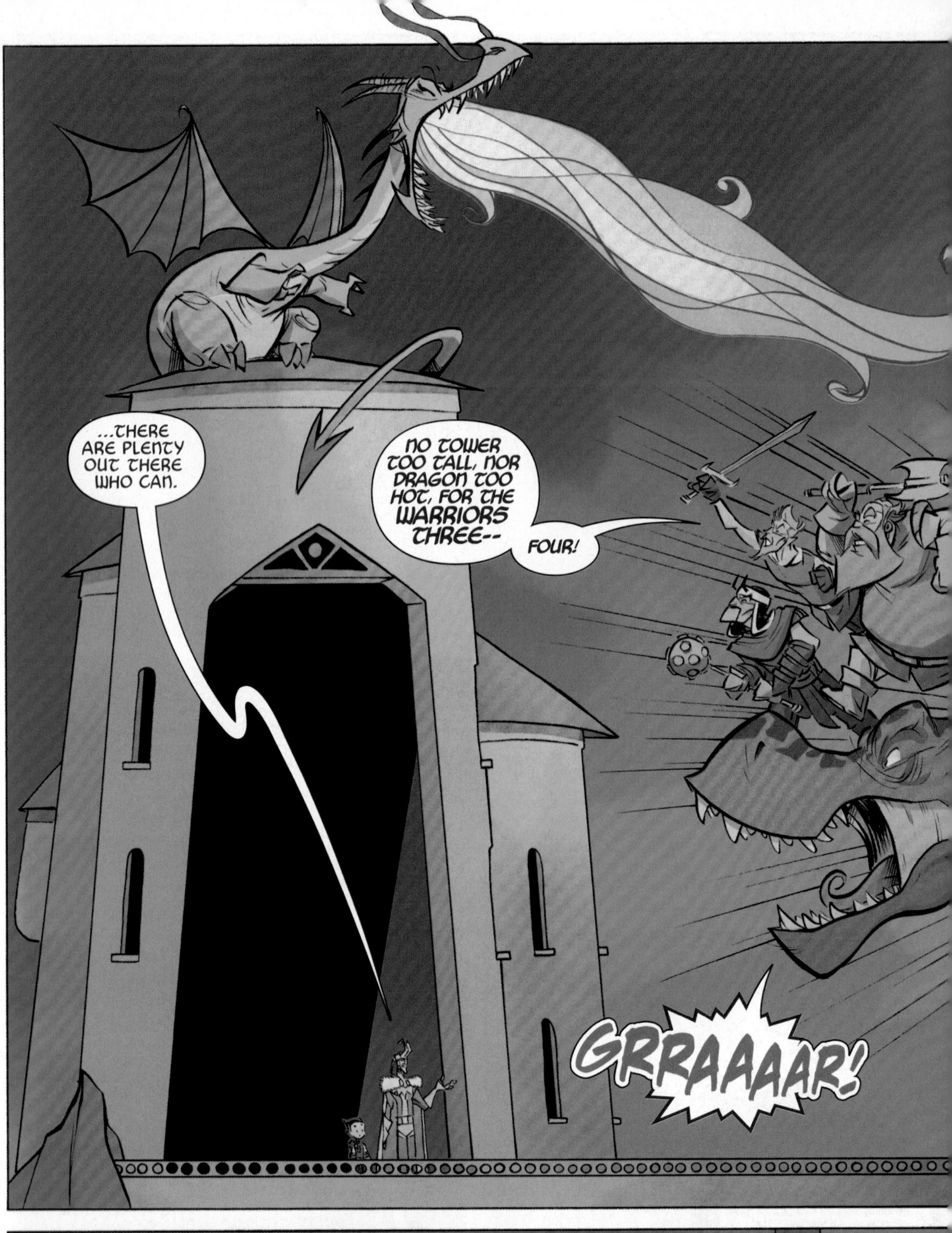
...THERE ARE PLENTY OUT THERE WHO CAN.
NO TOWER TOO TALL, NOR DRAGON TOO HOT, FOR THE WARRIORS THREE--
FOUR!
GRRAAAAR!
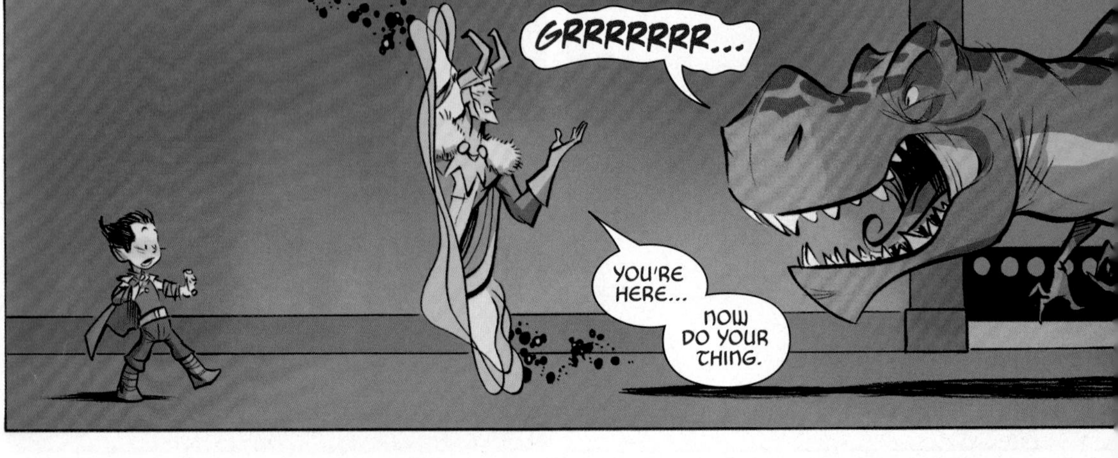
GRRRRRRR...
YOU'RE HERE...
NOW DO YOUR THING.

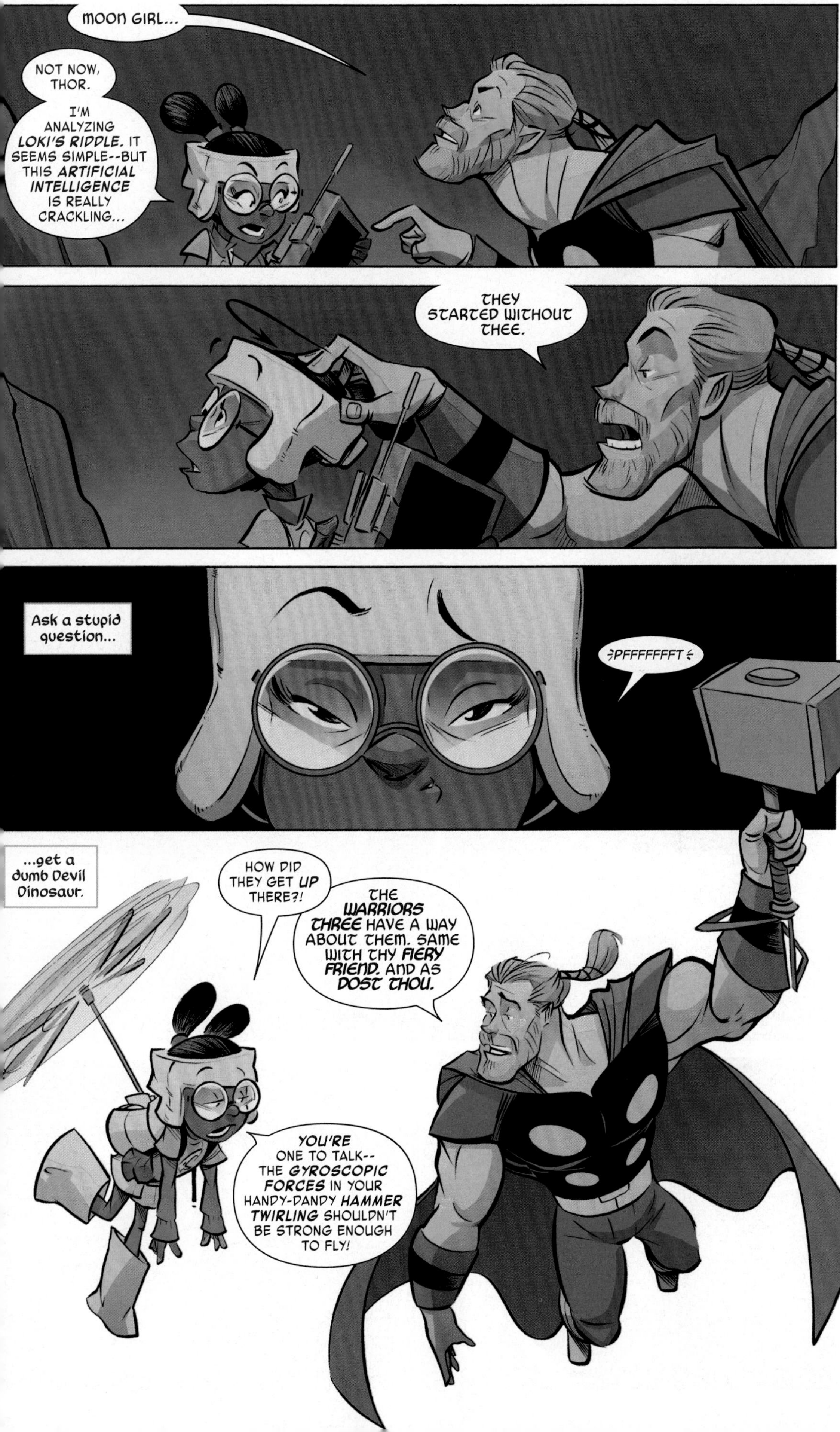

MOON GIRL...
NOT NOW, THOR.
I'M ANALYZING LOKI'S RIDDLE. IT SEEMS SIMPLE--BUT THIS ARTIFICIAL INTELLIGENCE IS REALLY CRACKLING...
THEY STARTED WITHOUT THEE.
Ask a stupid question...
PFFFFFFFT
...get a dumb Devil Dinosaur.
HOW DID THEY GET UP THERE?!
THE WARRIORS THREE HAVE A WAY ABOUT THEM. SAME WITH THY FIERY FRIEND. AND AS DOST THOU.
YOU'RE ONE TO TALK-- THE GYROSCOPIC FORCES IN YOUR HANDY-DANDY HAMMER TWIRLING SHOULDN'T BE STRONG ENOUGH TO FLY!

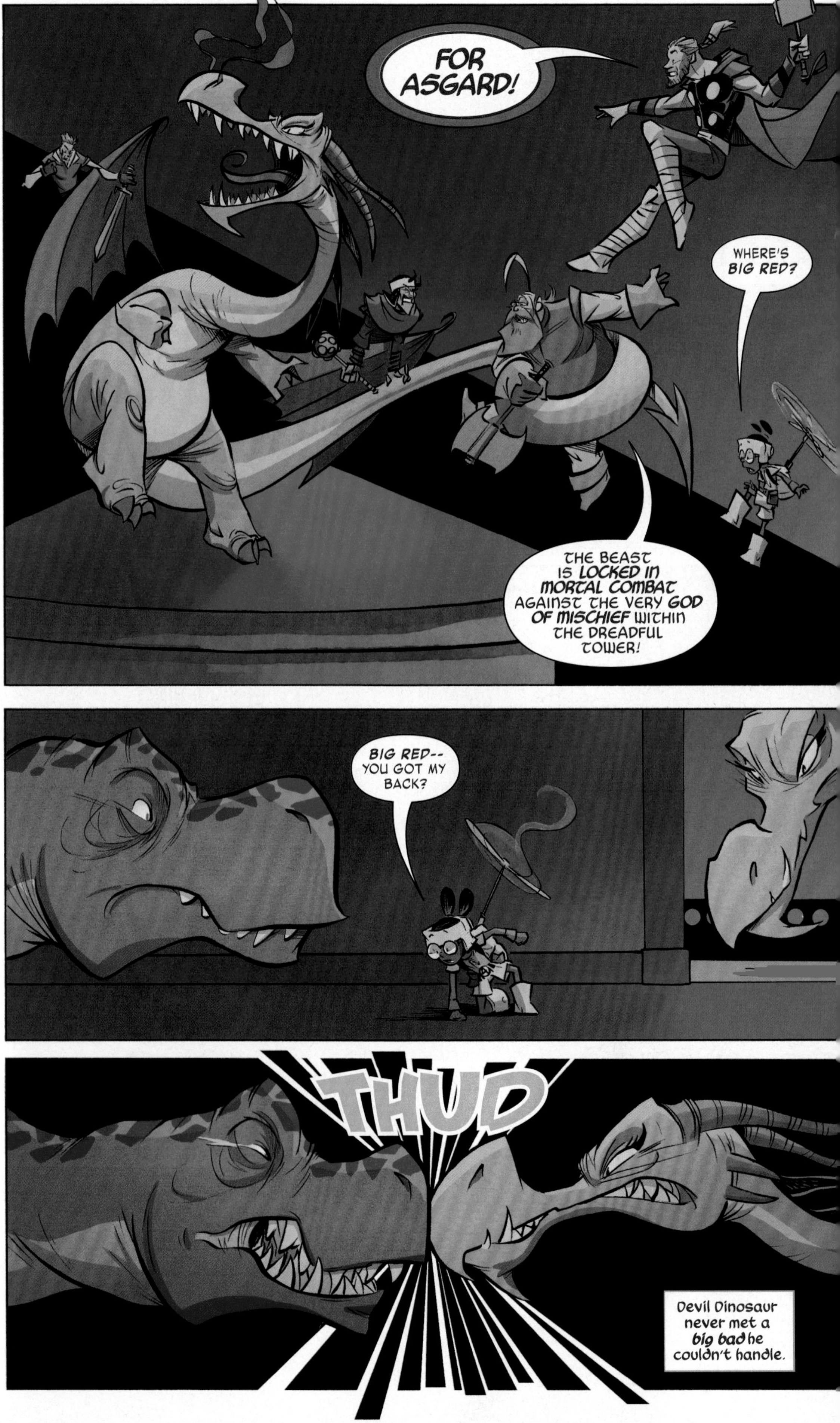
FOR ASGARD!
WHERE'S BIG RED?
THE BEAST IS LOCKED IN MORTAL COMBAT AGAINST THE VERY GOD OF MISCHIEF WITHIN THE DREADFUL TOWER!
BIG RED-- YOU GOT MY BACK?
THUD
Devil Dinosaur never met a big bad he couldn't handle.

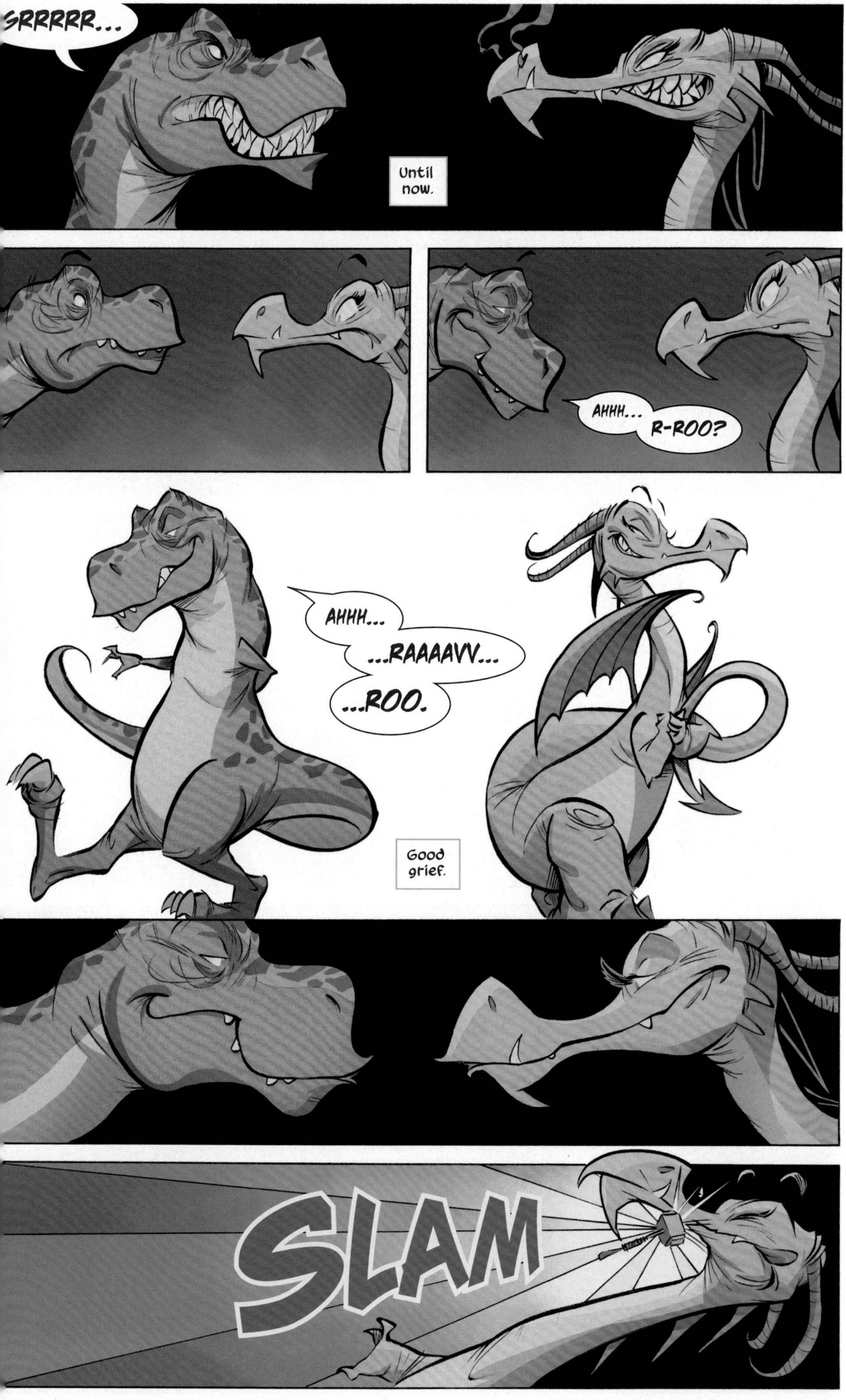

SRRRRR...
Until now.
AHHH... R-ROO?
AHHH...
...RAAAAVV...
...ROO.
Good grief.
SLAM

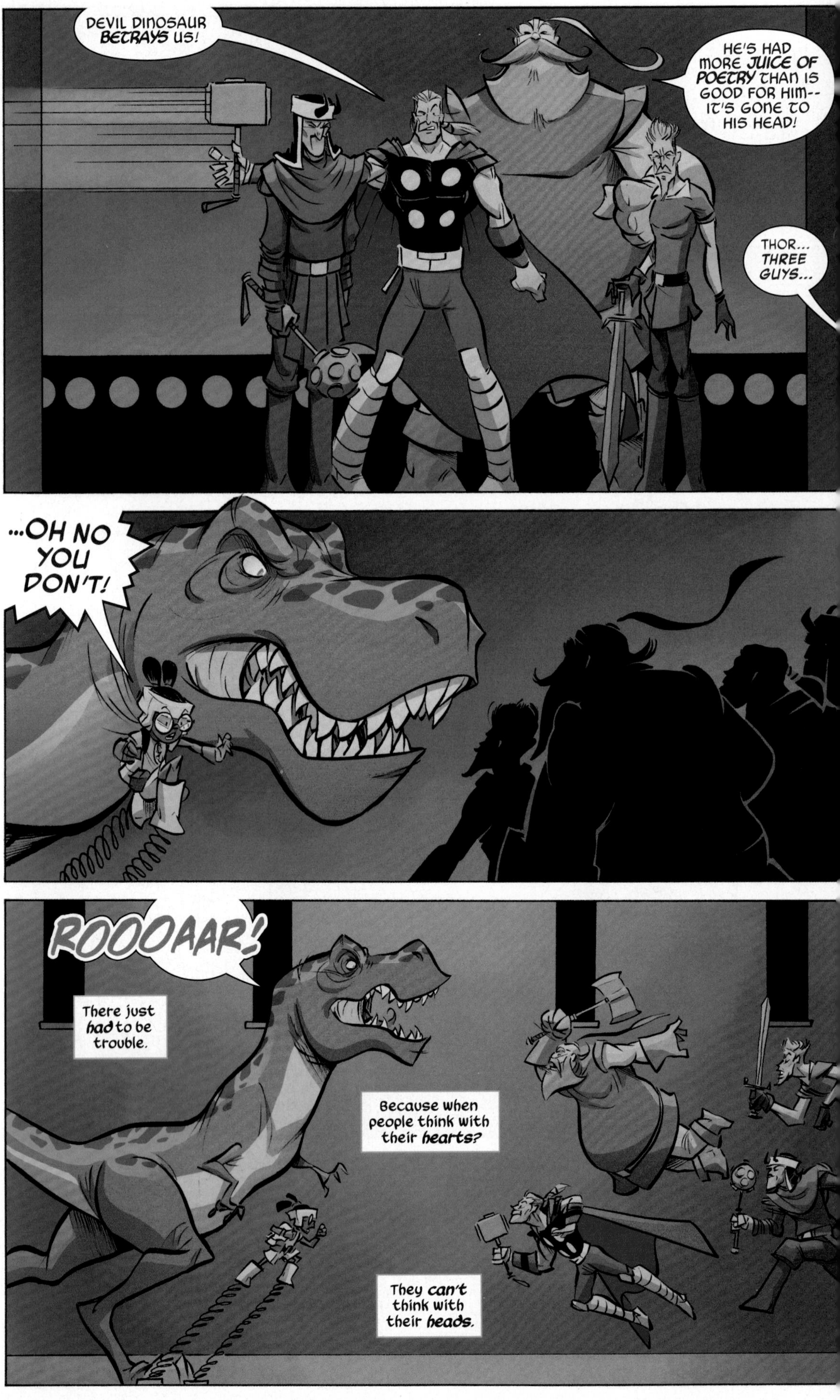
DEVIL DINOSAUR **BETRAYS** US!
HE'S HAD MORE **JUICE OF POETRY** THAN IS GOOD FOR HIM--IT'S GONE TO HIS HEAD!
THOR... **THREE GUYS...**
...OH NO YOU DON'T!
ROOOAAR!
There just *had* to be trouble.
Because when people think with their *hearts?*
They *can't* think with their *heads.*

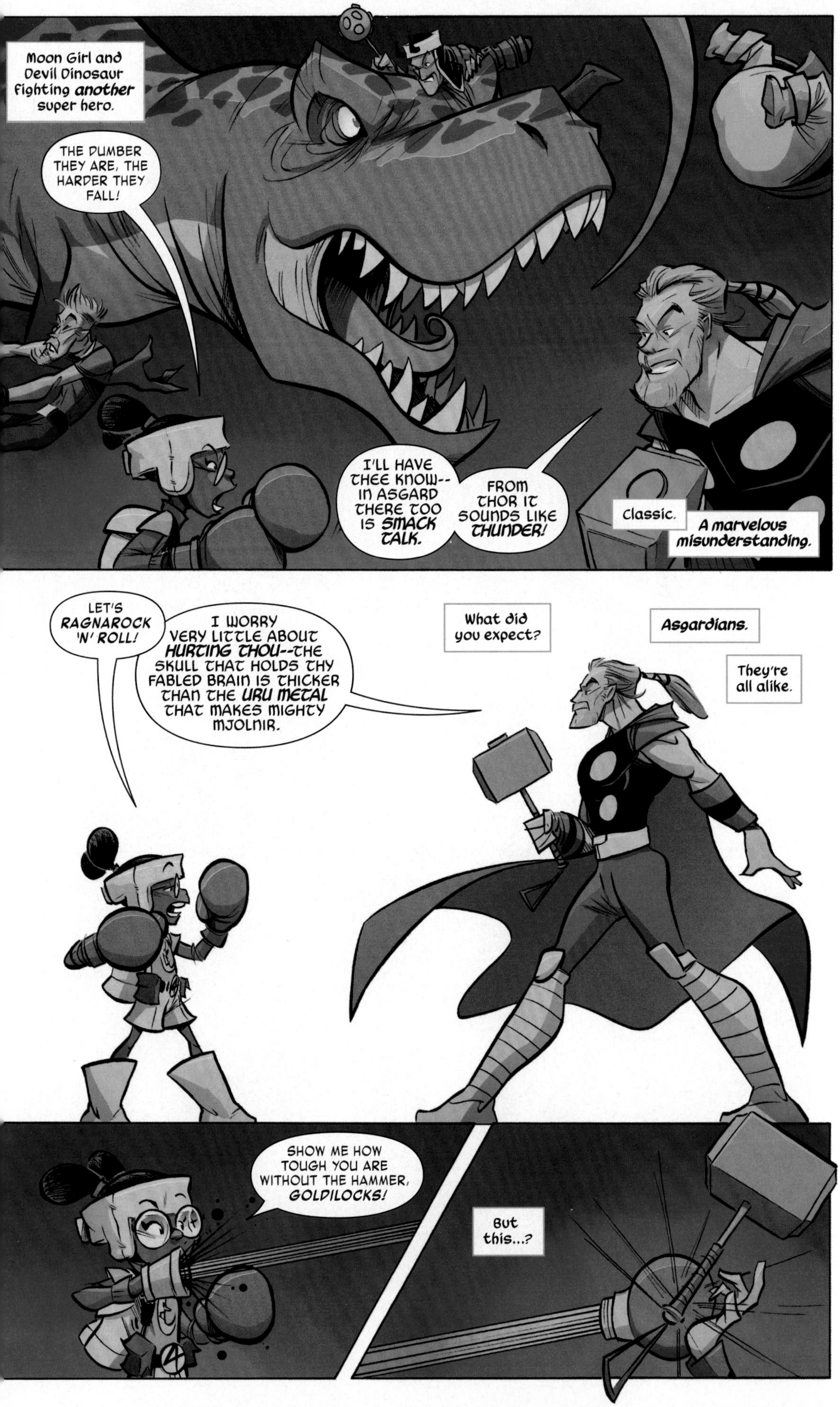
Moon Girl and Devil Dinosaur fighting another super hero.
THE DUMBER THEY ARE, THE HARDER THEY FALL!
I'LL HAVE THEE KNOW--IN ASGARD THERE TOO IS SMACK TALK.
FROM THOR IT SOUNDS LIKE THUNDER!
Classic.
A marvelous misunderstanding.
LET'S RAGNAROCK 'N' ROLL!
I WORRY VERY LITTLE ABOUT HURTING THOU--THE SKULL THAT HOLDS THY FABLED BRAIN IS THICKER THAN THE URU METAL THAT MAKES MIGHTY MJOLNIR.
What did you expect?
Asgardians.
They're all alike.
SHOW ME HOW TOUGH YOU ARE WITHOUT THE HAMMER, GOLDILOCKS!
But this...?

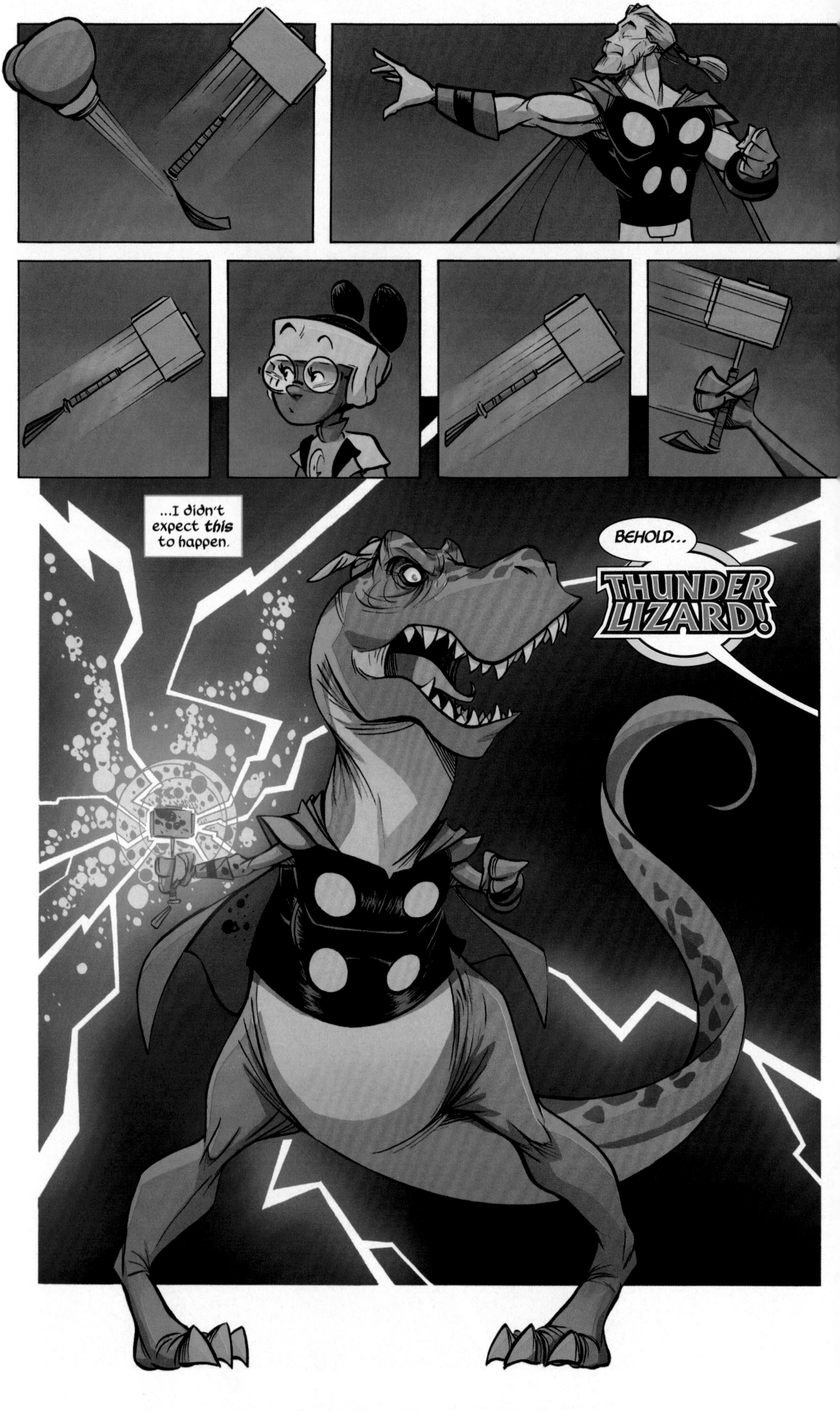
...I didn't expect **this** to happen.
BEHOLD...
THUNDER LIZARD!

GET THIS...

IT'S DINO-THOR.

GOT IT?

MOON GIRL...

THOU ART SMART...

LET US BE REASONABLE.

GYAAAA!

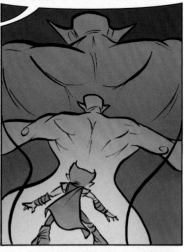

LOOKS LIKE ASGARD'S TRICKSTER IN CHIEF PLAYED US FOR FOOLS.

IN THE TOWER... INNOCENT...

SOMETHING SOMETHING TO SET HIM FREE...

SOMETHING SOMETHING...

...PURE OF HEART...

Oh!

That **does** make sense.

I guess.

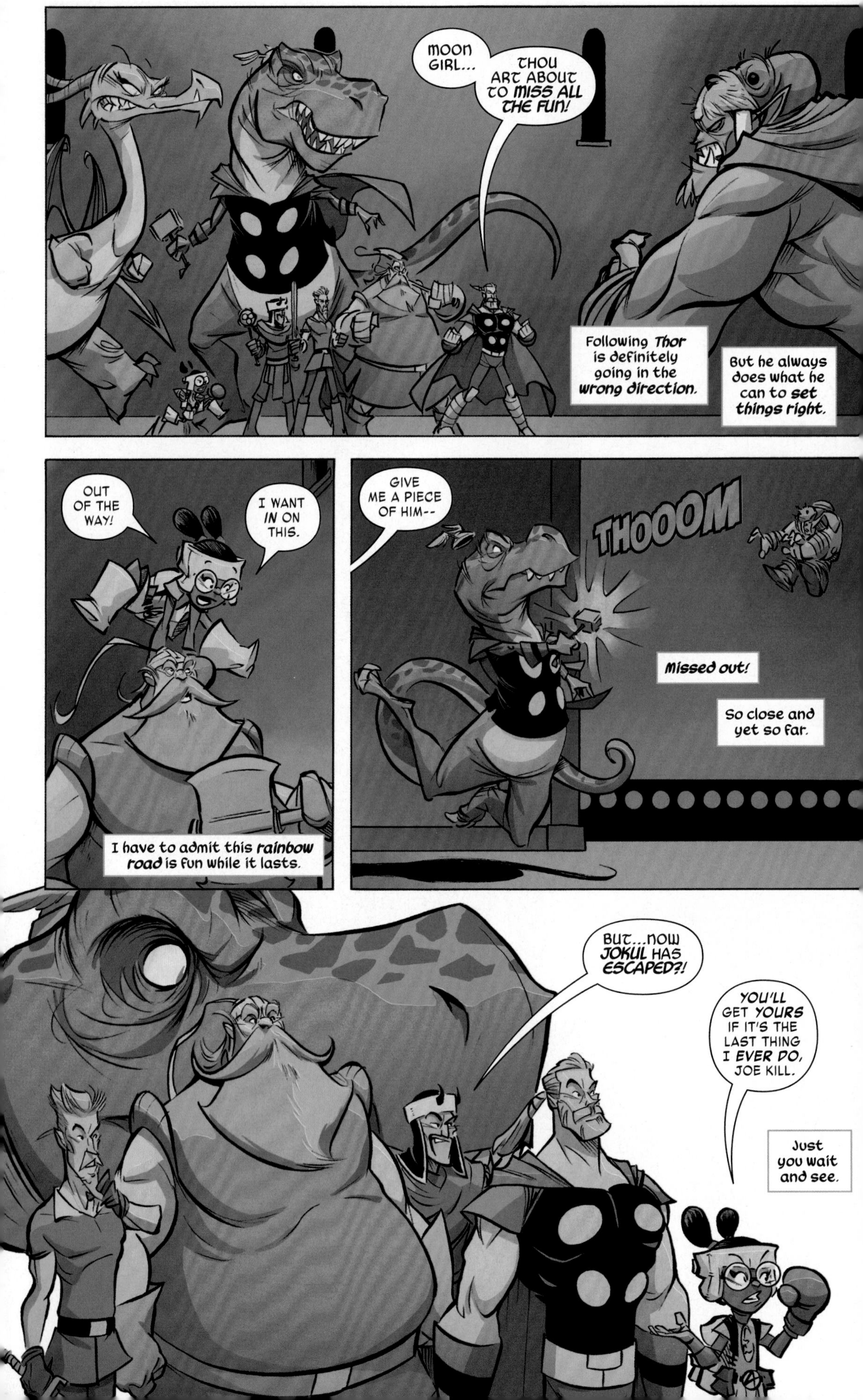
MOON GIRL...
THOU ART ABOUT TO MISS ALL THE FUN!
Following Thor is definitely going in the wrong direction.
But he always does what he can to set things right.
OUT OF THE WAY!
I WANT IN ON THIS.
I have to admit this rainbow road is fun while it lasts.
GIVE ME A PIECE OF HIM--
THOOOM
Missed out!
So close and yet so far.
BUT...NOW JOKUL HAS ESCAPED?!
YOU'LL GET YOURS IF IT'S THE LAST THING I EVER DO, JOE KILL.
Just you wait and see.

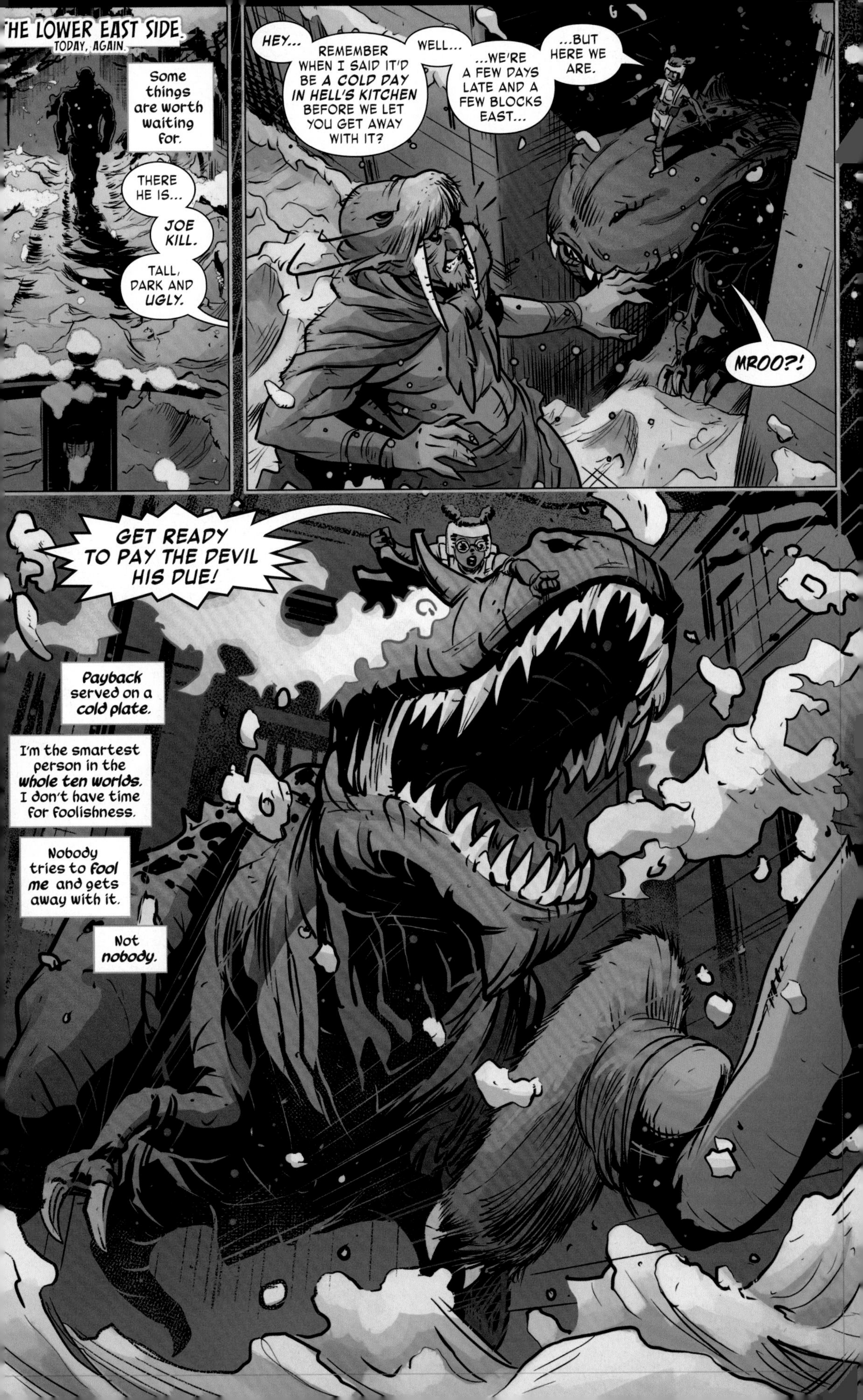
THE LOWER EAST SIDE.
TODAY, AGAIN.
Some things are worth waiting for.
THERE HE IS...
JOE KILL.
TALL, DARK AND UGLY.
HEY...
REMEMBER WHEN I SAID IT'D BE A COLD DAY IN HELL'S KITCHEN BEFORE WE LET YOU GET AWAY WITH IT?
WELL...
...WE'RE A FEW DAYS LATE AND A FEW BLOCKS EAST...
...BUT HERE WE ARE.
MROO?!
GET READY TO PAY THE DEVIL HIS DUE!
Payback served on a cold plate.
I'm the smartest person in the whole ten worlds. I don't have time for foolishness.
Nobody tries to fool me and gets away with it.
Not nobody.

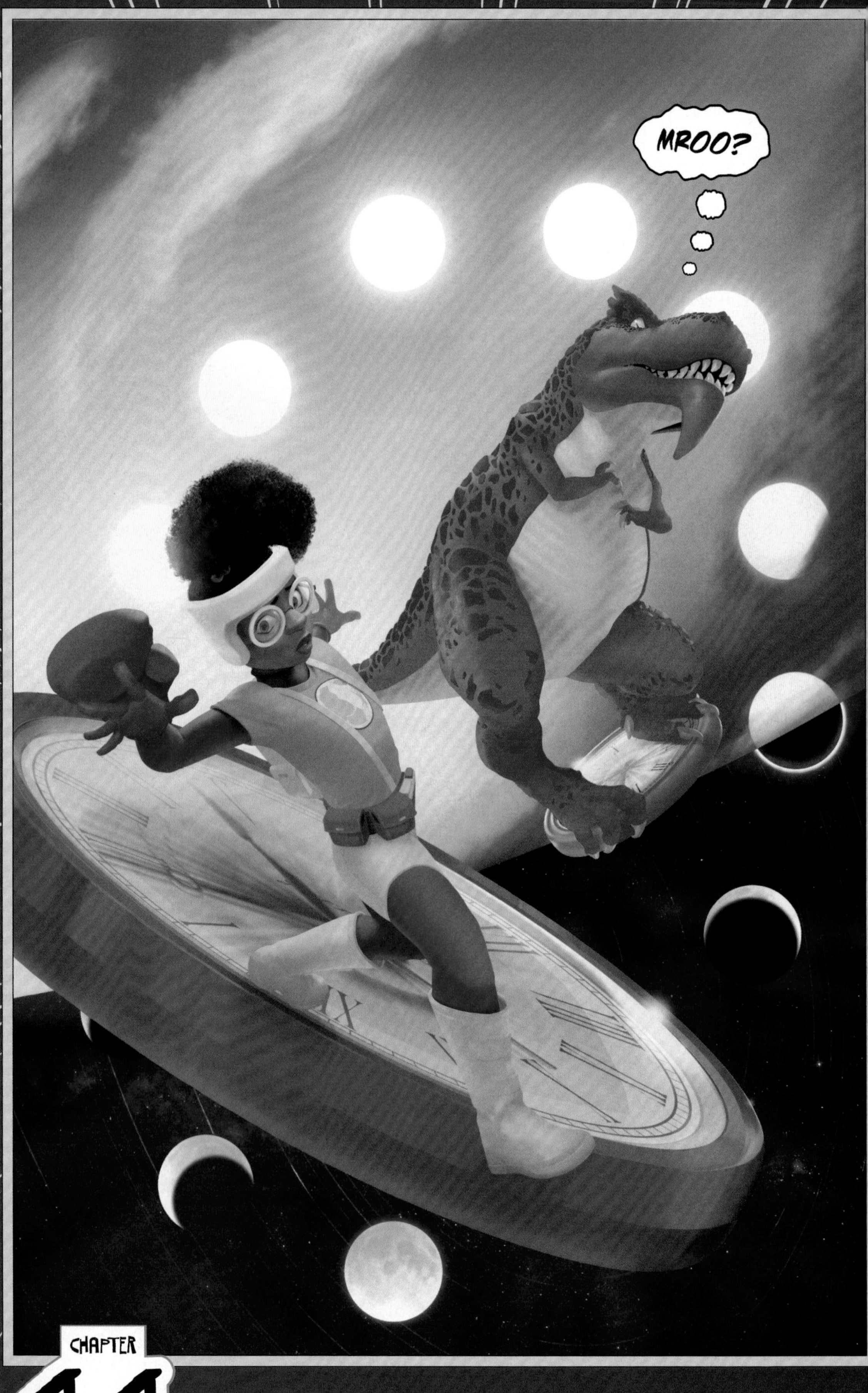
MROO?

CHAPTER 44

"YOUR PLACE IN THE WORLD"

YOUR PLACE IN THE WORLD

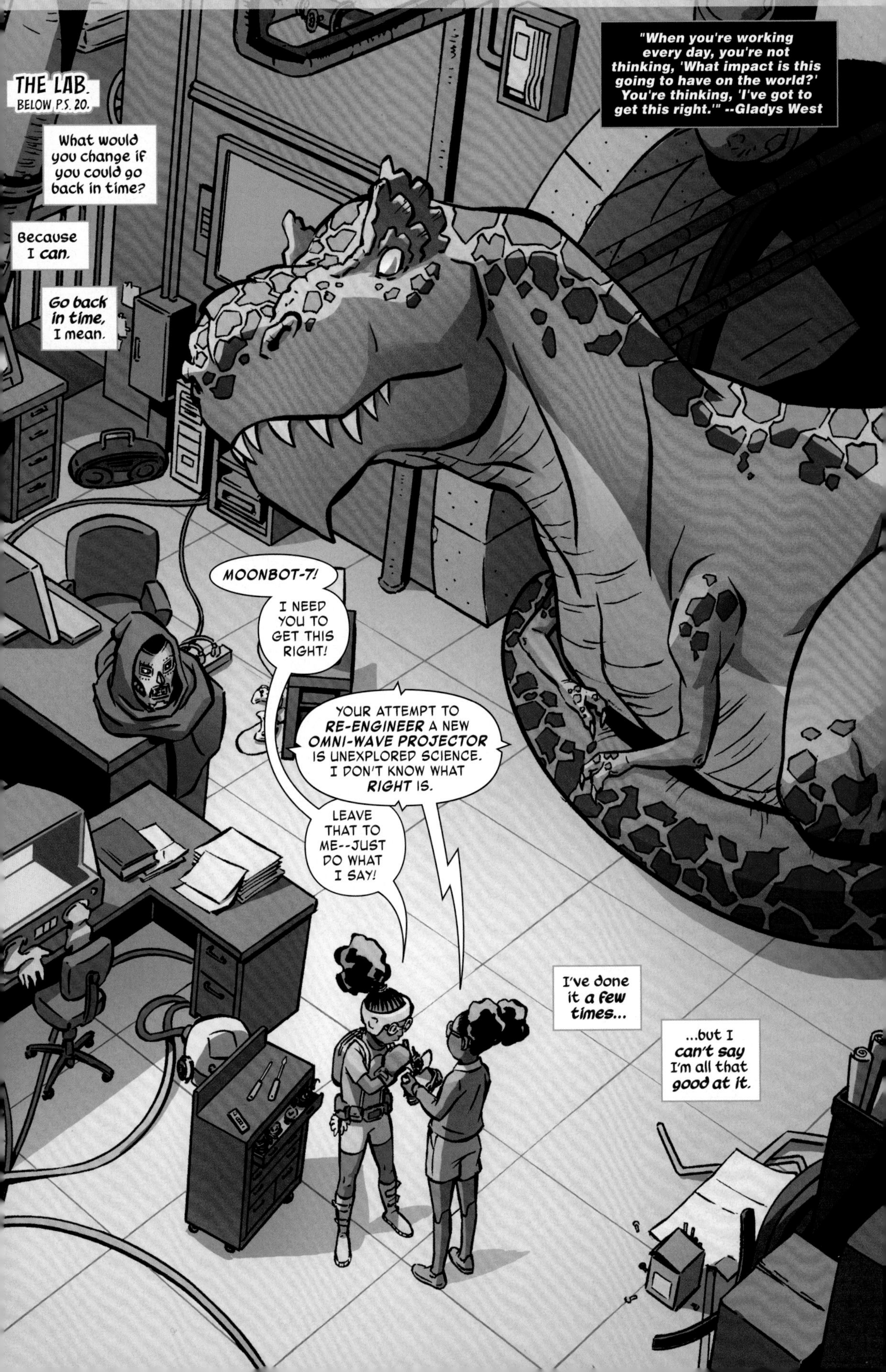

THE LAB.
BELOW P.S. 20.
"When you're working every day, you're not thinking, 'What impact is this going to have on the world?' You're thinking, 'I've got to get this right.'" --Gladys West
What would you change if you could go back in time?
Because I can.
Go back in time, I mean.
MOONBOT-7!
I NEED YOU TO GET THIS RIGHT!
YOUR ATTEMPT TO RE-ENGINEER A NEW OMNI-WAVE PROJECTOR IS UNEXPLORED SCIENCE. I DON'T KNOW WHAT RIGHT IS.
LEAVE THAT TO ME--JUST DO WHAT I SAY!
I've done it a few times...
...but I can't say I'm all that good at it.

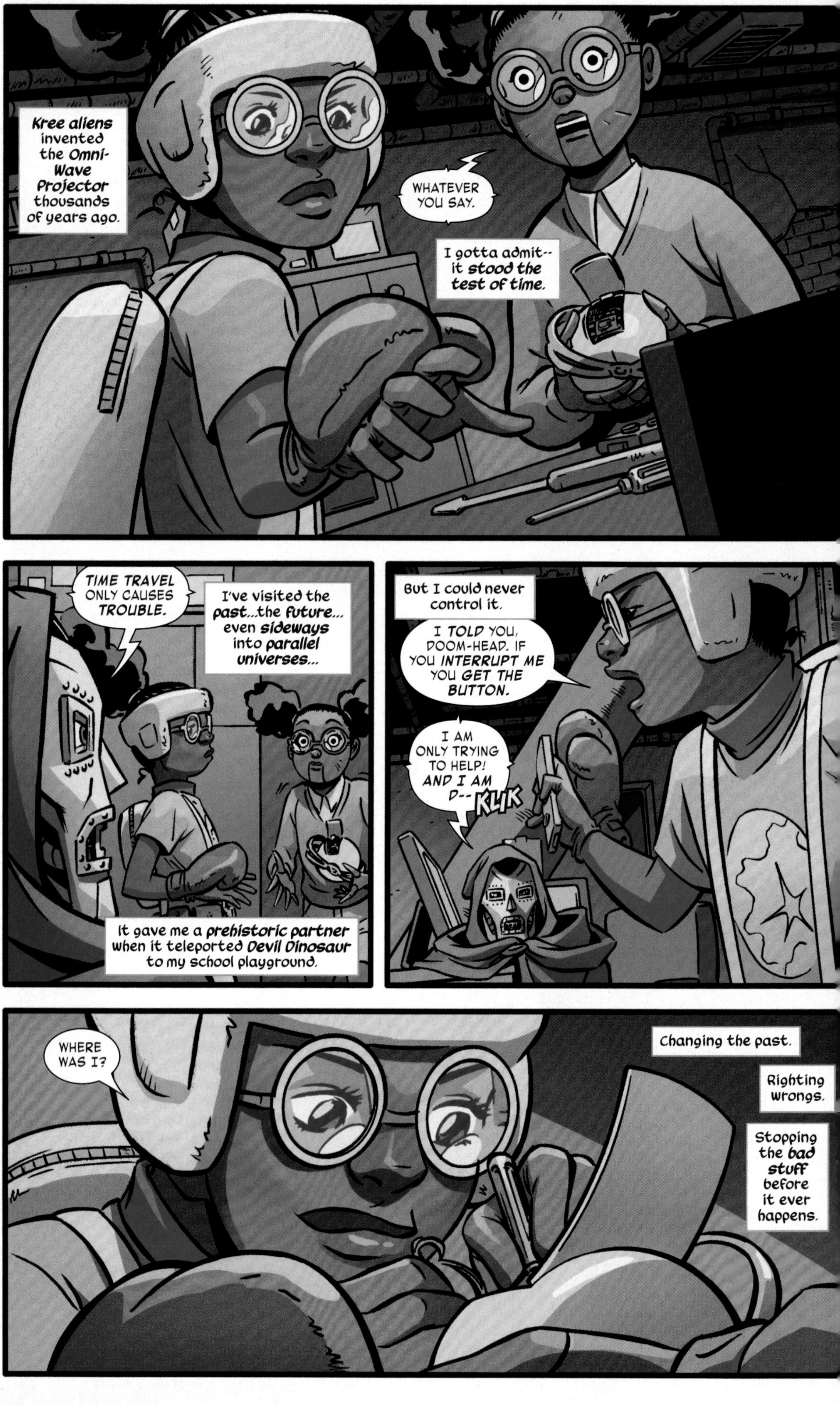

Kree aliens invented the Omni-Wave Projector thousands of years ago.
WHATEVER YOU SAY.
I gotta admit-- it stood the test of time.
TIME TRAVEL ONLY CAUSES TROUBLE.
I've visited the past...the future... even sideways into parallel universes...
It gave me a prehistoric partner when it teleported Devil Dinosaur to my school playground.
But I could never control it.
I TOLD YOU, DOOM-HEAD. IF YOU INTERRUPT ME YOU GET THE BUTTON.
I AM ONLY TRYING TO HELP! AND I AM D--
KLIK
WHERE WAS I?
Changing the past.
Righting wrongs.
Stopping the bad stuff before it ever happens.

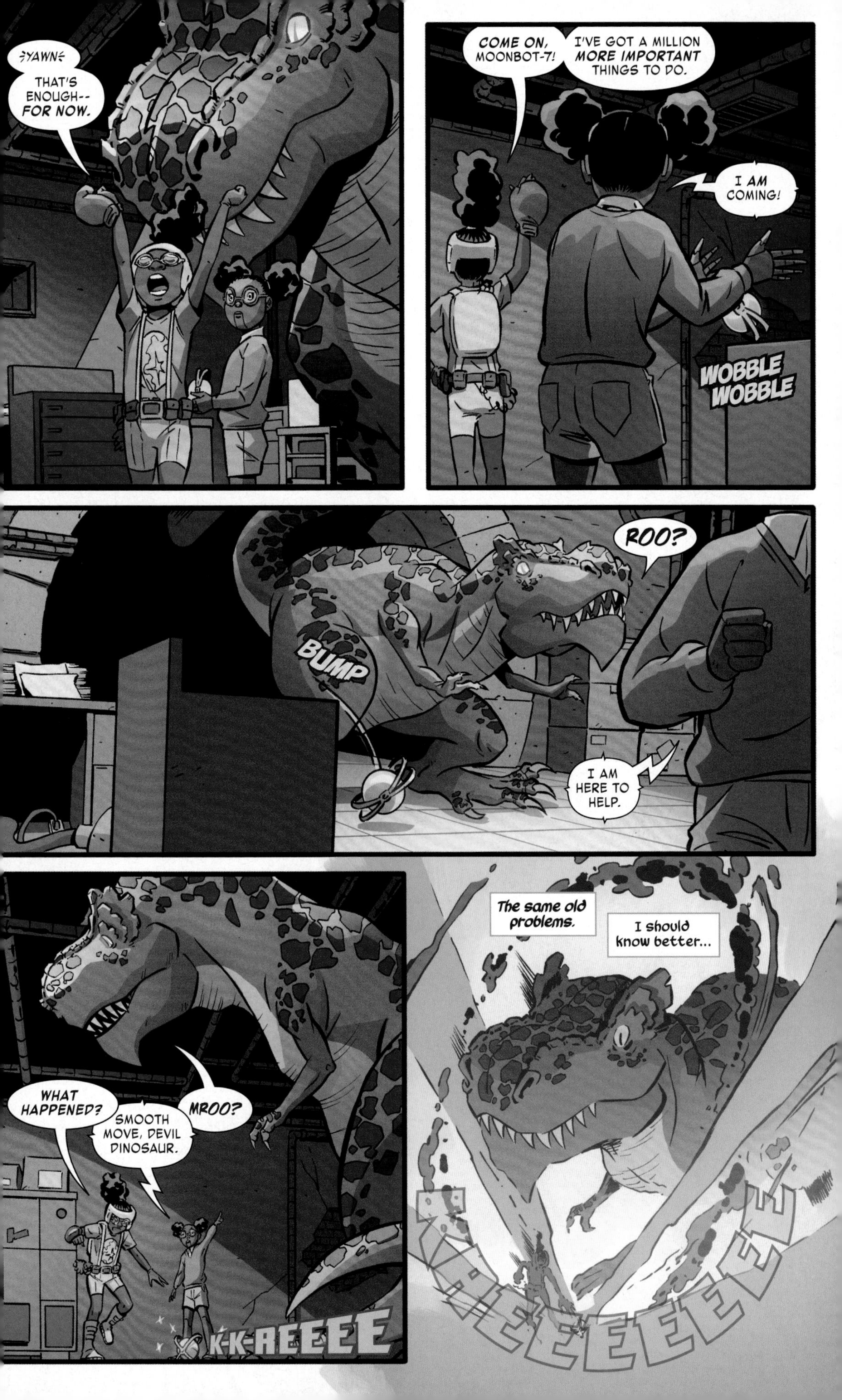

YAWN
THAT'S ENOUGH-- FOR NOW.
COME ON, MOONBOT-7!
I'VE GOT A MILLION MORE IMPORTANT THINGS TO DO.
I AM COMING!
WOBBLE WOBBLE
ROO?
BUMP
I AM HERE TO HELP.
WHAT HAPPENED?
SMOOTH MOVE, DEVIL DINOSAUR.
MROO?
K-K-REEEE
The same old problems.
I should know better...

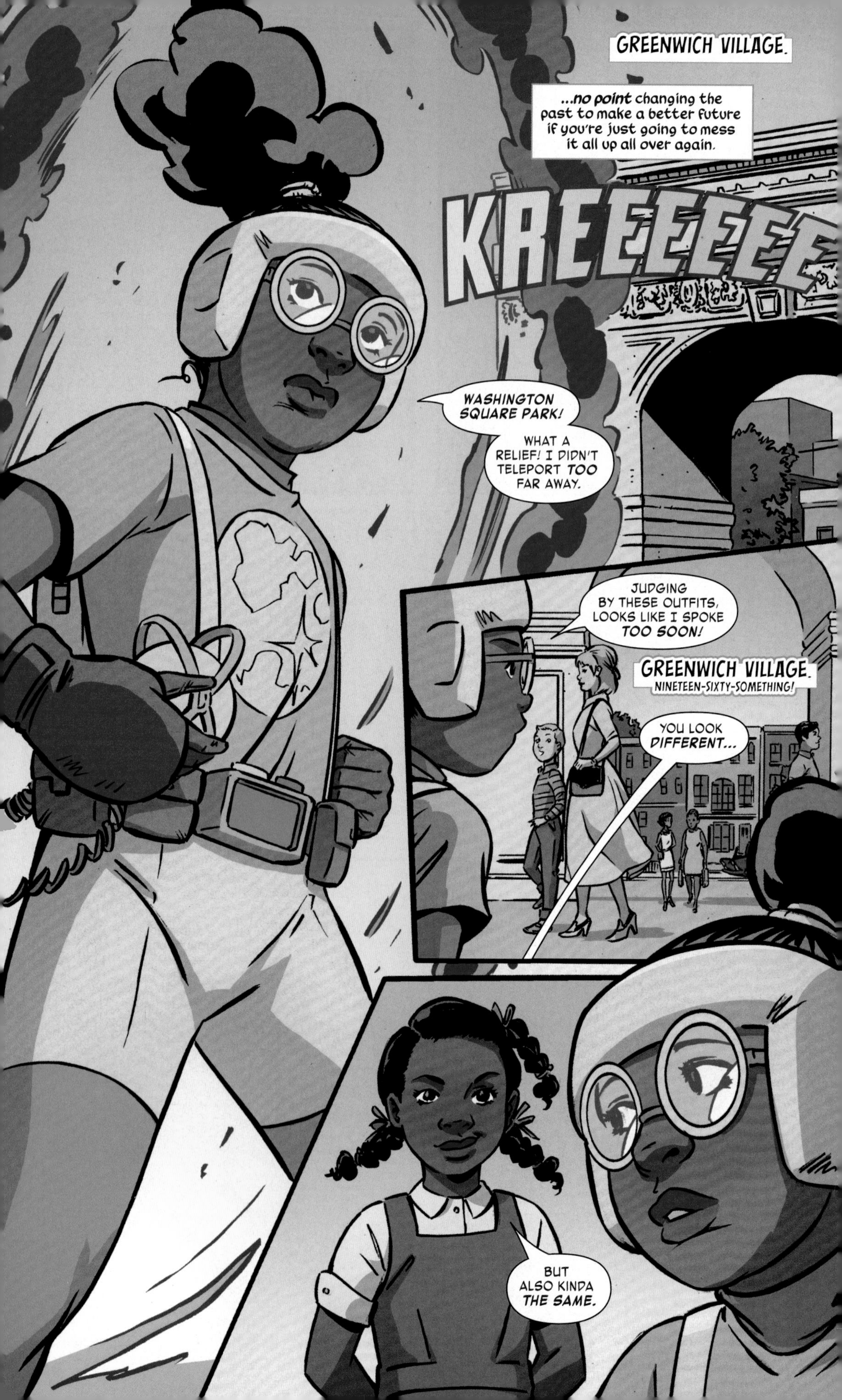
GREENWICH VILLAGE.
...no point changing the past to make a better future if you're just going to mess it all up all over again.
KREEEEEE
WASHINGTON SQUARE PARK!
WHAT A RELIEF! I DIDN'T TELEPORT TOO FAR AWAY.
JUDGING BY THESE OUTFITS, LOOKS LIKE I SPOKE TOO SOON!
GREENWICH VILLAGE. NINETEEN-SIXTY-SOMETHING!
YOU LOOK DIFFERENT...
BUT ALSO KINDA THE SAME.

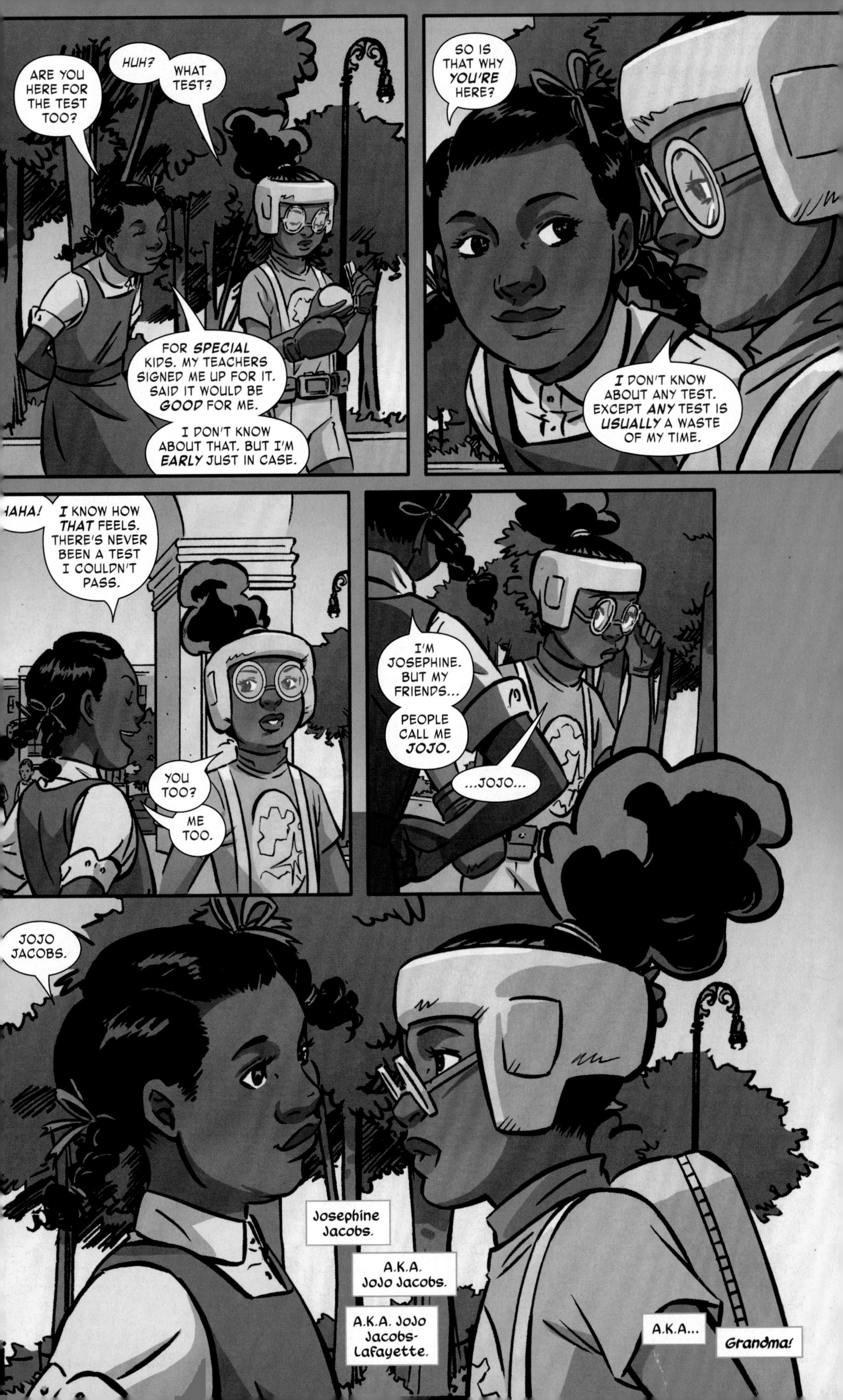
ARE YOU HERE FOR THE TEST TOO?
HUH?
WHAT TEST?
FOR SPECIAL KIDS. MY TEACHERS SIGNED ME UP FOR IT. SAID IT WOULD BE GOOD FOR ME.
I DON'T KNOW ABOUT THAT. BUT I'M EARLY JUST IN CASE.
SO IS THAT WHY YOU'RE HERE?
I DON'T KNOW ABOUT ANY TEST. EXCEPT ANY TEST IS USUALLY A WASTE OF MY TIME.
HAHA!
I KNOW HOW THAT FEELS. THERE'S NEVER BEEN A TEST I COULDN'T PASS.
YOU TOO?
ME TOO.
I'M JOSEPHINE. BUT MY FRIENDS...
PEOPLE CALL ME JOJO.
...JOJO...
JOJO JACOBS.
Josephine Jacobs.
A.K.A. JoJo Jacobs.
A.K.A. JoJo Jacobs-Lafayette.
A.K.A...
Grandma!

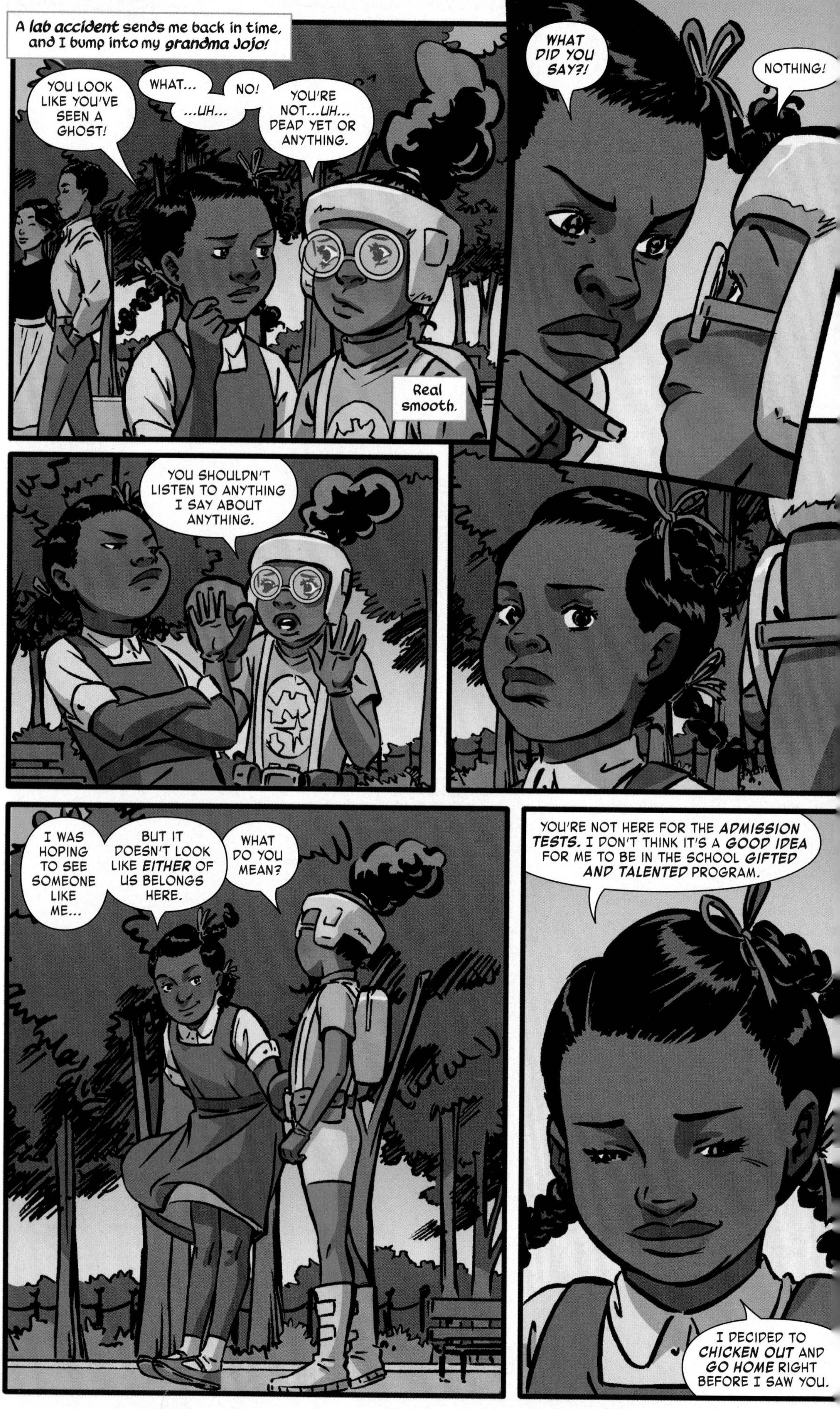

A *lab accident* sends me back in time, and I bump into my *grandma Jojo!*
YOU LOOK LIKE YOU'VE SEEN A GHOST!
WHAT...
...UH...
NO!
YOU'RE NOT...UH... DEAD YET OR ANYTHING.
Real smooth.
WHAT DID YOU SAY?!
NOTHING!
YOU SHOULDN'T LISTEN TO ANYTHING I SAY ABOUT ANYTHING.
I WAS HOPING TO SEE SOMEONE LIKE ME...
BUT IT DOESN'T LOOK LIKE *EITHER* OF US BELONGS HERE.
WHAT DO YOU MEAN?
YOU'RE NOT HERE FOR THE *ADMISSION TESTS.* I DON'T THINK IT'S A *GOOD IDEA* FOR ME TO BE IN THE SCHOOL *GIFTED AND TALENTED* PROGRAM.
I DECIDED TO *CHICKEN OUT* AND *GO HOME* RIGHT BEFORE I SAW YOU.

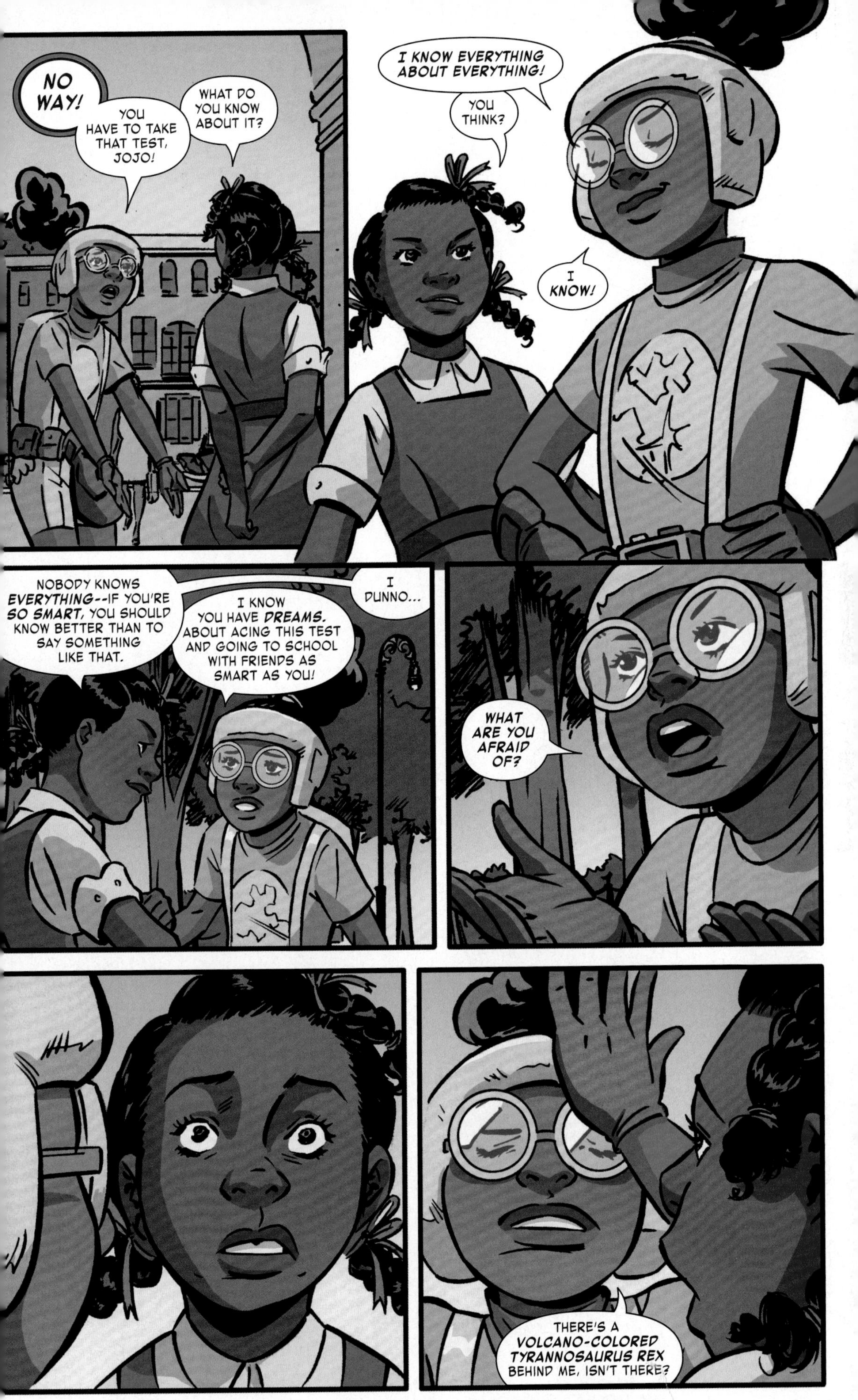
NO WAY!
YOU HAVE TO TAKE THAT TEST, JOJO!
WHAT DO YOU KNOW ABOUT IT?
I KNOW EVERYTHING ABOUT EVERYTHING!
YOU THINK?
I KNOW!
NOBODY KNOWS EVERYTHING--IF YOU'RE SO SMART, YOU SHOULD KNOW BETTER THAN TO SAY SOMETHING LIKE THAT.
I DUNNO...
I KNOW YOU HAVE DREAMS. ABOUT ACING THIS TEST AND GOING TO SCHOOL WITH FRIENDS AS SMART AS YOU!
WHAT ARE YOU AFRAID OF?
THERE'S A VOLCANO-COLORED TYRANNOSAURUS REX BEHIND ME, ISN'T THERE?

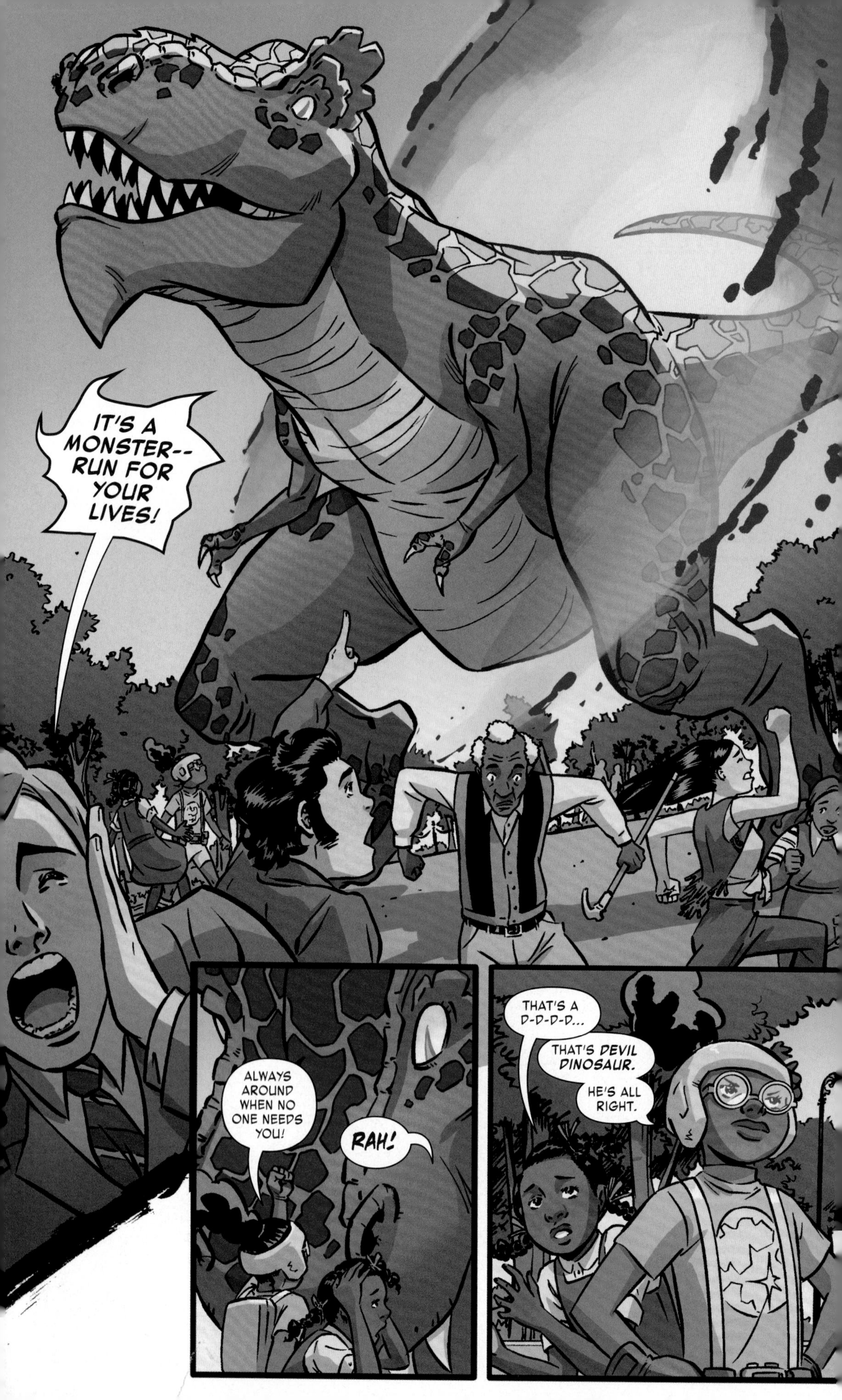
IT'S A MONSTER-- RUN FOR YOUR LIVES!
ALWAYS AROUND WHEN NO ONE NEEDS YOU!
RAH!
THAT'S A D-D-D-D...
THAT'S DEVIL DINOSAUR.
HE'S ALL RIGHT.

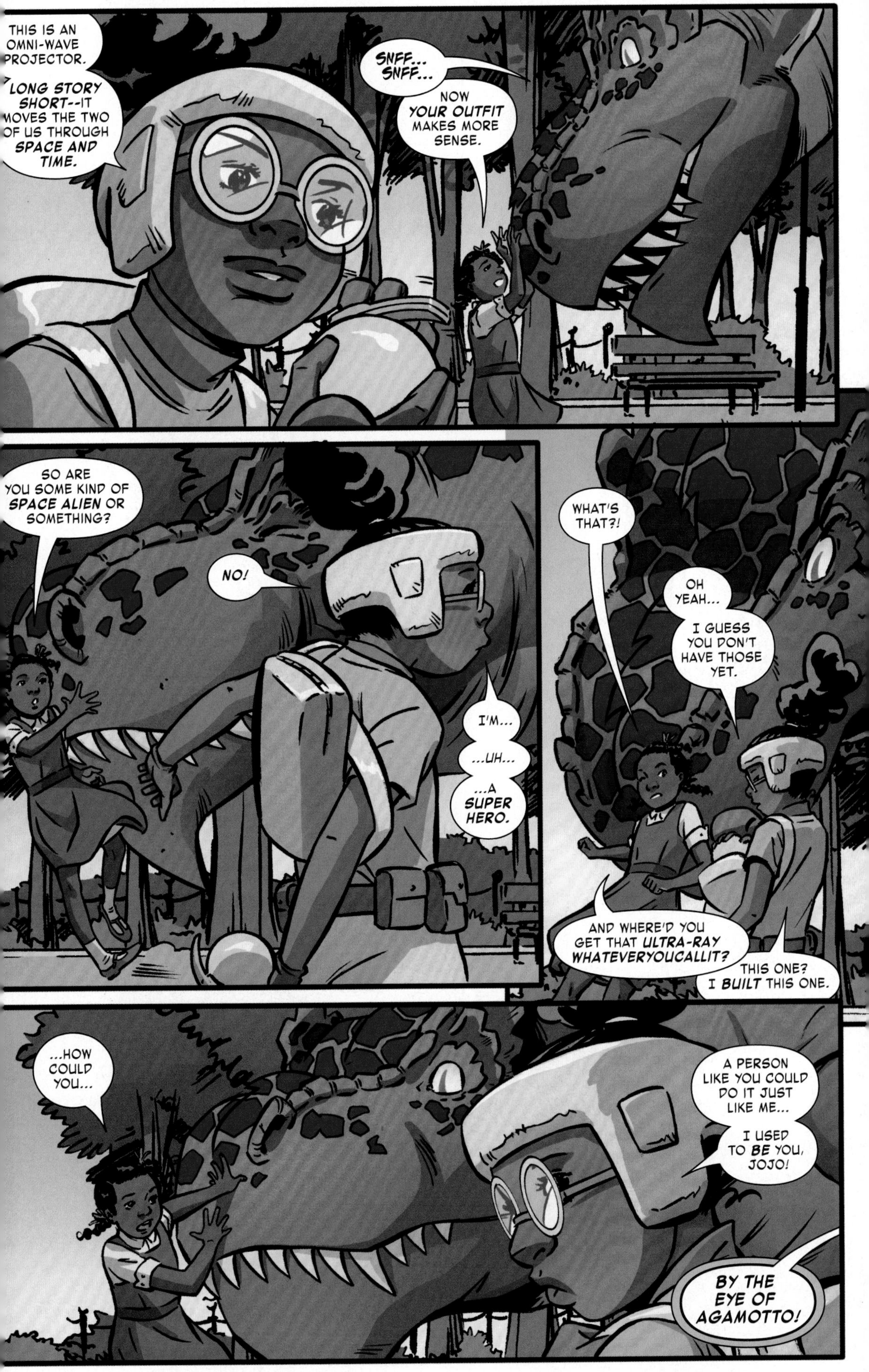
THIS IS AN OMNI-WAVE PROJECTOR.
LONG STORY SHORT--IT MOVES THE TWO OF US THROUGH SPACE AND TIME.
SNFF... SNFF...
NOW YOUR OUTFIT MAKES MORE SENSE.
SO ARE YOU SOME KIND OF SPACE ALIEN OR SOMETHING?
NO!
I'M...
...UH...
...A SUPER HERO.
WHAT'S THAT?!
OH YEAH...
I GUESS YOU DON'T HAVE THOSE YET.
AND WHERE'D YOU GET THAT ULTRA-RAY WHATEVERYOUCALLIT?
THIS ONE? I BUILT THIS ONE.
...HOW COULD YOU...
A PERSON LIKE YOU COULD DO IT JUST LIKE ME...
I USED TO BE YOU, JOJO!
BY THE EYE OF AGAMOTTO!

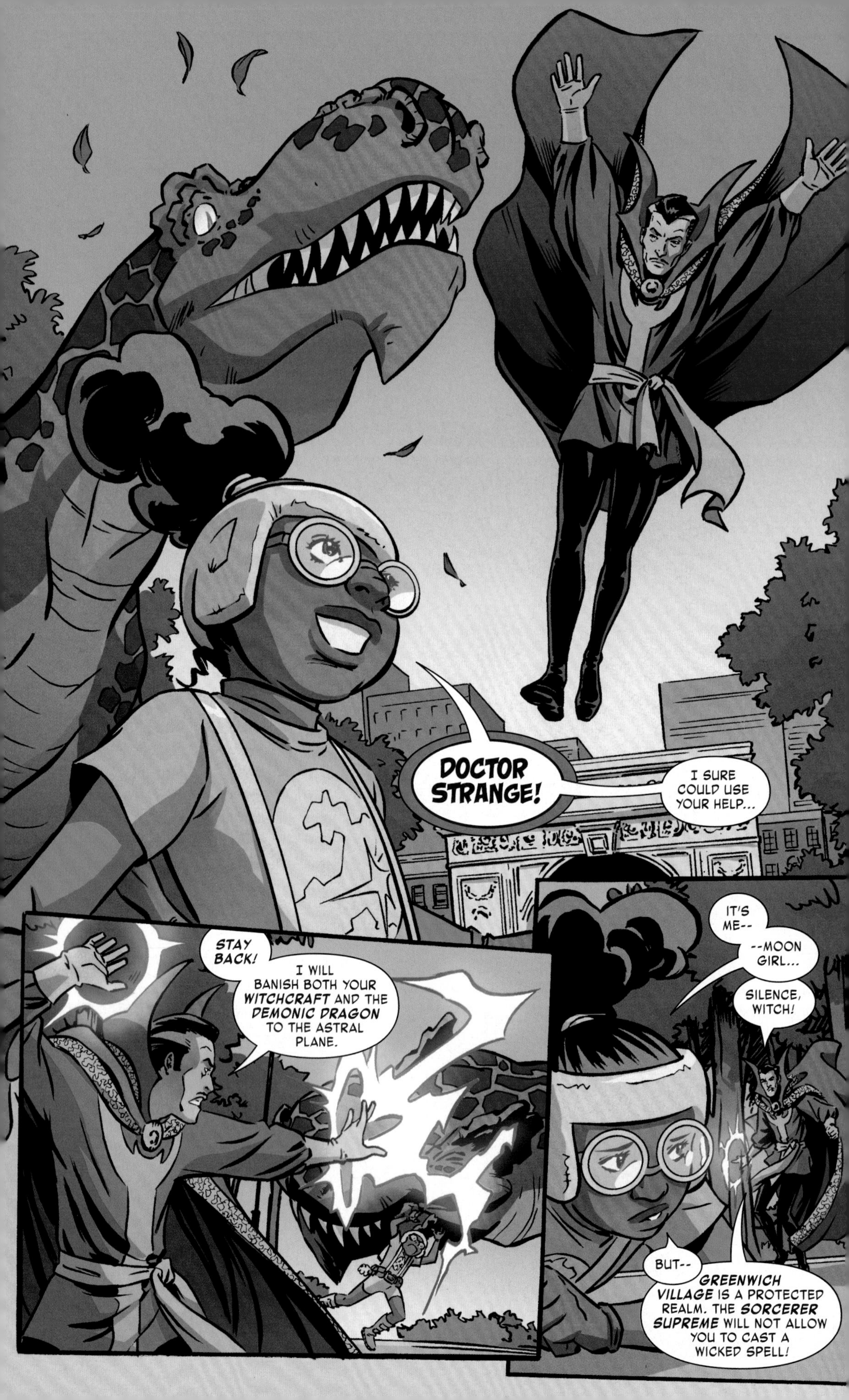
DOCTOR STRANGE!
I SURE COULD USE YOUR HELP...
STAY BACK!
I WILL BANISH BOTH YOUR WITCHCRAFT AND THE DEMONIC DRAGON TO THE ASTRAL PLANE.
IT'S ME--
--MOON GIRL...
SILENCE, WITCH!
BUT--
GREENWICH VILLAGE IS A PROTECTED REALM. THE SORCERER SUPREME WILL NOT ALLOW YOU TO CAST A WICKED SPELL!

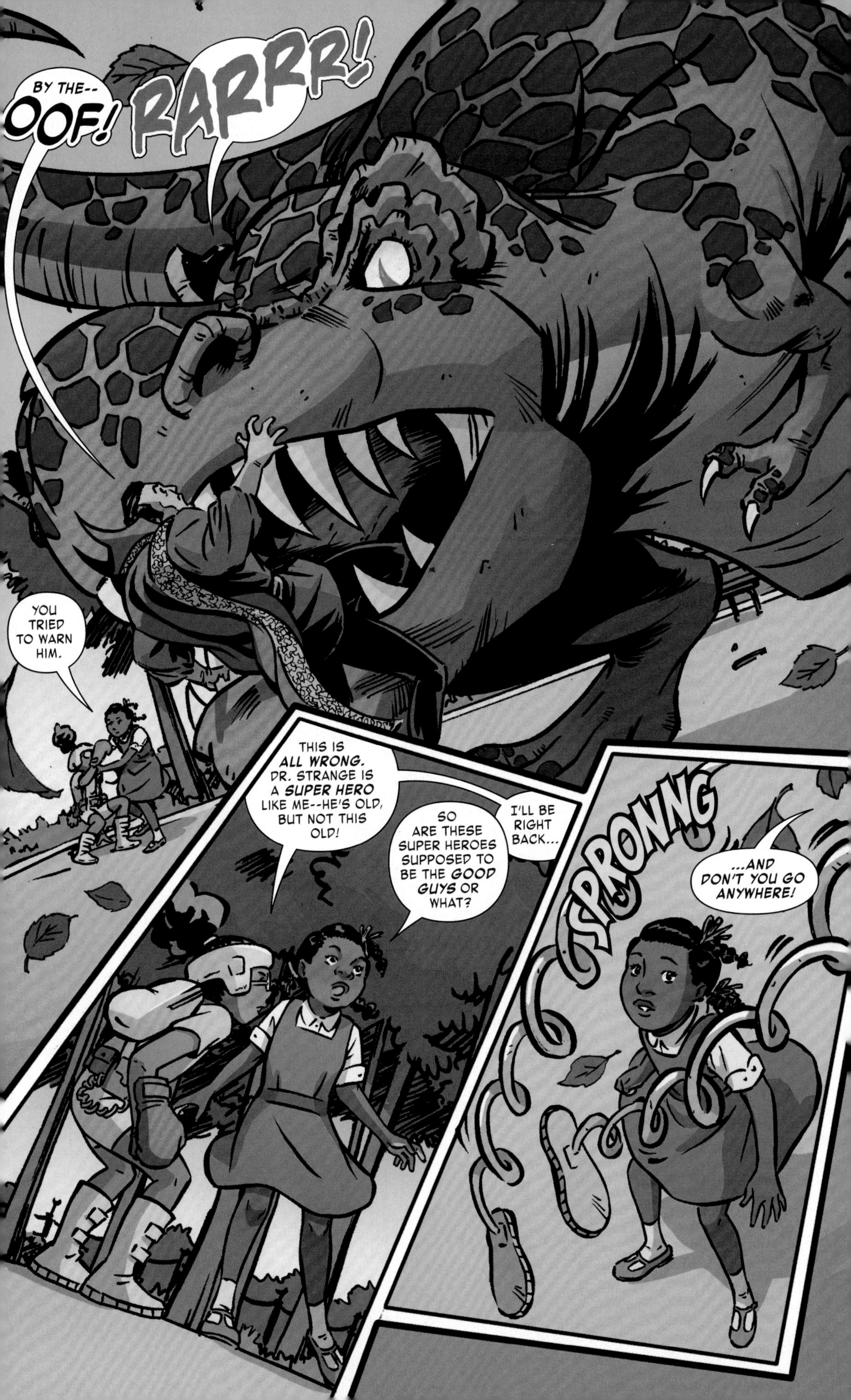
BY THE--
OOF!
RARRR!
YOU TRIED TO WARN HIM.
THIS IS ALL WRONG. DR. STRANGE IS A SUPER HERO LIKE ME--HE'S OLD, BUT NOT THIS OLD!
SO ARE THESE SUPER HEROES SUPPOSED TO BE THE GOOD GUYS OR WHAT?
I'LL BE RIGHT BACK...
SPRONNG
...AND DON'T YOU GO ANYWHERE!

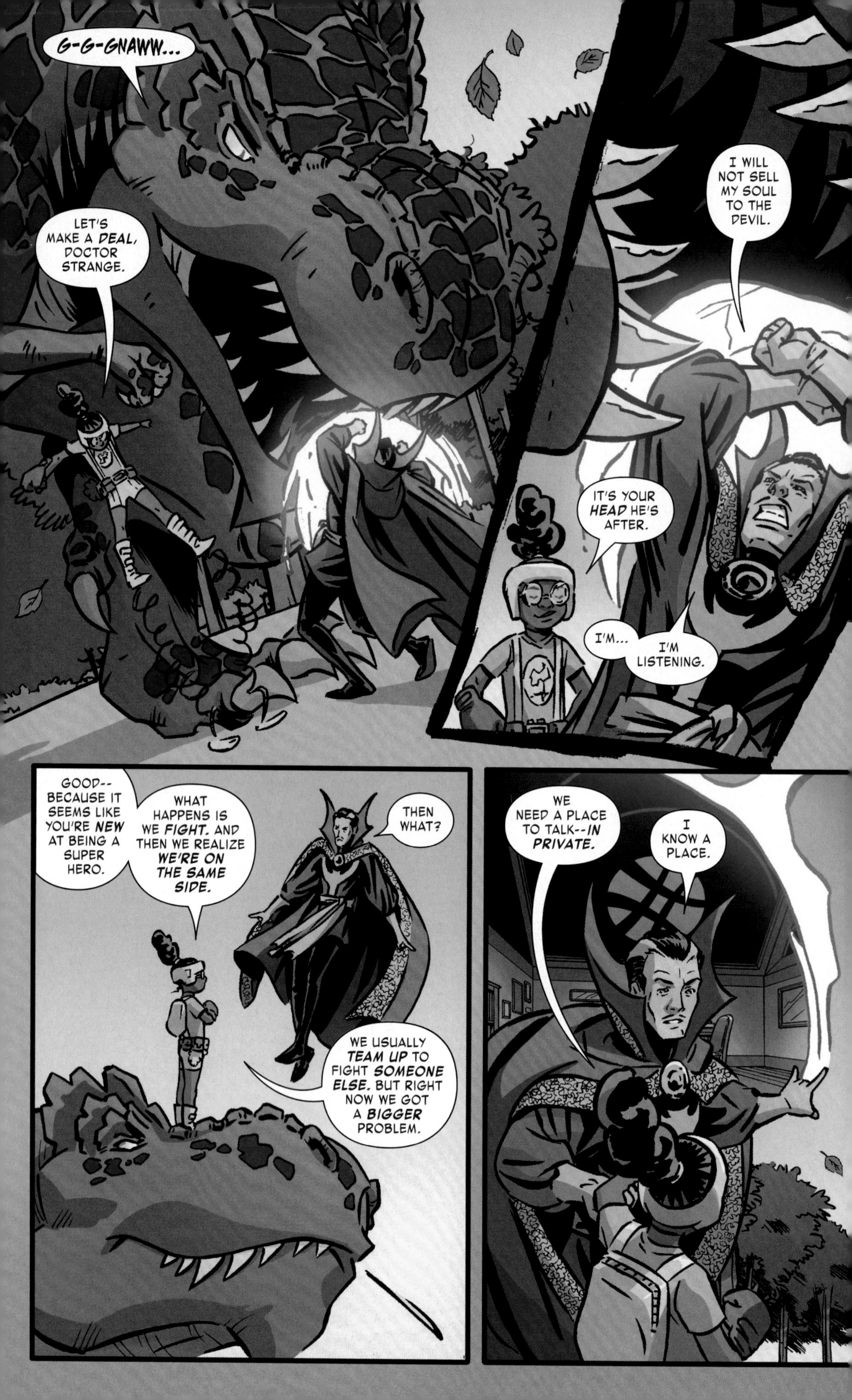
G-G-GNAWW...
LET'S MAKE A DEAL, DOCTOR STRANGE.
I WILL NOT SELL MY SOUL TO THE DEVIL.
IT'S YOUR HEAD HE'S AFTER.
I'M...
I'M LISTENING.
GOOD-- BECAUSE IT SEEMS LIKE YOU'RE NEW AT BEING A SUPER HERO.
WHAT HAPPENS IS WE FIGHT. AND THEN WE REALIZE WE'RE ON THE SAME SIDE.
THEN WHAT?
WE USUALLY TEAM UP TO FIGHT SOMEONE ELSE. BUT RIGHT NOW WE GOT A BIGGER PROBLEM.
WE NEED A PLACE TO TALK--IN PRIVATE.
I KNOW A PLACE.

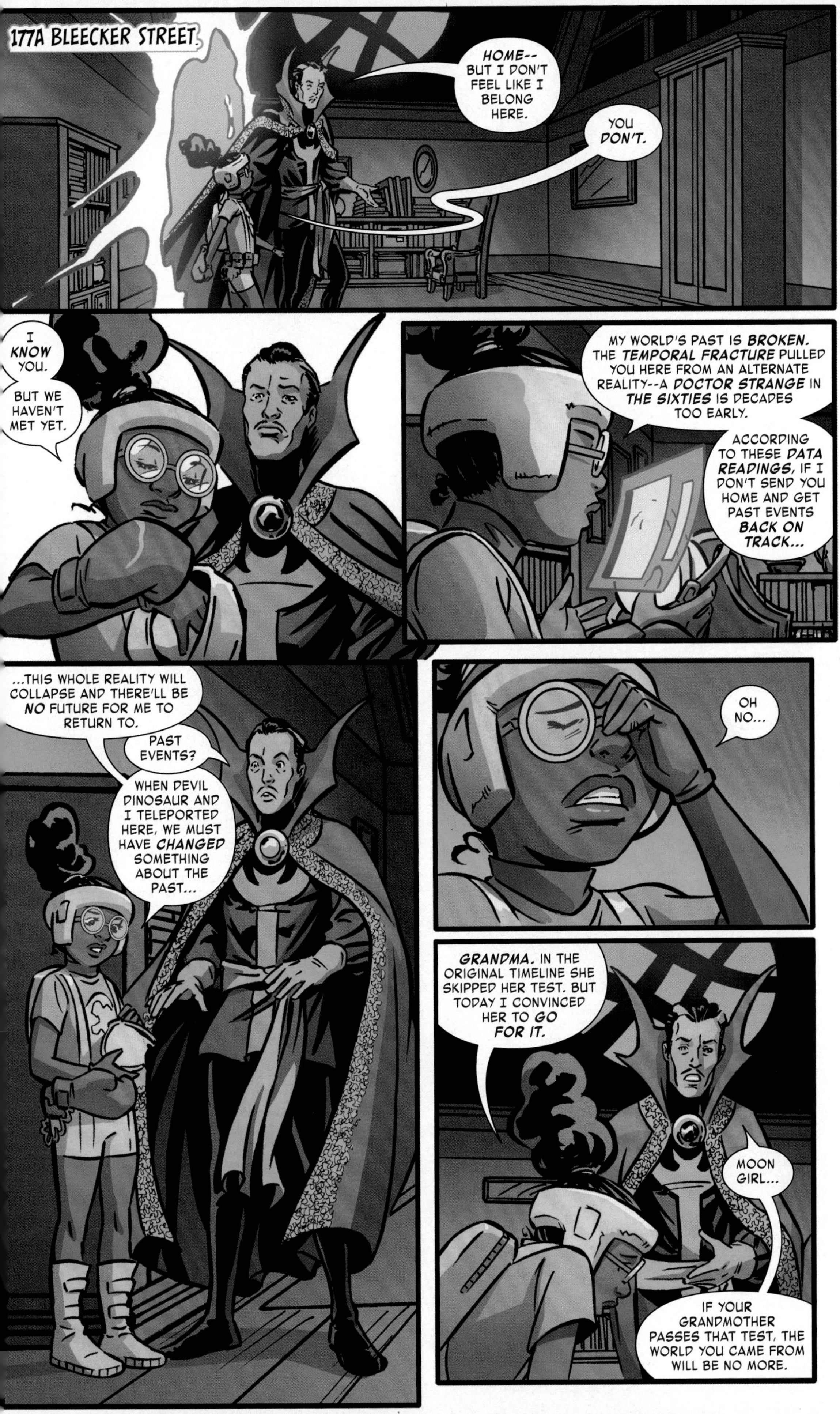
177A BLEECKER STREET.
HOME-- BUT I DON'T FEEL LIKE I BELONG HERE.
YOU DON'T.
I KNOW YOU.
BUT WE HAVEN'T MET YET.
MY WORLD'S PAST IS BROKEN. THE TEMPORAL FRACTURE PULLED YOU HERE FROM AN ALTERNATE REALITY--A DOCTOR STRANGE IN THE SIXTIES IS DECADES TOO EARLY.
ACCORDING TO THESE DATA READINGS, IF I DON'T SEND YOU HOME AND GET PAST EVENTS BACK ON TRACK...
...THIS WHOLE REALITY WILL COLLAPSE AND THERE'LL BE NO FUTURE FOR ME TO RETURN TO.
PAST EVENTS?
WHEN DEVIL DINOSAUR AND I TELEPORTED HERE, WE MUST HAVE CHANGED SOMETHING ABOUT THE PAST...
OH NO...
GRANDMA. IN THE ORIGINAL TIMELINE SHE SKIPPED HER TEST. BUT TODAY I CONVINCED HER TO GO FOR IT.
MOON GIRL...
IF YOUR GRANDMOTHER PASSES THAT TEST, THE WORLD YOU CAME FROM WILL BE NO MORE.

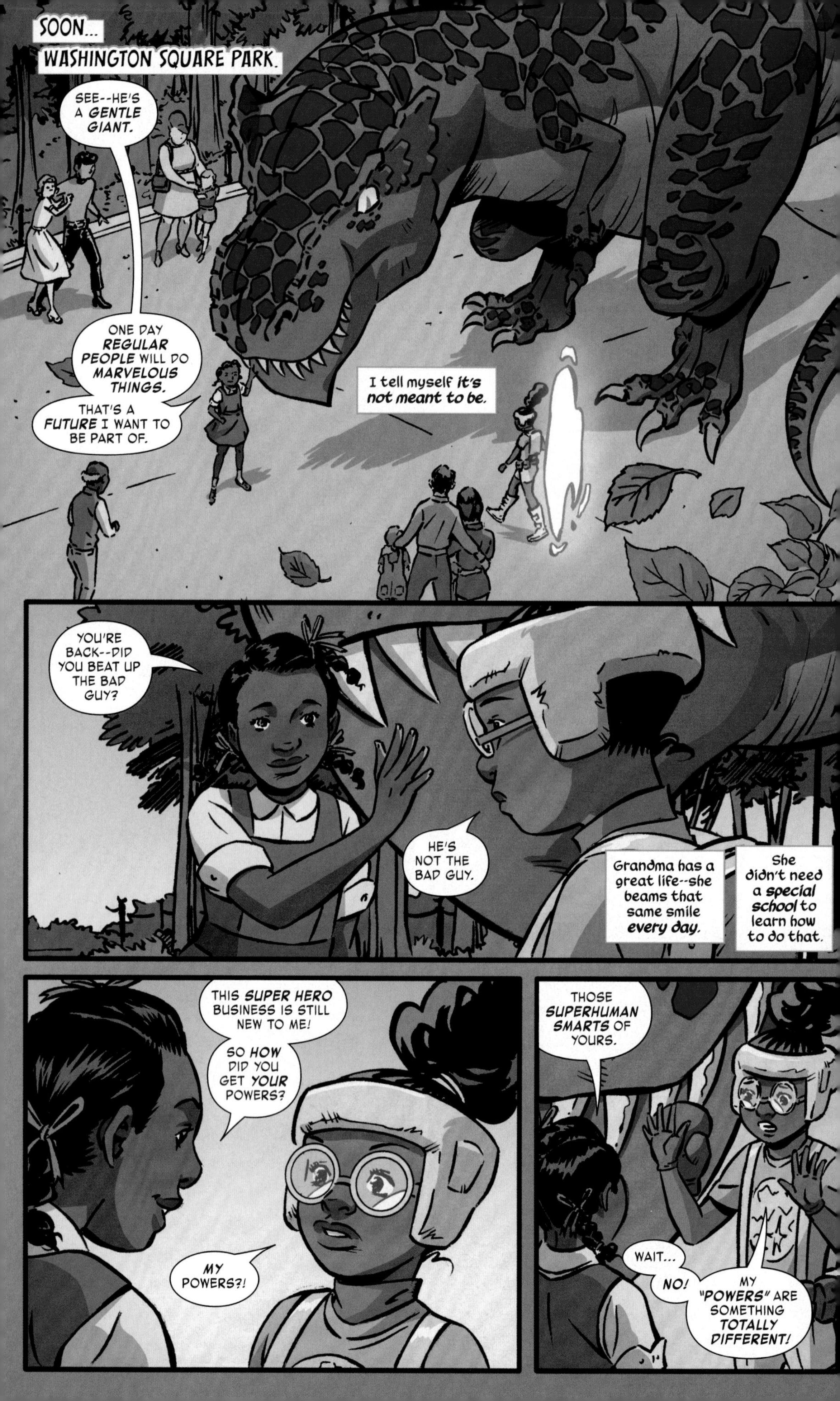
SOON...
WASHINGTON SQUARE PARK.
SEE--HE'S A GENTLE GIANT.
ONE DAY REGULAR PEOPLE WILL DO MARVELOUS THINGS.
THAT'S A FUTURE I WANT TO BE PART OF.
I tell myself it's not meant to be.
YOU'RE BACK--DID YOU BEAT UP THE BAD GUY?
HE'S NOT THE BAD GUY.
Grandma has a great life--she beams that same smile every day.
She didn't need a special school to learn how to do that.
THIS SUPER HERO BUSINESS IS STILL NEW TO ME!
SO HOW DID YOU GET YOUR POWERS?
MY POWERS?!
THOSE SUPERHUMAN SMARTS OF YOURS.
WAIT...
NO!
MY "POWERS" ARE SOMETHING TOTALLY DIFFERENT!

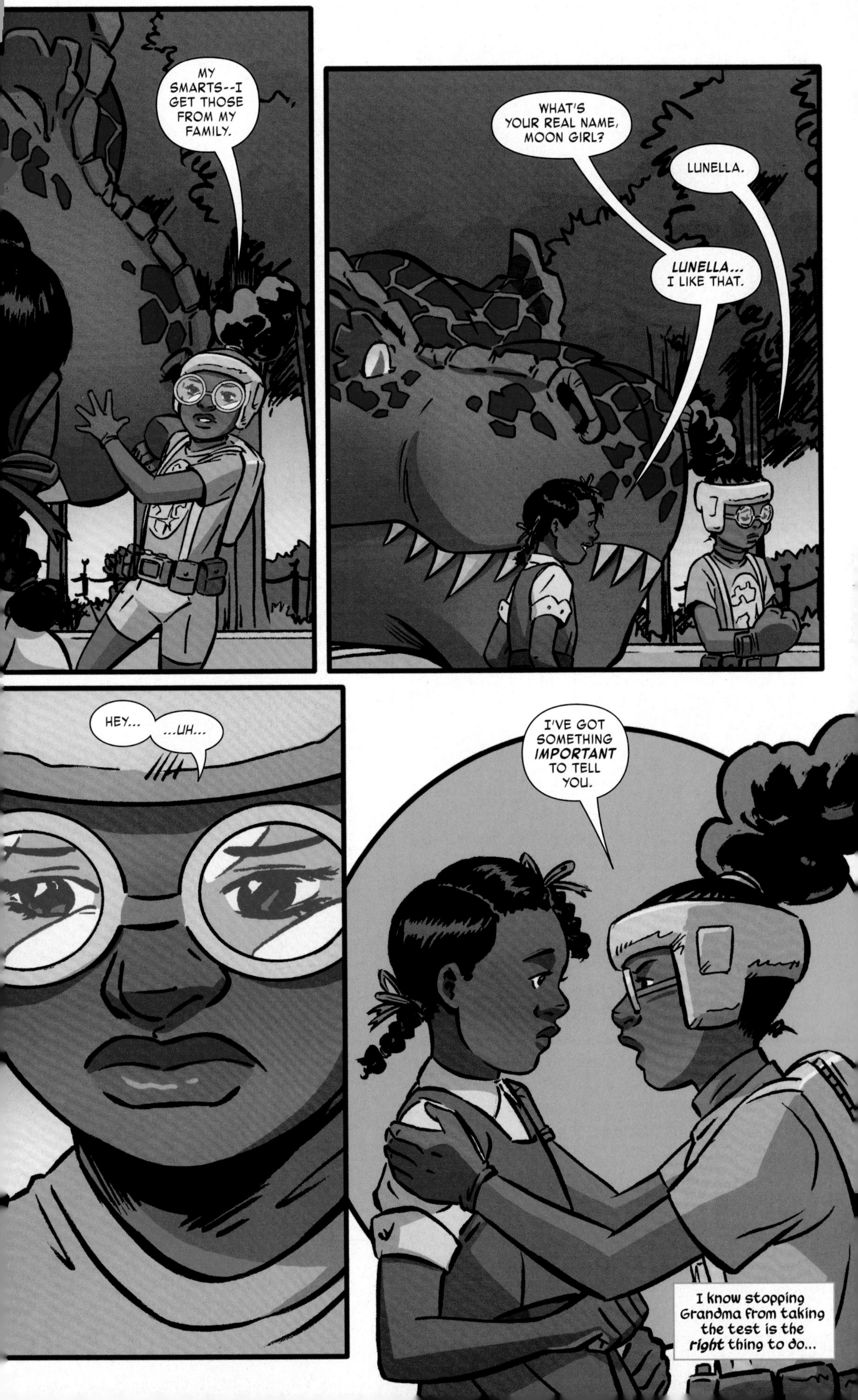
MY SMARTS--I GET THOSE FROM MY FAMILY.
WHAT'S YOUR REAL NAME, MOON GIRL?
LUNELLA.
LUNELLA... I LIKE THAT.
HEY...
...UH...
I'VE GOT SOMETHING IMPORTANT TO TELL YOU.
I know stopping Grandma from taking the test is the right thing to do...

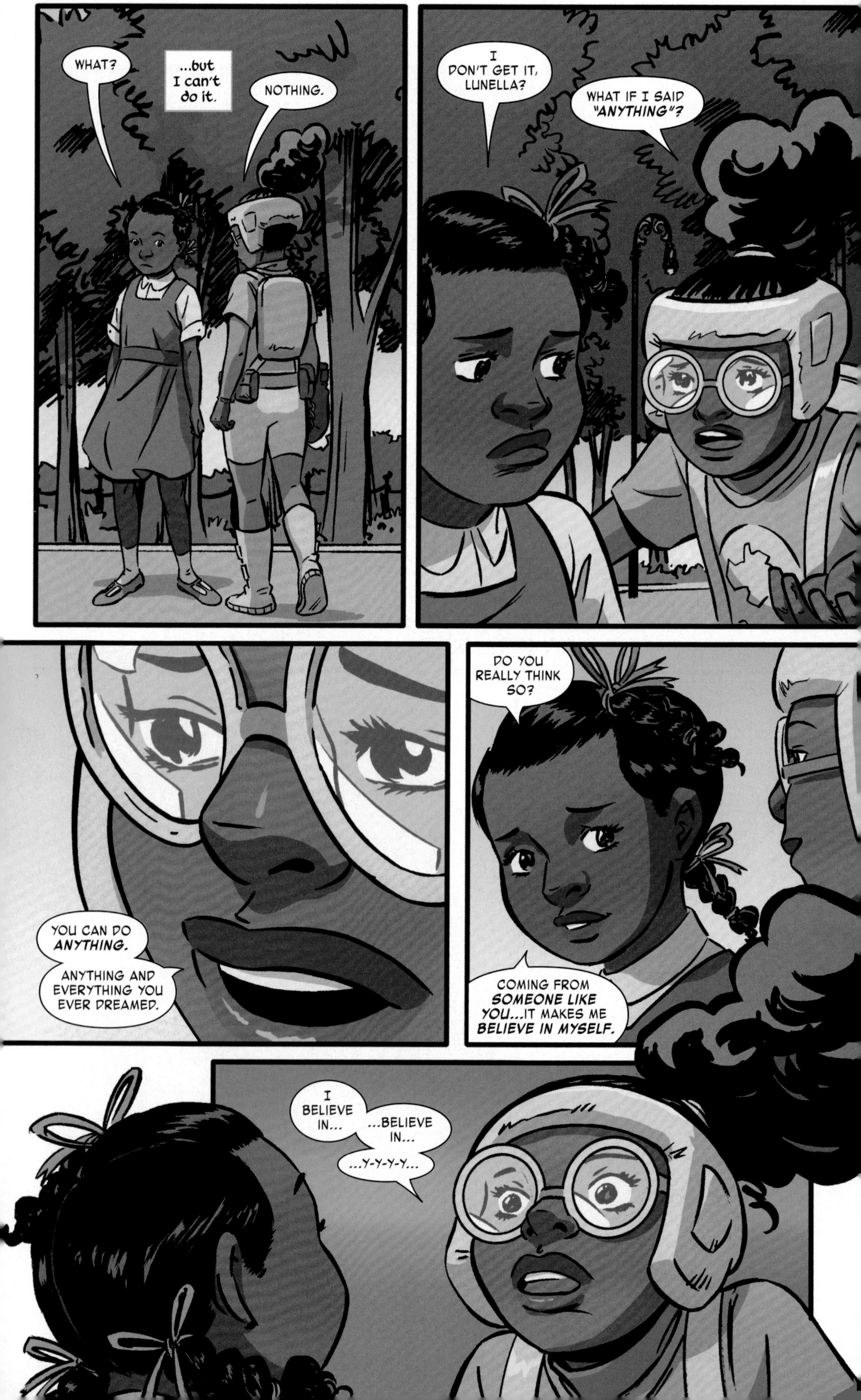
WHAT?
...but I can't do it.
NOTHING.
I DON'T GET IT, LUNELLA?
WHAT IF I SAID "ANYTHING"?
YOU CAN DO ANYTHING.
ANYTHING AND EVERYTHING YOU EVER DREAMED.
DO YOU REALLY THINK SO?
COMING FROM SOMEONE LIKE YOU...IT MAKES ME BELIEVE IN MYSELF.
I BELIEVE IN...
...BELIEVE IN...
...Y-Y-Y-Y...

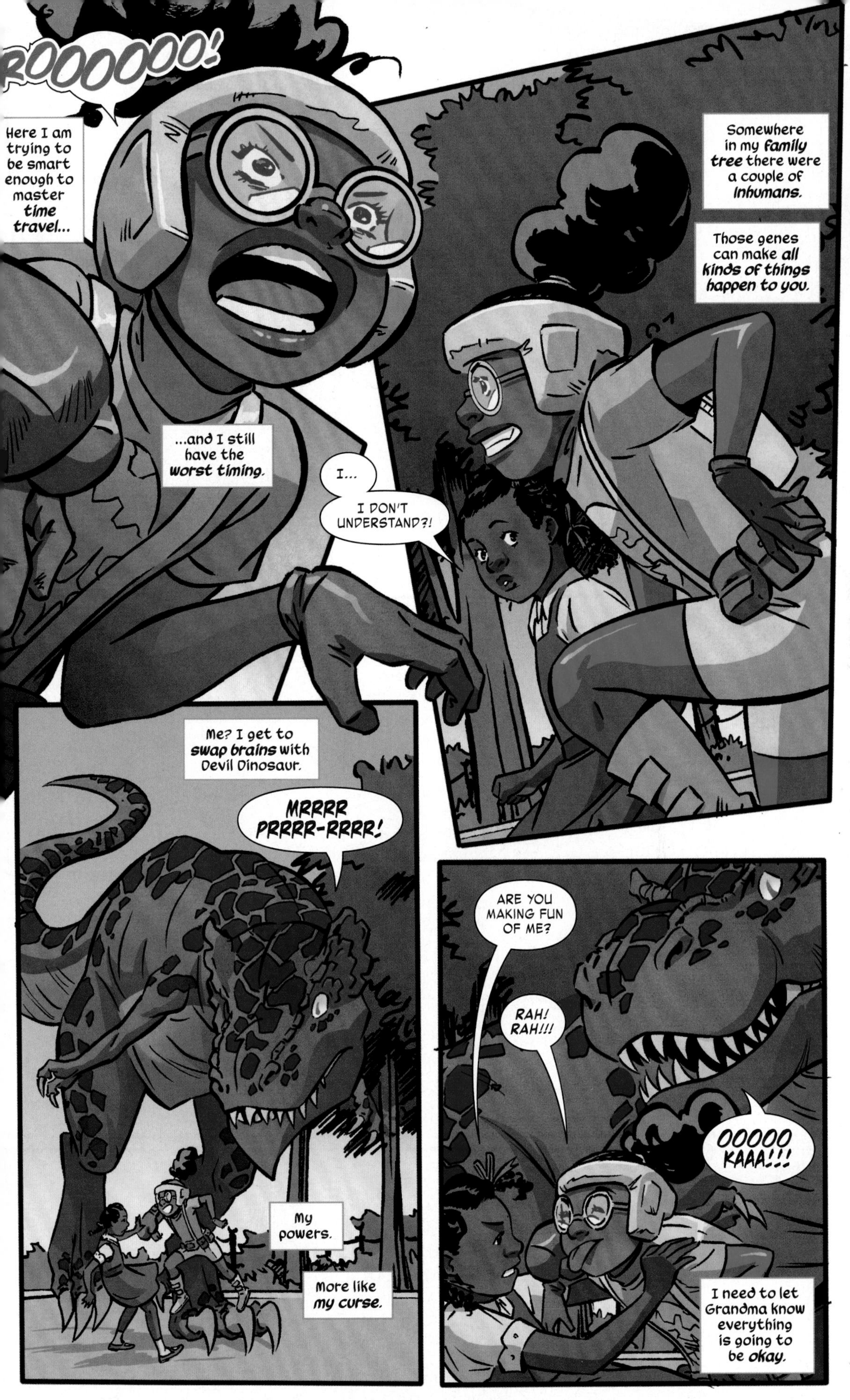
ROOOOOO!
Here I am trying to be smart enough to master *time travel...*
...and I still have the *worst timing.*
Somewhere in my *family tree* there were a couple of *Inhumans.*
Those genes can make *all kinds of things happen to you.*
I... I DON'T UNDERSTAND?!
Me? I get to *swap brains* with Devil Dinosaur.
MRRRR PRRRR-RRRR!
My powers.
More like *my curse.*
ARE YOU MAKING FUN OF ME?
RAH! RAH!!!
OOOOO KAAA!!!
I need to let Grandma know everything is going to be *okay.*

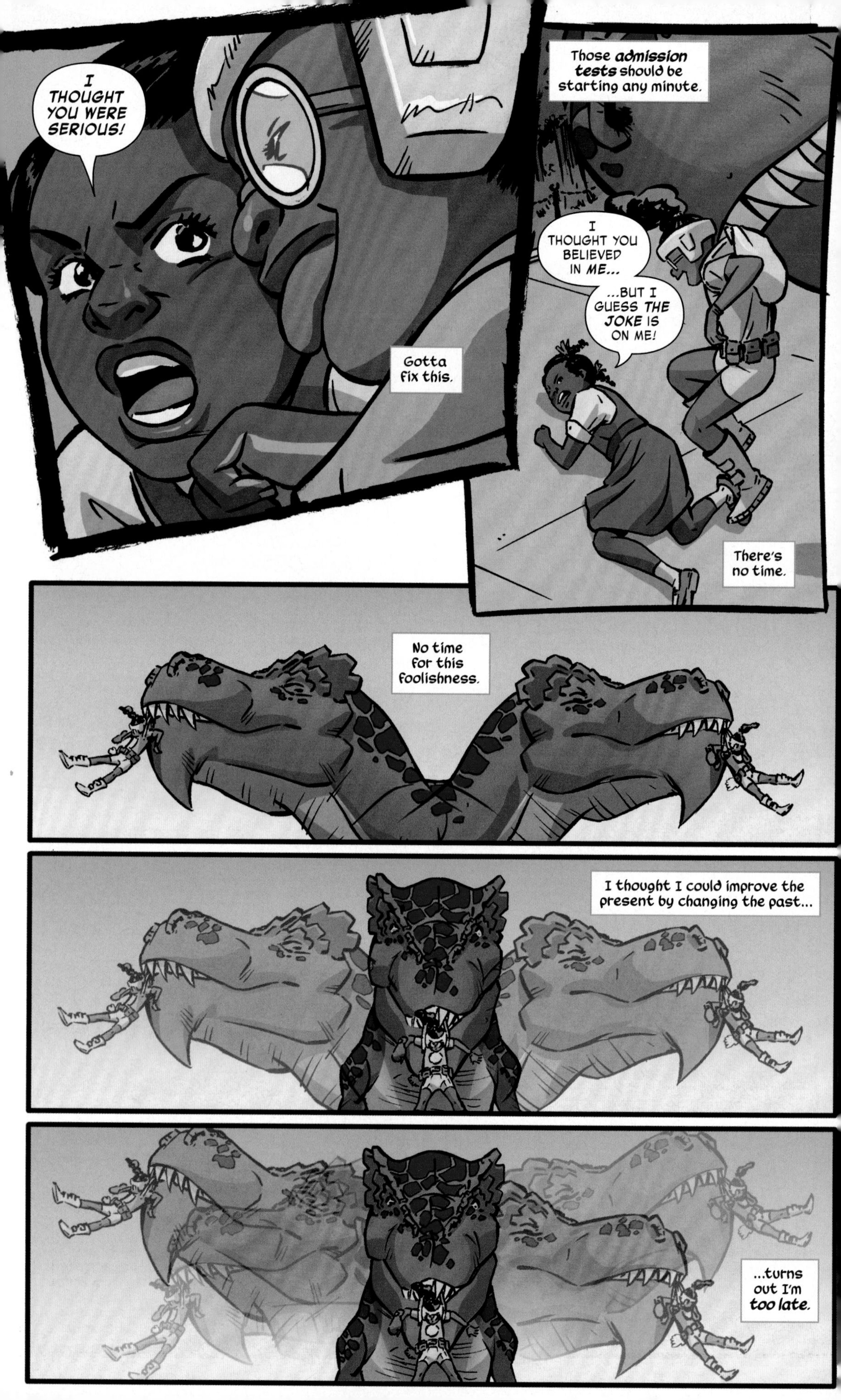

I THOUGHT YOU WERE SERIOUS!
Gotta fix this.
Those admission tests should be starting any minute.
I THOUGHT YOU BELIEVED IN ME...
...BUT I GUESS THE JOKE IS ON ME!
There's no time.
No time for this foolishness.
I thought I could improve the present by changing the past...
...turns out I'm too late.

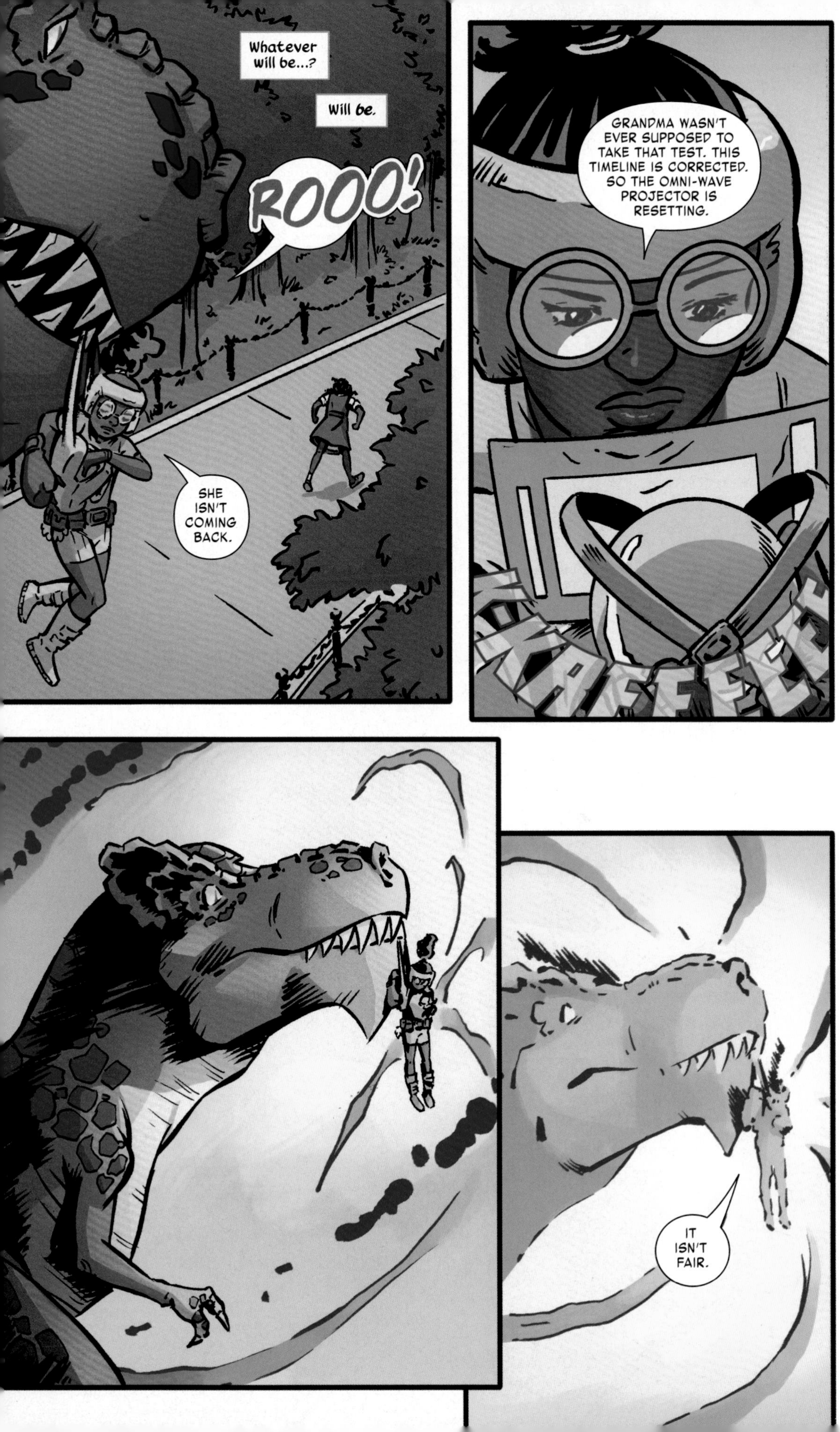
Whatever will be...?
Will be.
ROOO!
SHE ISN'T COMING BACK.
GRANDMA WASN'T EVER SUPPOSED TO TAKE THAT TEST. THIS TIMELINE IS CORRECTED. SO THE OMNI-WAVE PROJECTOR IS RESETTING.
IT ISN'T FAIR.

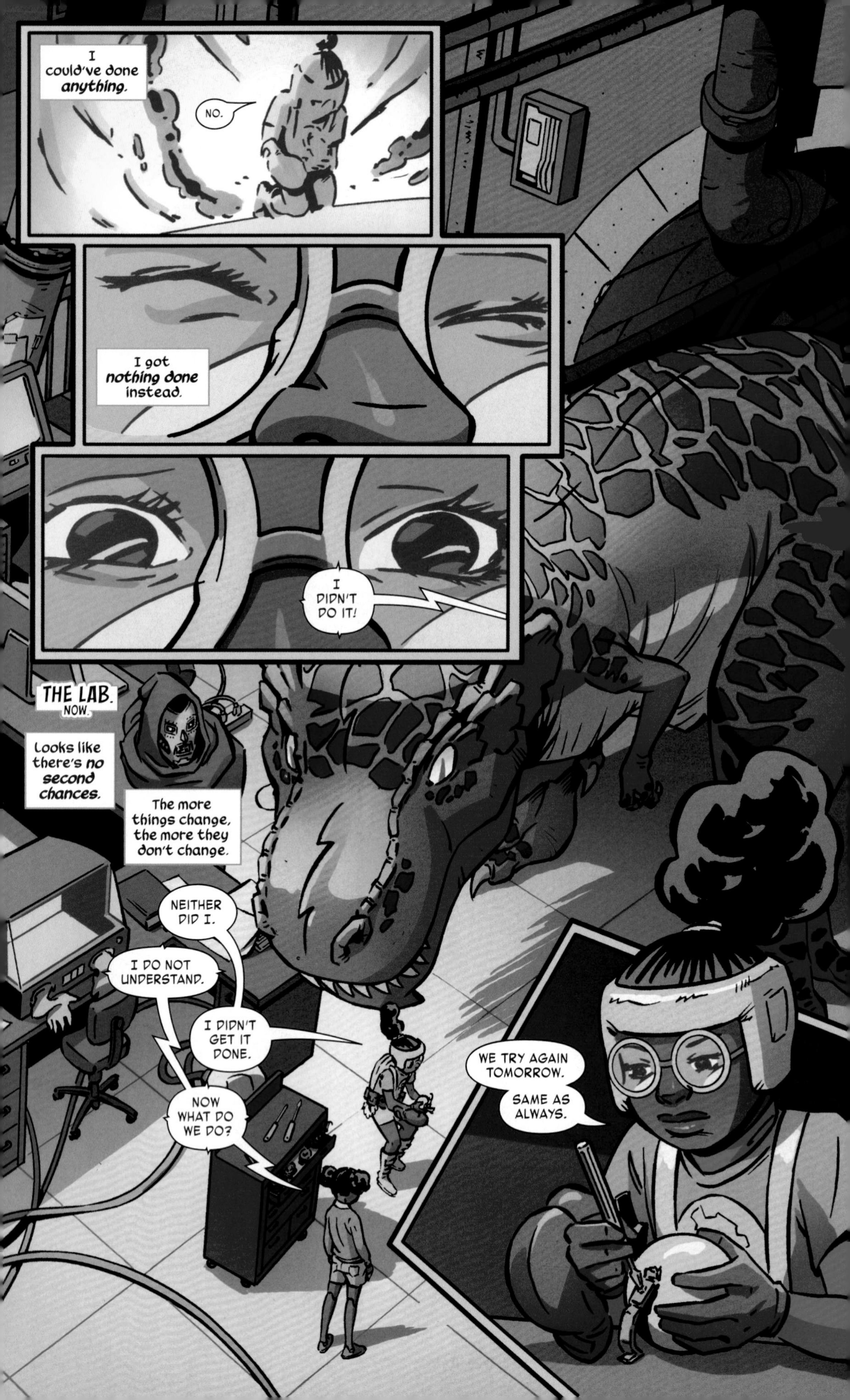
I could've done *anything.*
NO.
I got *nothing done* instead.
I DIDN'T DO IT!
THE LAB. NOW.
Looks like there's *no second chances.*
The more things change, the more they don't change.
NEITHER DID I.
I DO NOT UNDERSTAND.
I DIDN'T GET IT DONE.
NOW WHAT DO WE DO?
WE TRY AGAIN TOMORROW.
SAME AS ALWAYS.

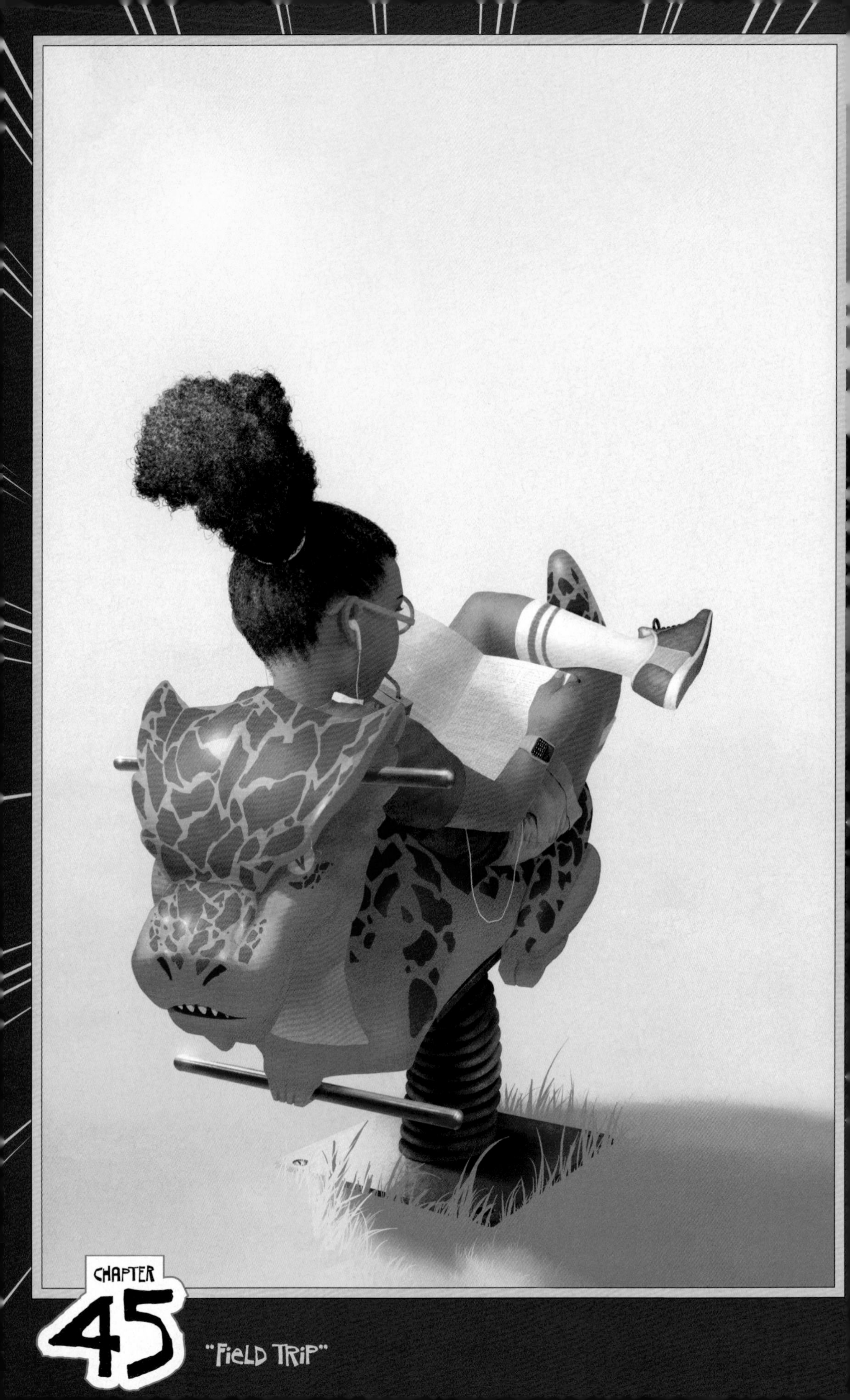
CHAPTER
45
"FIELD TRIP"

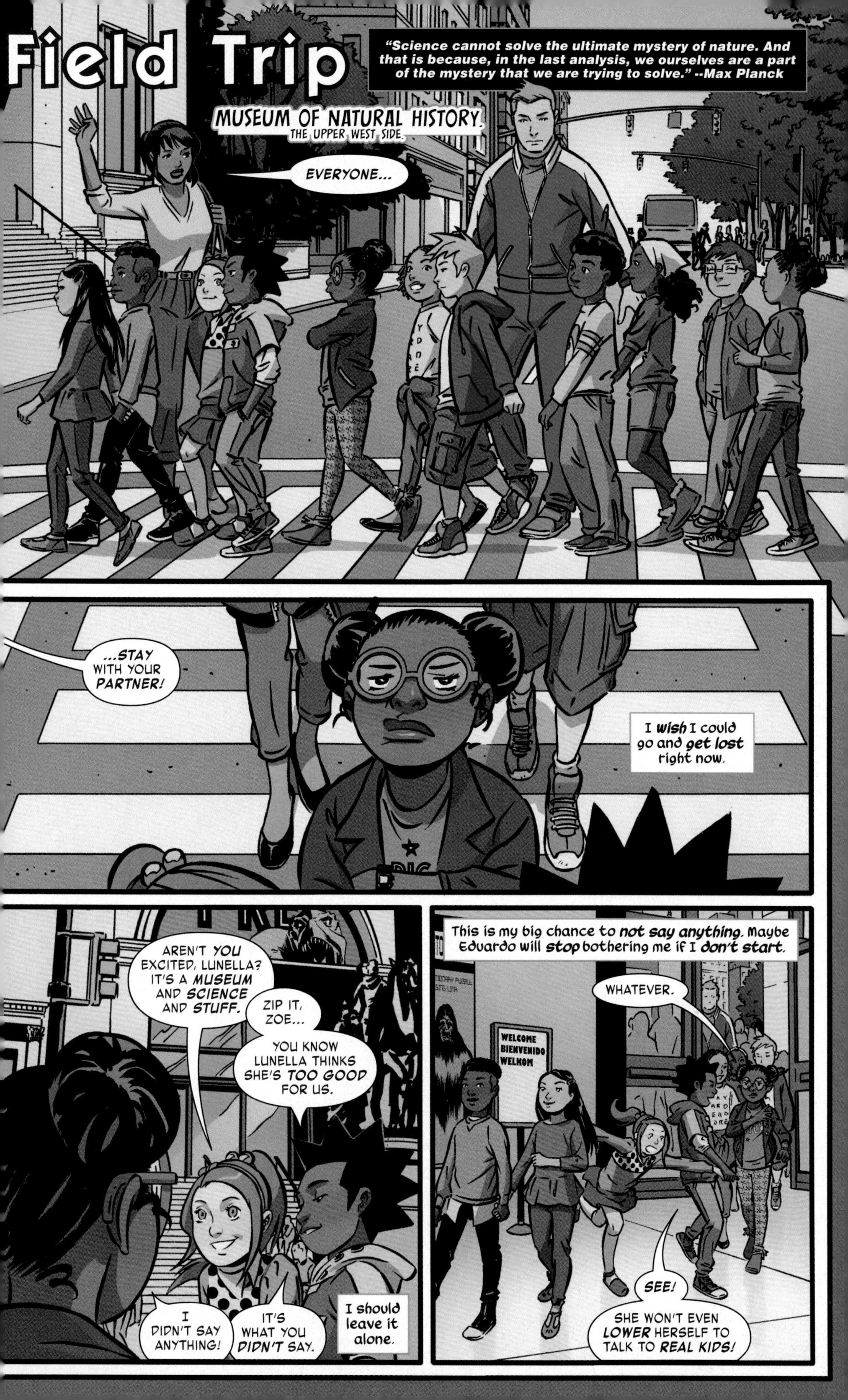
Field Trip
"Science cannot solve the ultimate mystery of nature. And that is because, in the last analysis, we ourselves are a part of the mystery that we are trying to solve." --Max Planck
MUSEUM OF NATURAL HISTORY. THE UPPER WEST SIDE.
EVERYONE...
...STAY WITH YOUR PARTNER!
I wish I could go and get lost right now.
AREN'T YOU EXCITED, LUNELLA? IT'S A MUSEUM AND SCIENCE AND STUFF.
ZIP IT, ZOE...
YOU KNOW LUNELLA THINKS SHE'S TOO GOOD FOR US.
I DIDN'T SAY ANYTHING!
IT'S WHAT YOU DIDN'T SAY.
I should leave it alone.
This is my big chance to not say anything. Maybe Eduardo will stop bothering me if I don't start.
WELCOME BIENVENIDO WELKOM
WHATEVER.
SEE!
SHE WON'T EVEN LOWER HERSELF TO TALK TO REAL KIDS!

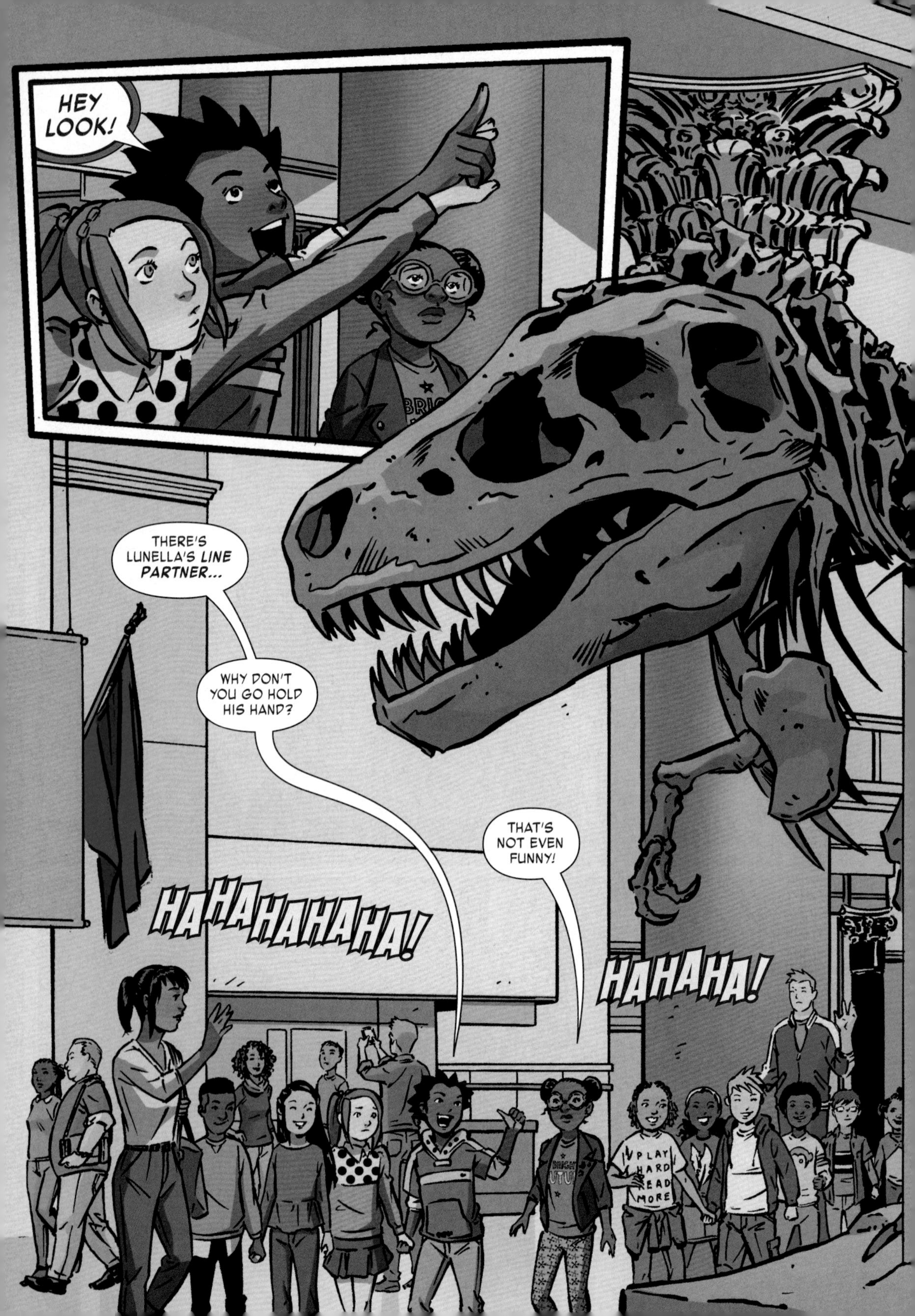
HEY LOOK!
THERE'S LUNELLA'S LINE PARTNER...
WHY DON'T YOU GO HOLD HIS HAND?
HAHAHAHAHAHA!
THAT'S NOT EVEN FUNNY!
HAHAHA!

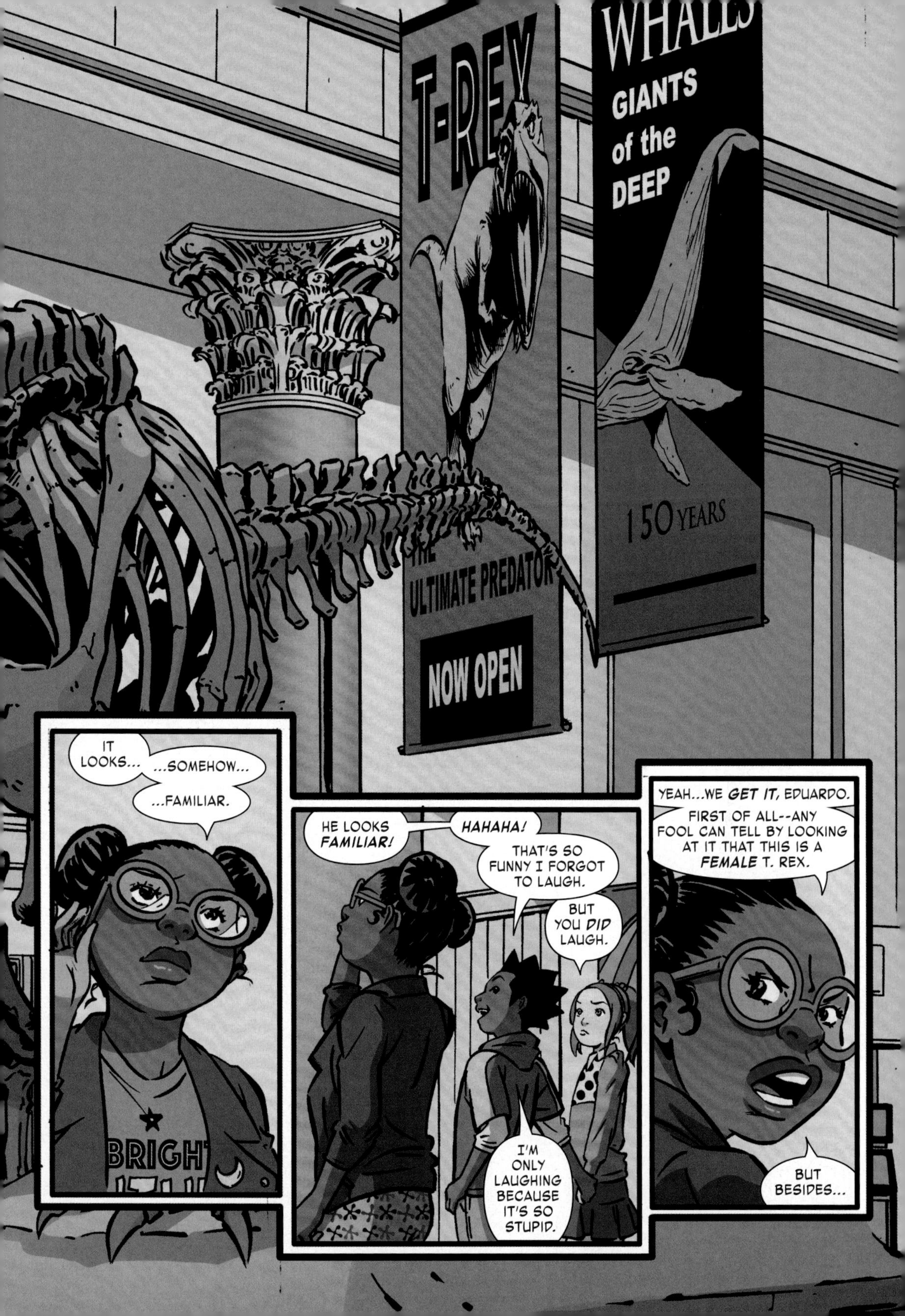
T-REX
ULTIMATE PREDATOR
NOW OPEN
GIANTS of the DEEP
150 YEARS
IT LOOKS...
...SOMEHOW...
...FAMILIAR.
HE LOOKS *FAMILIAR!*
HAHAHA!
THAT'S SO FUNNY I FORGOT TO LAUGH.
BUT YOU *DID* LAUGH.
I'M ONLY LAUGHING BECAUSE IT'S SO STUPID.
YEAH...WE *GET IT,* EDUARDO.
FIRST OF ALL--ANY FOOL CAN TELL BY LOOKING AT IT THAT THIS IS A *FEMALE* T. REX.
BUT BESIDES...

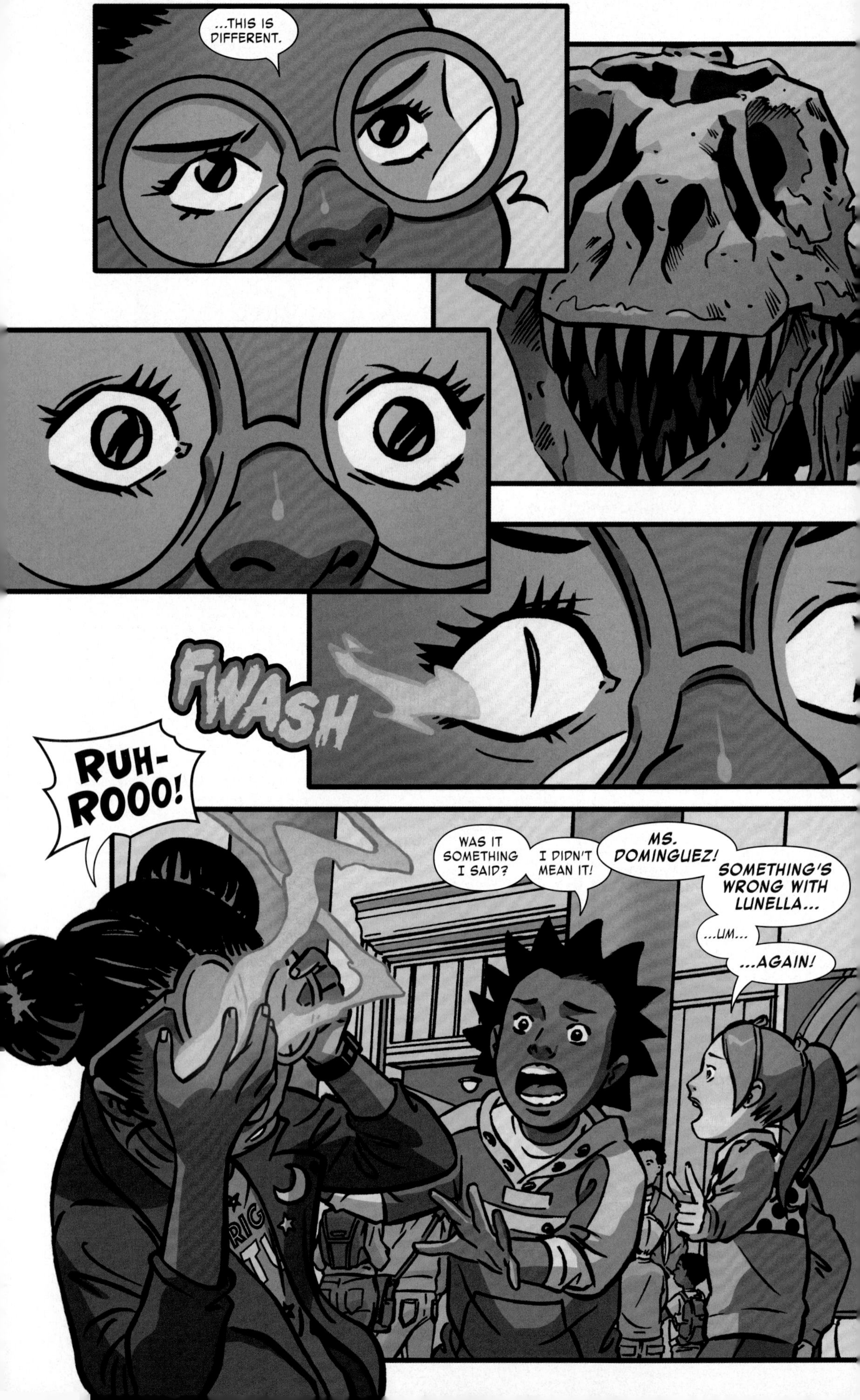
...THIS IS DIFFERENT.
FWASH
RUH-ROOO!
WAS IT SOMETHING I SAID?
I DIDN'T MEAN IT!
MS. DOMINGUEZ!
SOMETHING'S WRONG WITH LUNELLA...
...UM...
...AGAIN!

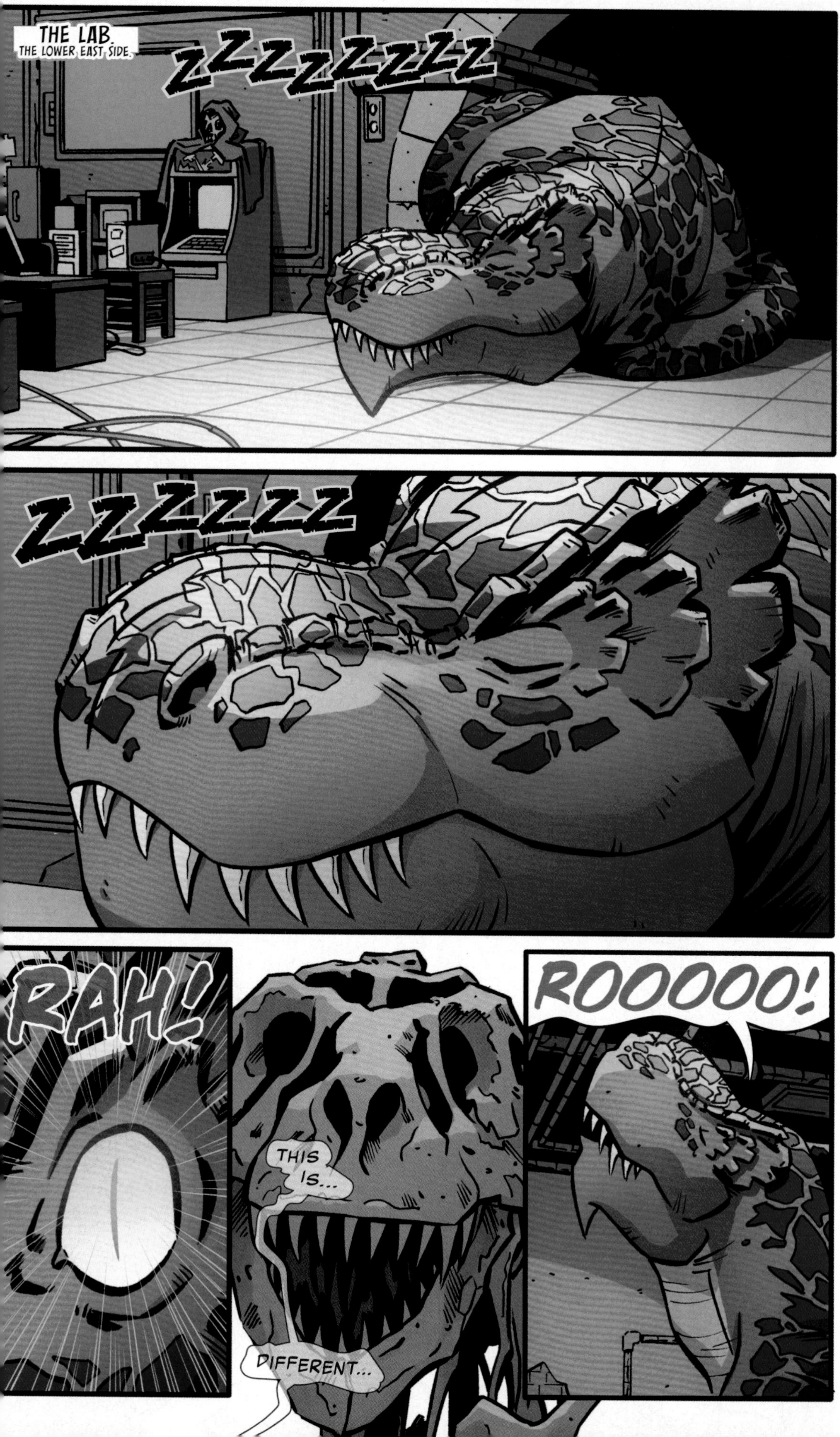
THE LAB.
THE LOWER EAST SIDE.
ZZZZZZZZZ
ZZZZZZZ
RAH!
THIS IS...
DIFFERENT...
ROOOOO!

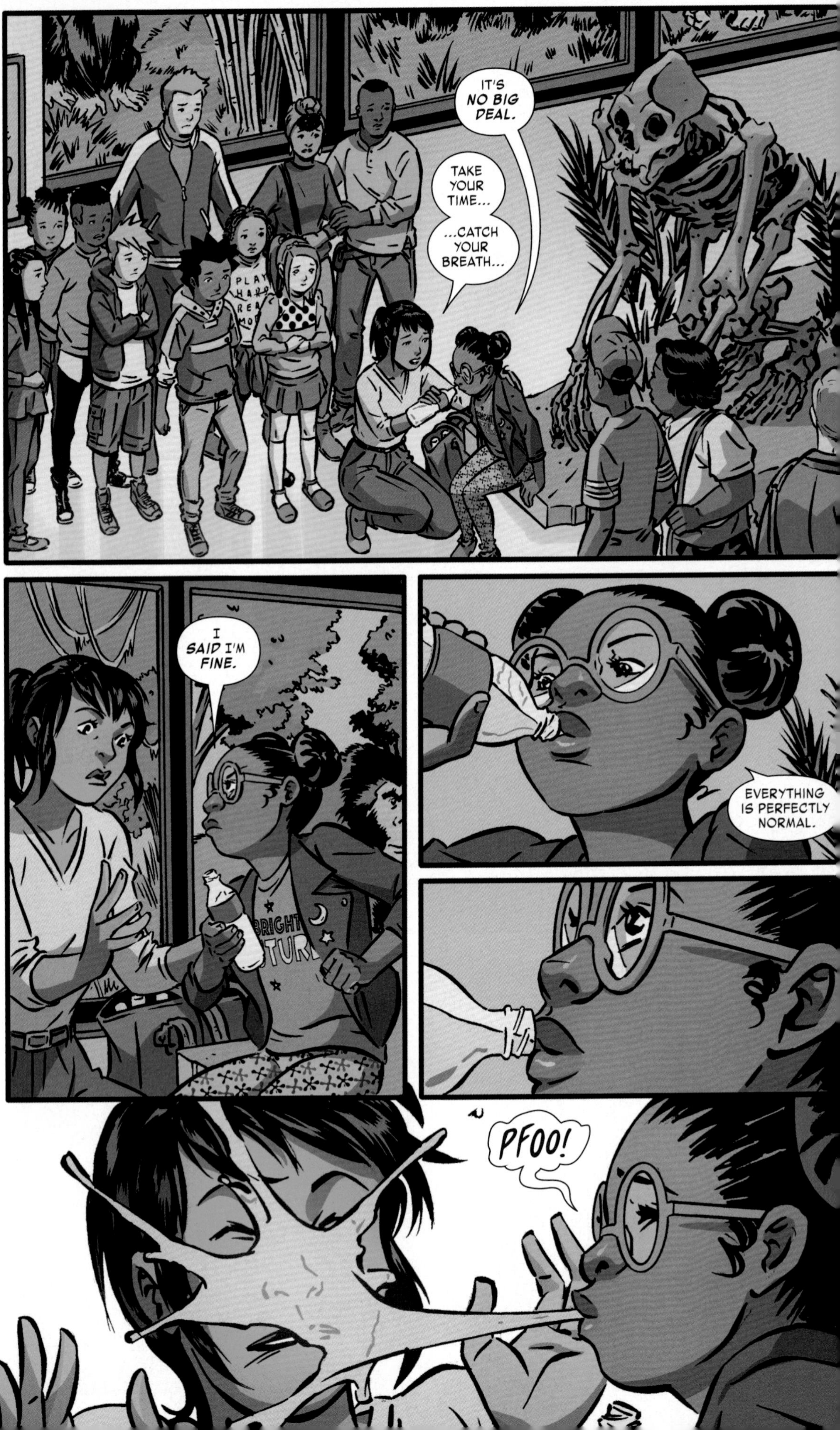

IT'S NO BIG DEAL.
TAKE YOUR TIME...
...CATCH YOUR BREATH...
I SAID I'M FINE.
EVERYTHING IS PERFECTLY NORMAL.
PFOO!

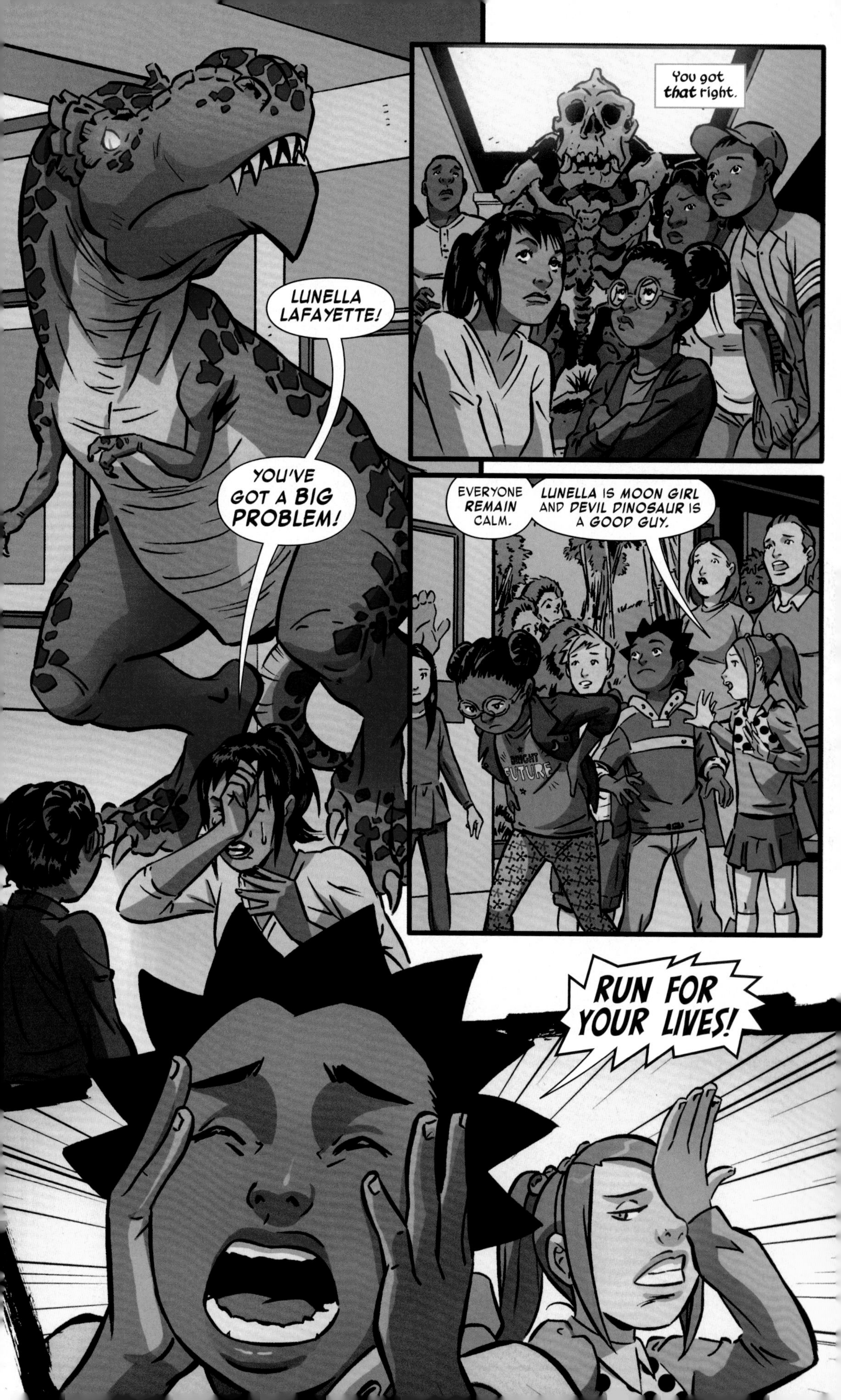
LUNELLA LAFAYETTE!
YOU'VE GOT A BIG PROBLEM!
You got that right.
EVERYONE REMAIN CALM.
LUNELLA IS MOON GIRL AND DEVIL DINOSAUR IS A GOOD GUY.
BRIGHT FUTURE
RUN FOR YOUR LIVES!

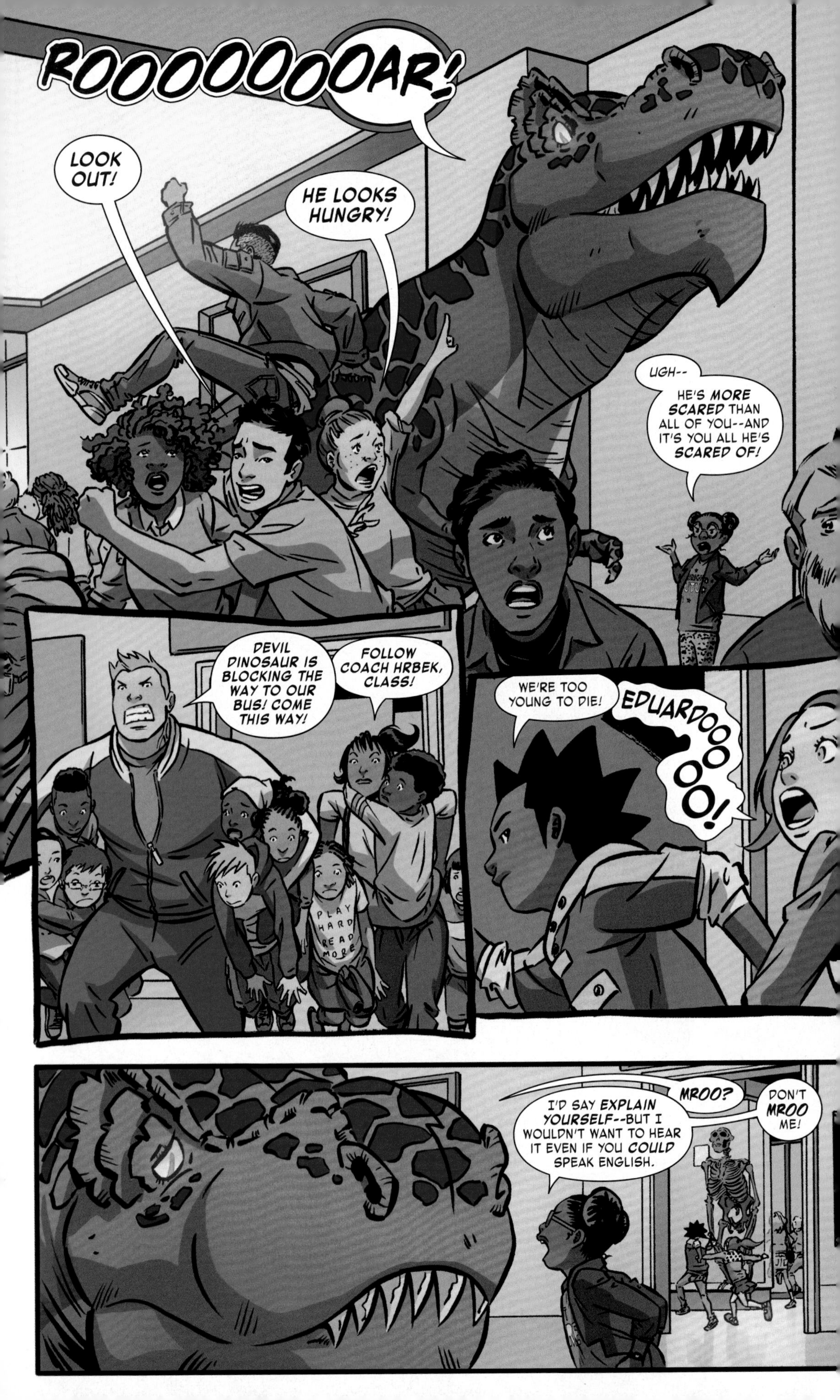
ROOOOOOOOAR!
LOOK OUT!
HE LOOKS HUNGRY!
UGH--
HE'S MORE SCARED THAN ALL OF YOU--AND IT'S YOU ALL HE'S SCARED OF!
DEVIL DINOSAUR IS BLOCKING THE WAY TO OUR BUS! COME THIS WAY!
FOLLOW COACH HRBEK, CLASS!
PLAY HARD READ MORE
WE'RE TOO YOUNG TO DIE!
EDUARDOOOOOO!
I'D SAY EXPLAIN YOURSELF--BUT I WOULDN'T WANT TO HEAR IT EVEN IF YOU COULD SPEAK ENGLISH.
MROO?
DON'T MROO ME!

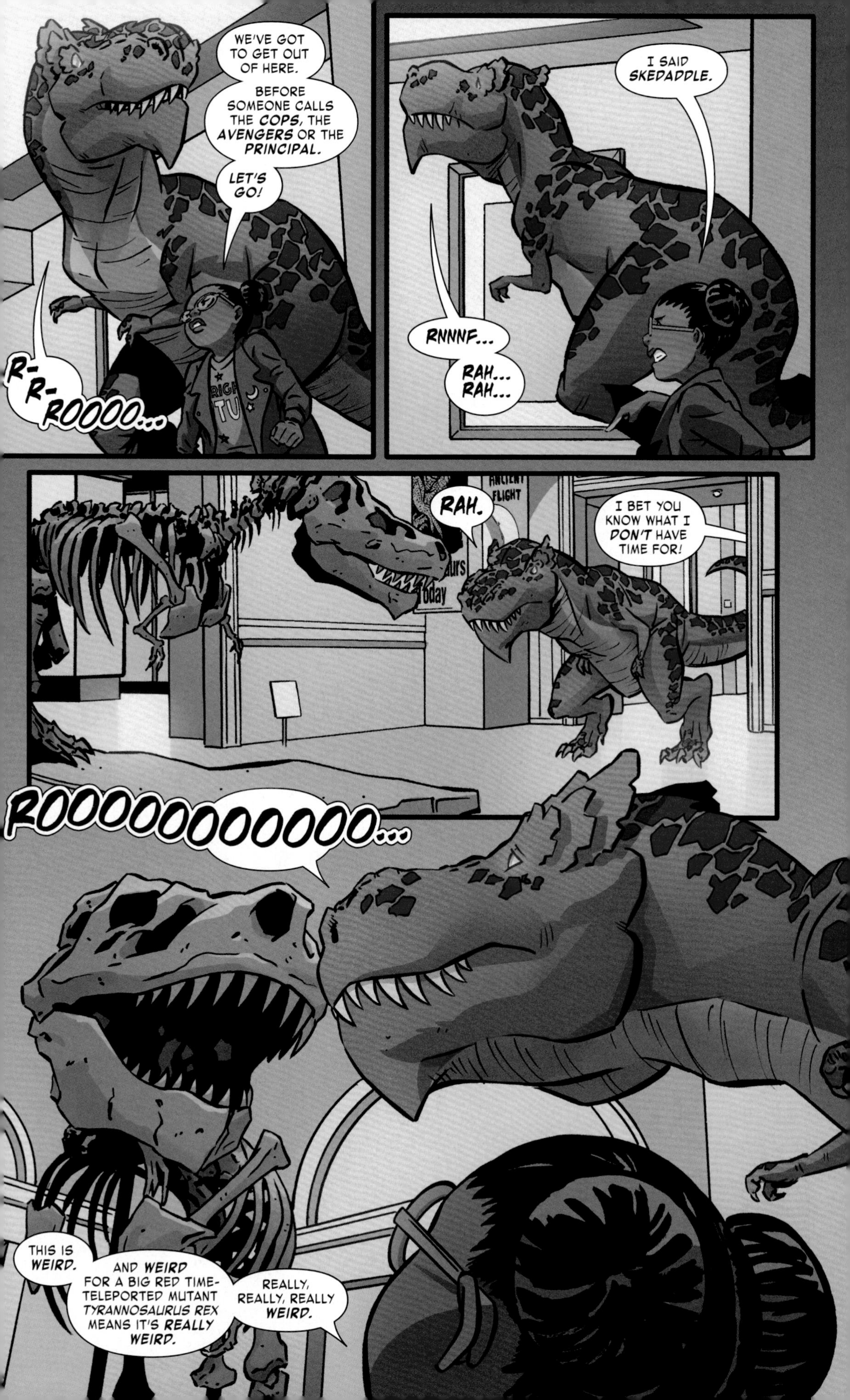
WE'VE GOT TO GET OUT OF HERE.
BEFORE SOMEONE CALLS THE COPS, THE AVENGERS OR THE PRINCIPAL.
LET'S GO!
R-R-ROOOO...
I SAID SKEDADDLE.
RNNNF...
RAH... RAH...
ANCIENT FLIGHT
RAH.
I BET YOU KNOW WHAT I DON'T HAVE TIME FOR!
ROOOOOOOOOOOO...
THIS IS WEIRD.
AND WEIRD FOR A BIG RED TIME-TELEPORTED MUTANT TYRANNOSAURUS REX MEANS IT'S REALLY WEIRD.
REALLY, REALLY, REALLY WEIRD.

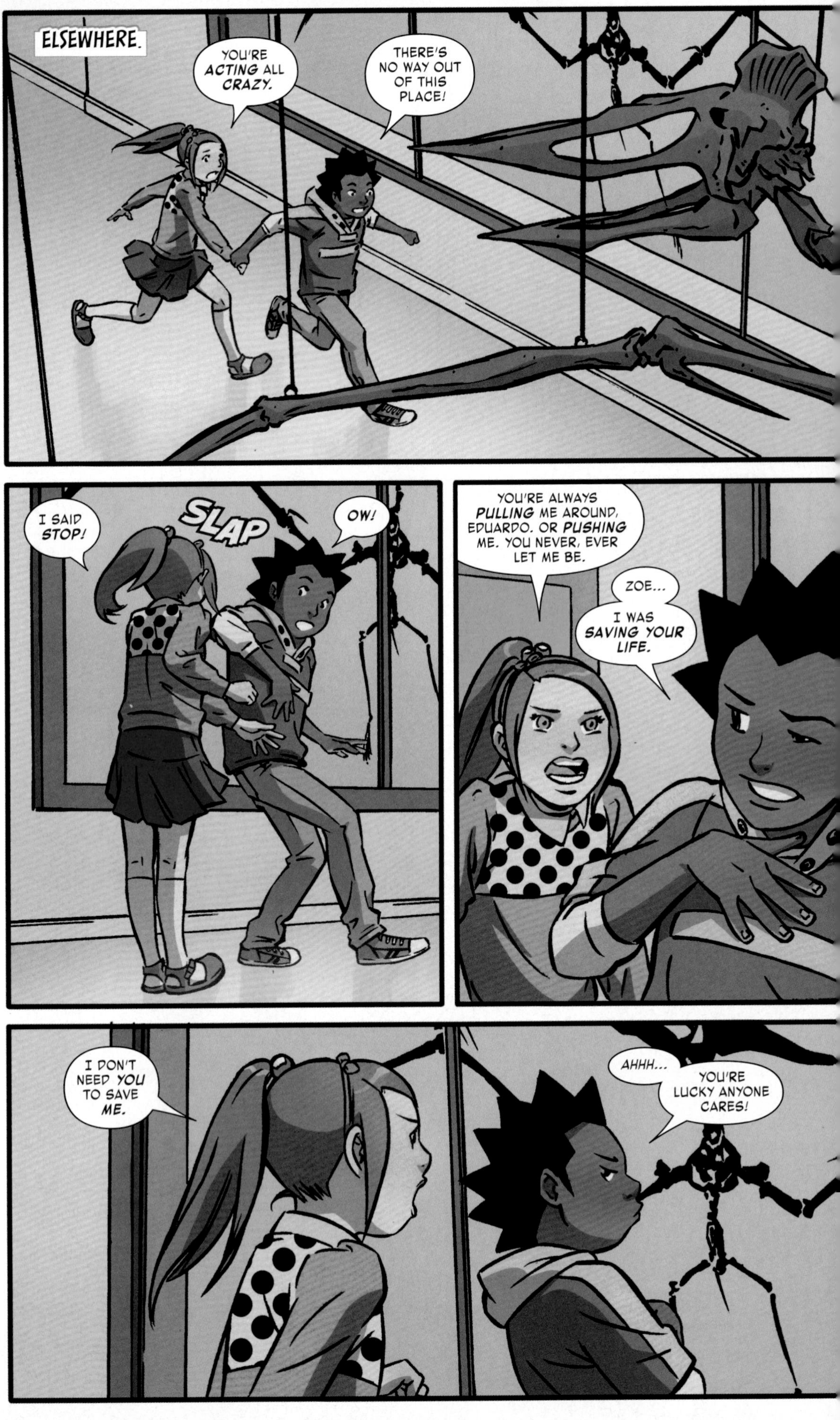
ELSEWHERE.
YOU'RE ACTING ALL CRAZY.
THERE'S NO WAY OUT OF THIS PLACE!
I SAID STOP!
SLAP
OW!
YOU'RE ALWAYS PULLING ME AROUND, EDUARDO. OR PUSHING ME. YOU NEVER, EVER LET ME BE.
ZOE...
I WAS SAVING YOUR LIFE.
I DON'T NEED YOU TO SAVE ME.
AHHH...
YOU'RE LUCKY ANYONE CARES!

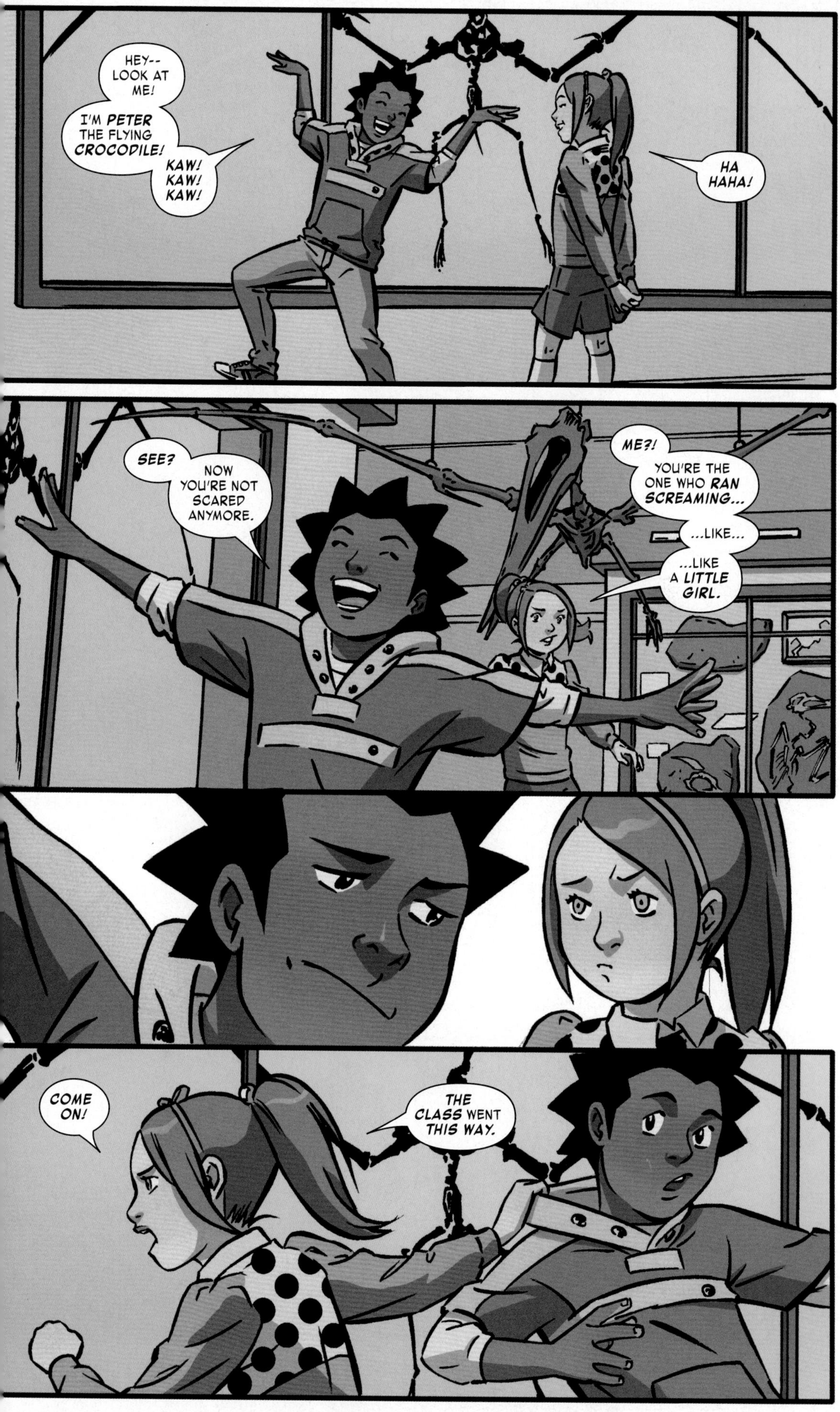
HEY-- LOOK AT ME!
I'M PETER THE FLYING CROCODILE!
KAW! KAW! KAW!
HA HAHA!
SEE?
NOW YOU'RE NOT SCARED ANYMORE.
ME?!
YOU'RE THE ONE WHO RAN SCREAMING...
...LIKE...
...LIKE A LITTLE GIRL.
COME ON!
THE CLASS WENT THIS WAY.

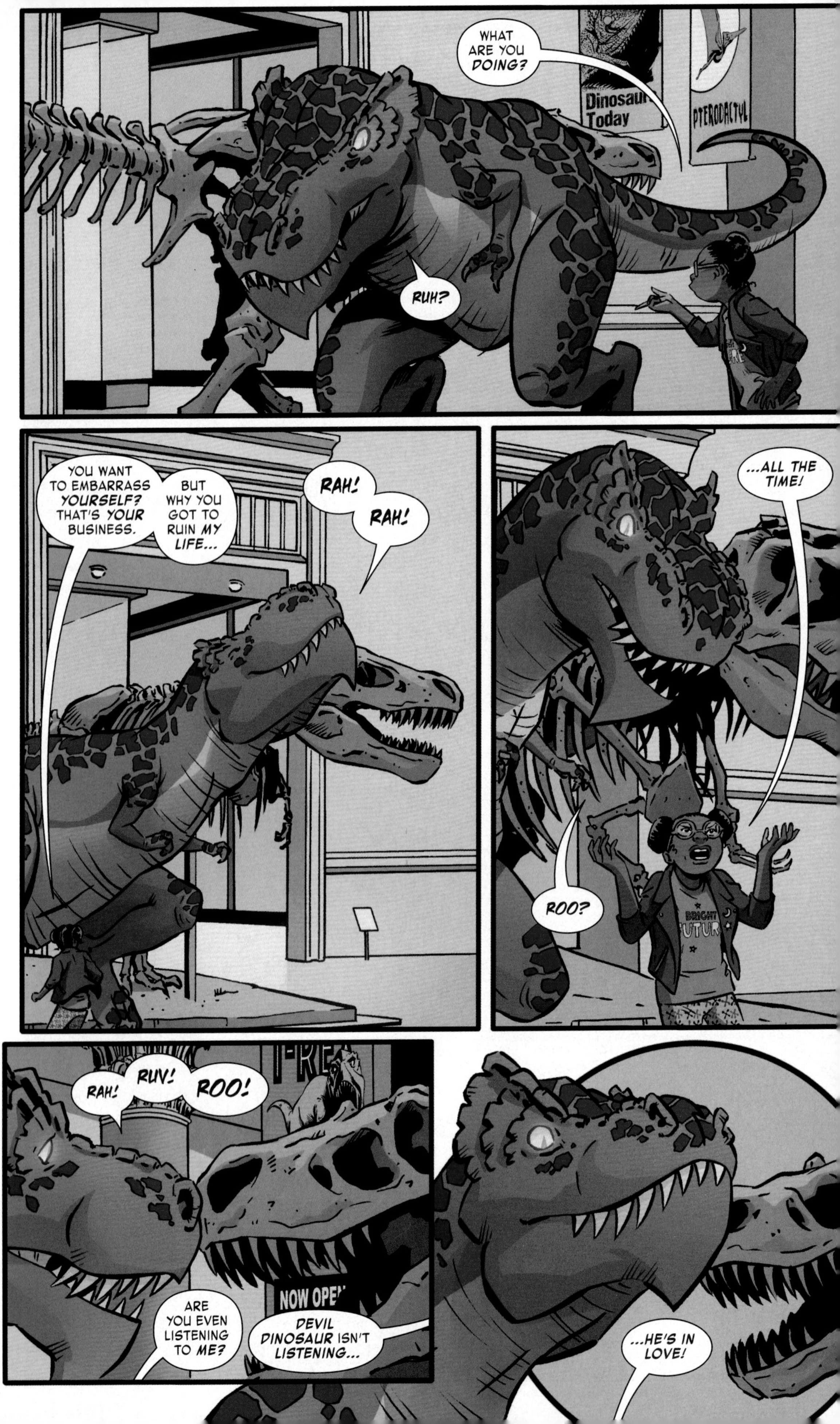
WHAT ARE YOU DOING?
Dinosaur Today
PTERODACTYL
RUH?
YOU WANT TO EMBARRASS YOURSELF? THAT'S YOUR BUSINESS.
BUT WHY YOU GOT TO RUIN MY LIFE...
RAH!
RAH!
...ALL THE TIME!
ROO?
RAH!
RUV!
ROO!
NOW OPEN
ARE YOU EVEN LISTENING TO ME?
DEVIL DINOSAUR ISN'T LISTENING...
...HE'S IN LOVE!

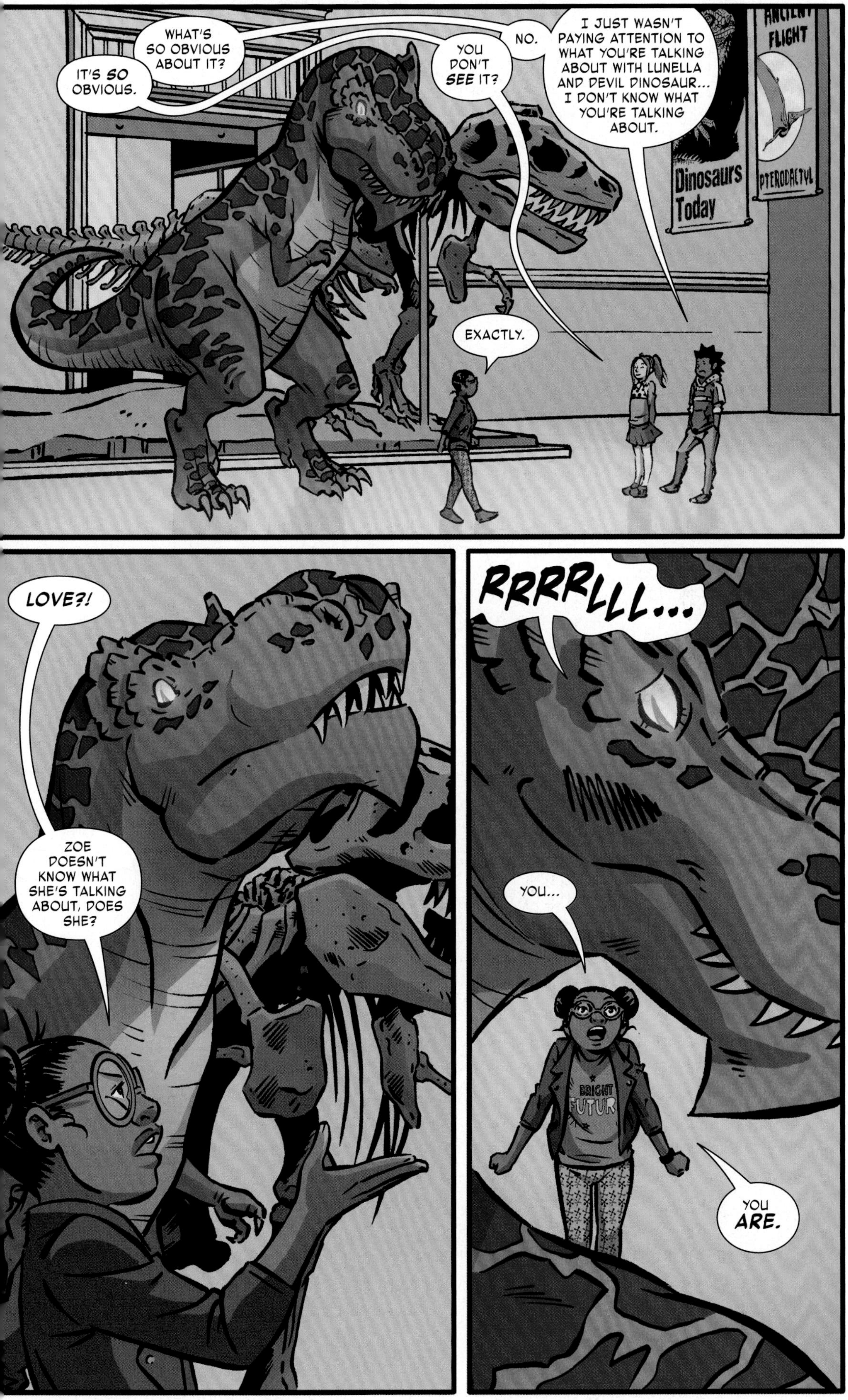
IT'S *SO* OBVIOUS.
WHAT'S SO OBVIOUS ABOUT IT?
YOU DON'T *SEE* IT?
NO.
I JUST WASN'T PAYING ATTENTION TO WHAT YOU'RE TALKING ABOUT WITH LUNELLA AND DEVIL DINOSAUR... I DON'T KNOW WHAT YOU'RE TALKING ABOUT.
ANCIENT FLIGHT
Dinosaurs Today
PTERODACTYL
EXACTLY.
LOVE?!
ZOE DOESN'T KNOW WHAT SHE'S TALKING ABOUT, DOES SHE?
RRRRLLL...
YOU...
BRIGHT FUTUR
YOU **ARE.**

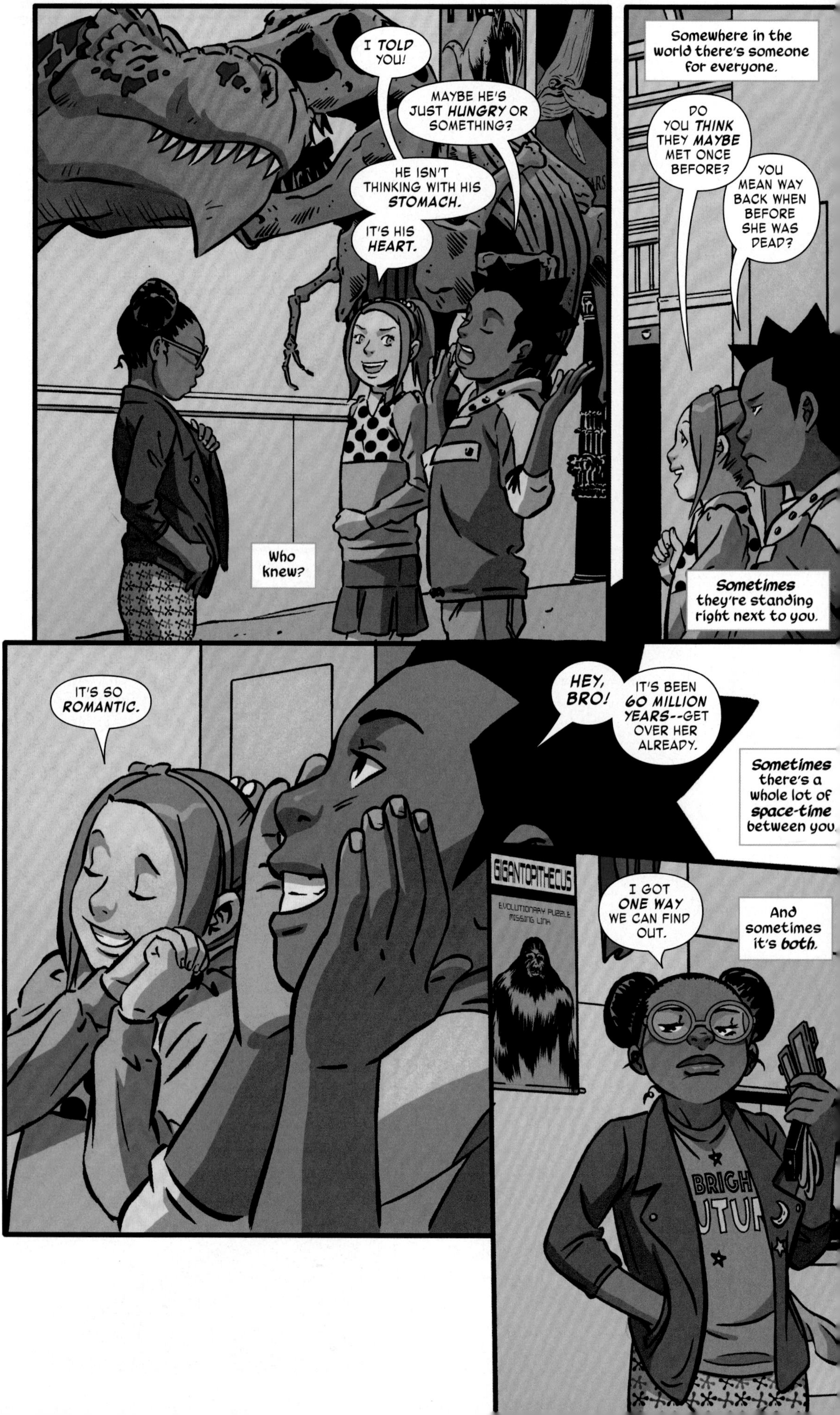
I TOLD YOU!
MAYBE HE'S JUST HUNGRY OR SOMETHING?
HE ISN'T THINKING WITH HIS STOMACH.
IT'S HIS HEART.
Who knew?
Somewhere in the world there's someone for everyone.
DO YOU THINK THEY MAYBE MET ONCE BEFORE?
YOU MEAN WAY BACK WHEN BEFORE SHE WAS DEAD?
Sometimes they're standing right next to you.
IT'S SO ROMANTIC.
HEY, BRO!
IT'S BEEN 60 MILLION YEARS--GET OVER HER ALREADY.
Sometimes there's a whole lot of space-time between you.
GIGANTOPITHECUS
EVOLUTIONARY PUZZLE
MISSING LINK
I GOT ONE WAY WE CAN FIND OUT.
And sometimes it's both.

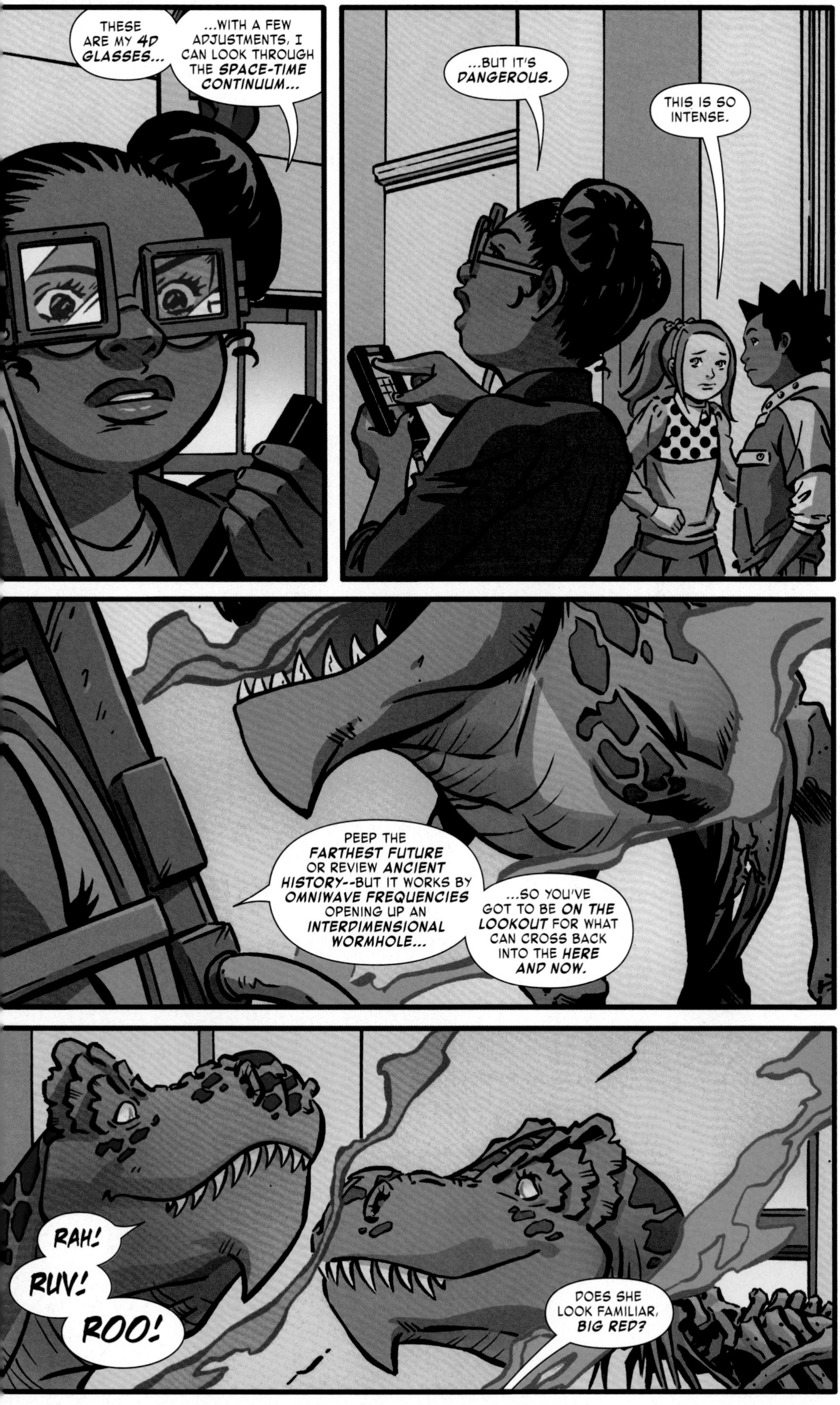
THESE ARE MY 4D GLASSES...
...WITH A FEW ADJUSTMENTS, I CAN LOOK THROUGH THE SPACE-TIME CONTINUUM...
...BUT IT'S DANGEROUS.
THIS IS SO INTENSE.
PEEP THE FARTHEST FUTURE OR REVIEW ANCIENT HISTORY--BUT IT WORKS BY OMNIWAVE FREQUENCIES OPENING UP AN INTERDIMENSIONAL WORMHOLE...
...SO YOU'VE GOT TO BE ON THE LOOKOUT FOR WHAT CAN CROSS BACK INTO THE HERE AND NOW.
RAH!
RUV!
ROO!
DOES SHE LOOK FAMILIAR, BIG RED?

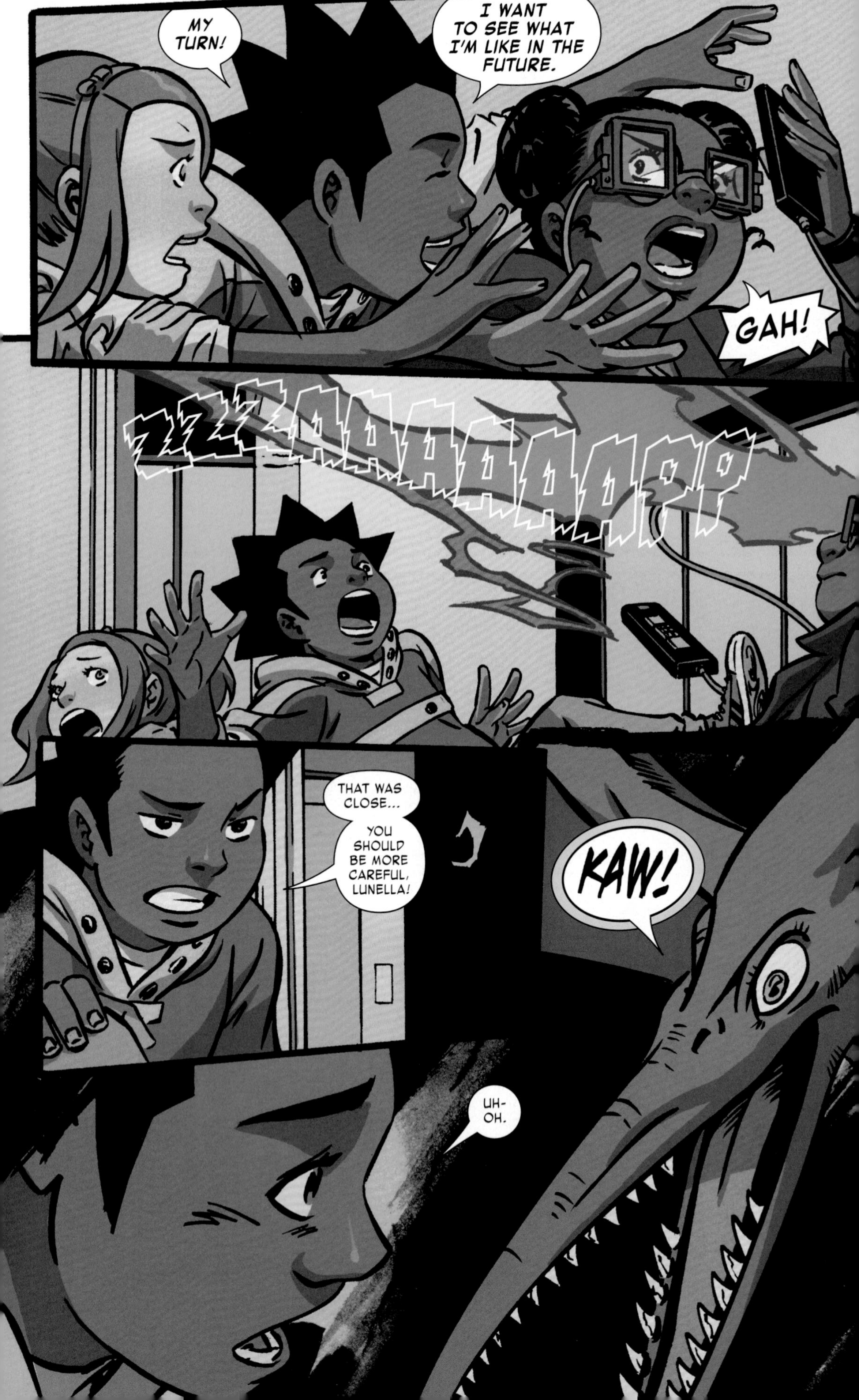
MY TURN!
I WANT TO SEE WHAT I'M LIKE IN THE FUTURE.
GAH!
ZZZZAAAAAAAPP
THAT WAS CLOSE...
YOU SHOULD BE MORE CAREFUL, LUNELLA!
KAW!
UH-OH.

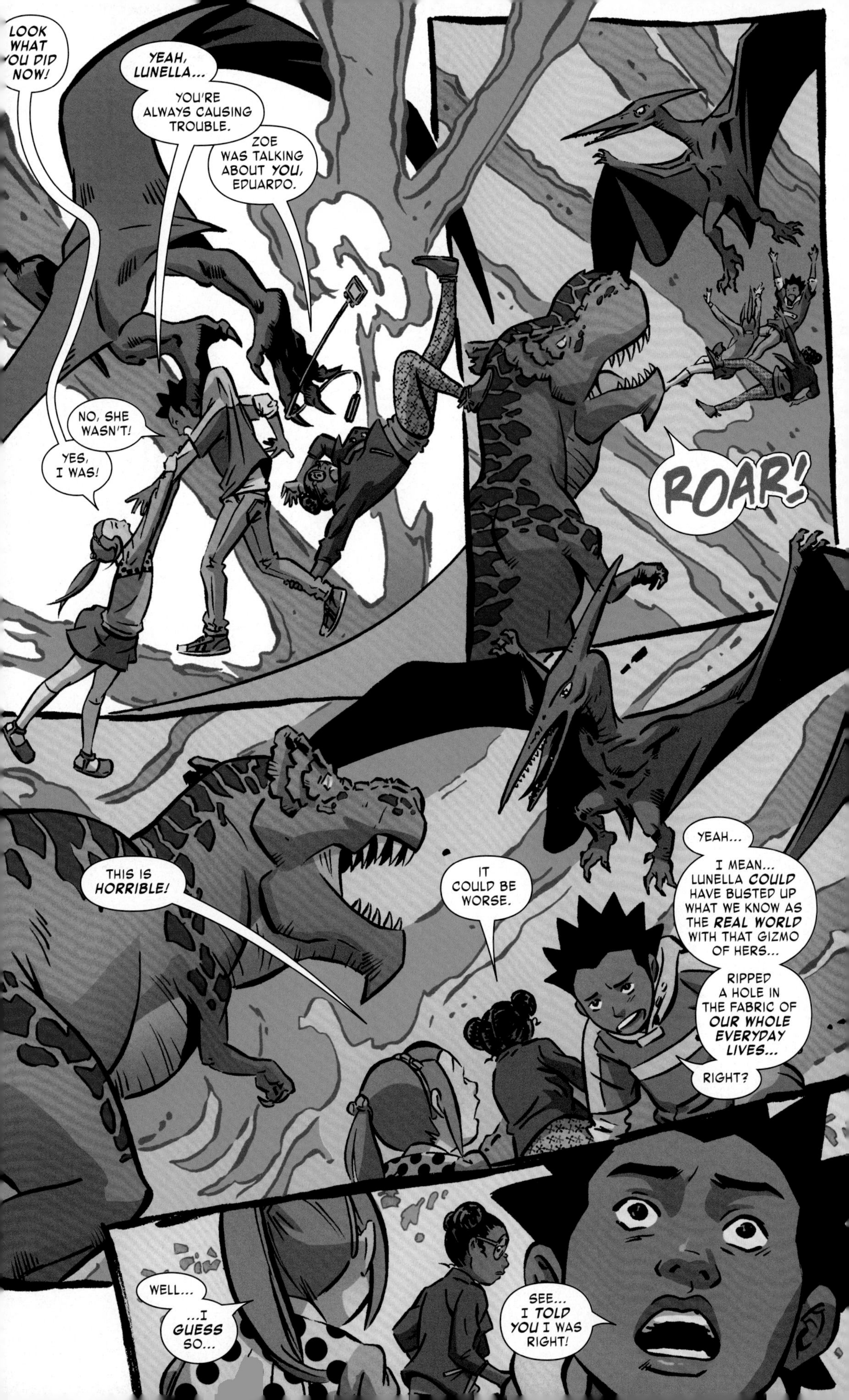
LOOK WHAT YOU DID NOW!
YEAH, LUNELLA...
YOU'RE ALWAYS CAUSING TROUBLE.
ZOE WAS TALKING ABOUT YOU, EDUARDO.
NO, SHE WASN'T!
YES, I WAS!
ROAR!
THIS IS HORRIBLE!
IT COULD BE WORSE.
YEAH...
I MEAN... LUNELLA COULD HAVE BUSTED UP WHAT WE KNOW AS THE REAL WORLD WITH THAT GIZMO OF HERS...
RIPPED A HOLE IN THE FABRIC OF OUR WHOLE EVERYDAY LIVES...
RIGHT?
WELL...
...I GUESS SO...
SEE... I TOLD YOU I WAS RIGHT!

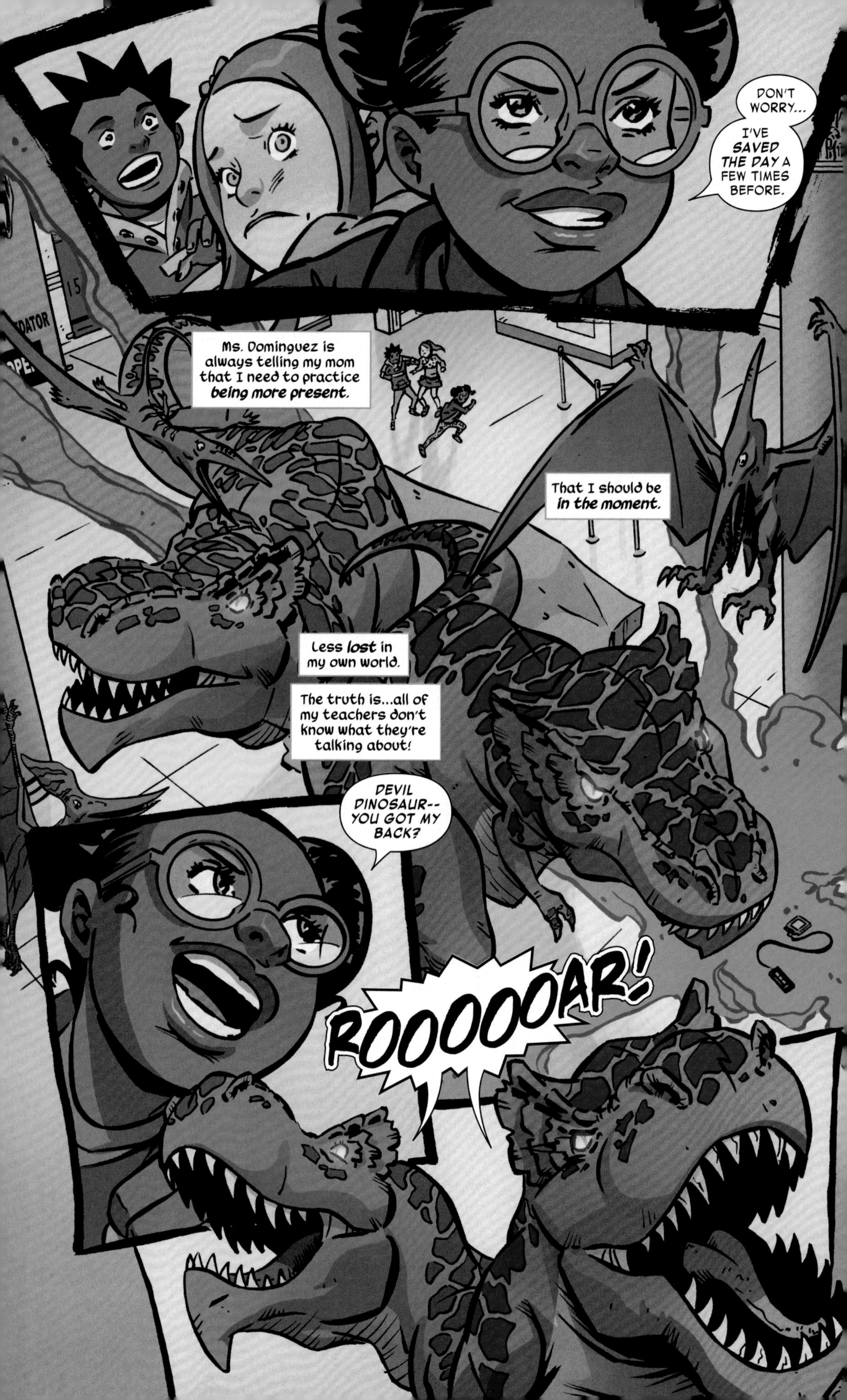
DON'T WORRY...
I'VE SAVED THE DAY A FEW TIMES BEFORE.
Ms. Dominguez is always telling my mom that I need to practice being more present.
That I should be in the moment.
Less lost in my own world.
The truth is...all of my teachers don't know what they're talking about!
DEVIL DINOSAUR-- YOU GOT MY BACK?
ROOOOOOAR!

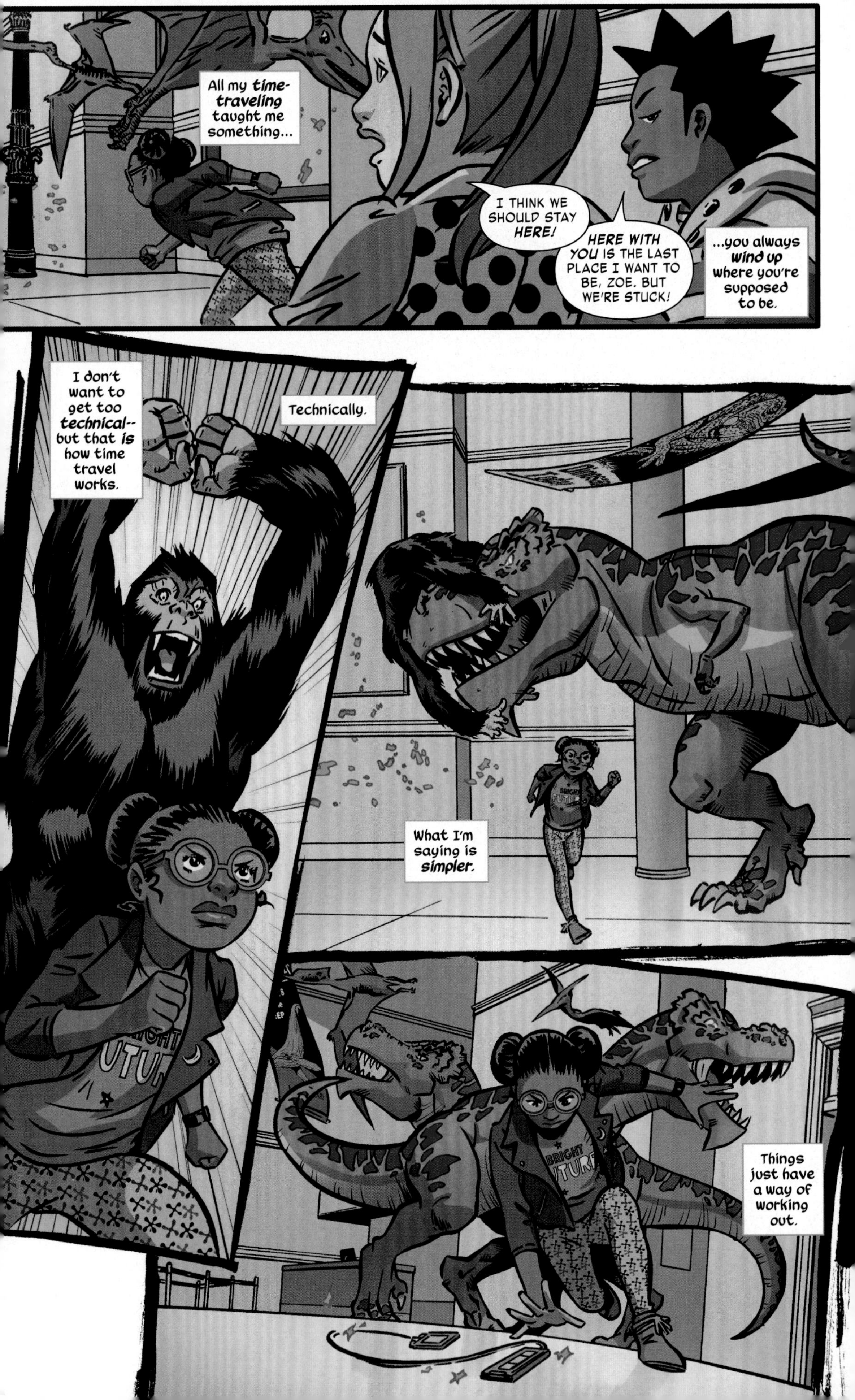
All my time-traveling taught me something...
I THINK WE SHOULD STAY HERE!
HERE WITH YOU IS THE LAST PLACE I WANT TO BE, ZOE. BUT WE'RE STUCK!
...you always wind up where you're supposed to be.
I don't want to get too technical--but that is how time travel works.
Technically.
What I'm saying is simpler.
Things just have a way of working out.

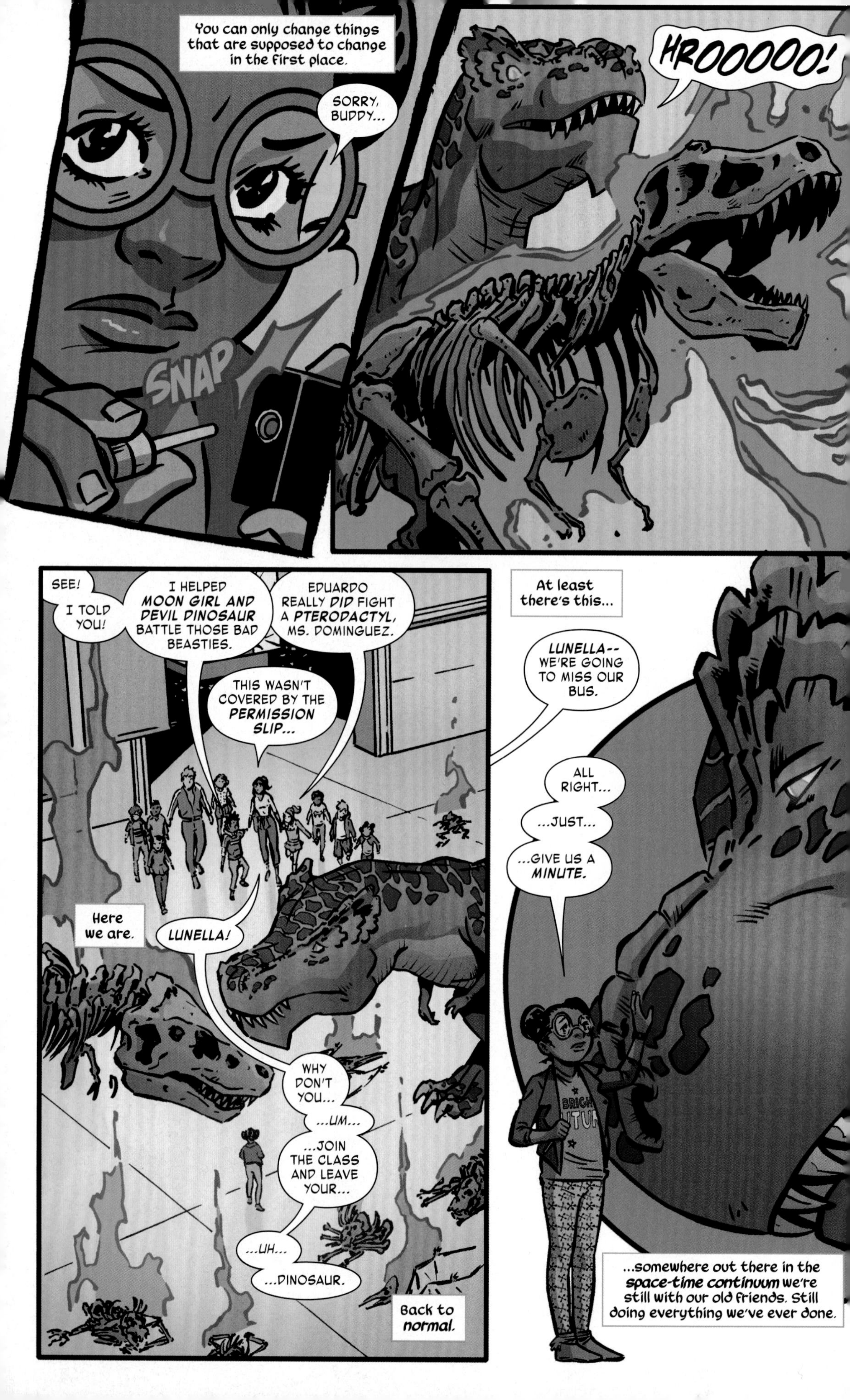

You can only change things that are supposed to change in the first place.
SORRY, BUDDY...
SNAP
HROOOOO!
SEE!
I TOLD YOU!
I HELPED MOON GIRL AND DEVIL DINOSAUR BATTLE THOSE BAD BEASTIES.
EDUARDO REALLY DID FIGHT A PTERODACTYL, MS. DOMINGUEZ.
THIS WASN'T COVERED BY THE PERMISSION SLIP...
Here we are.
LUNELLA!
WHY DON'T YOU...
...UM...
...JOIN THE CLASS AND LEAVE YOUR...
...UH...
...DINOSAUR.
Back to normal.
At least there's this...
LUNELLA-- WE'RE GOING TO MISS OUR BUS.
ALL RIGHT...
...JUST...
...GIVE US A MINUTE.
...somewhere out there in the space-time continuum we're still with our old friends. Still doing everything we've ever done.

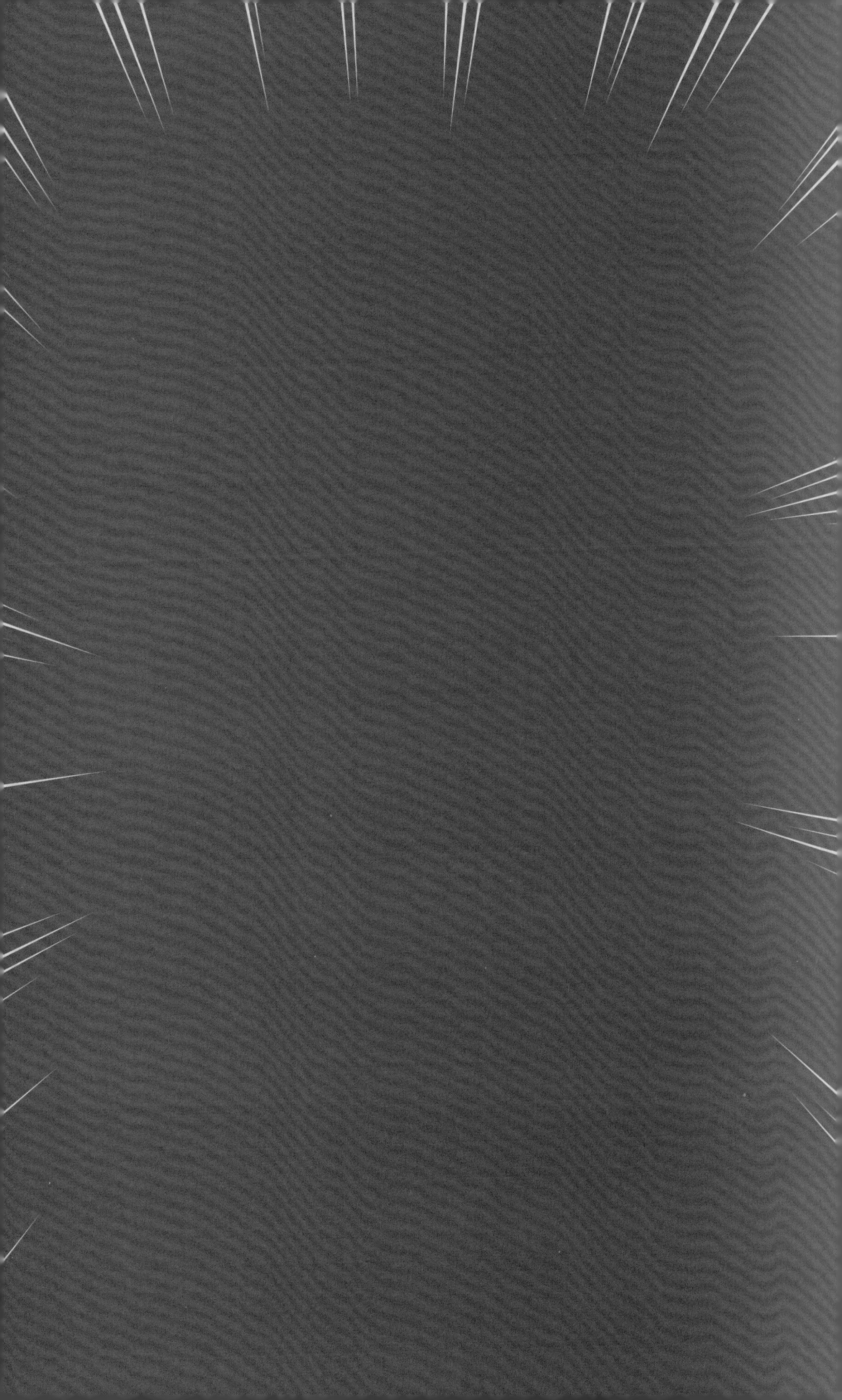

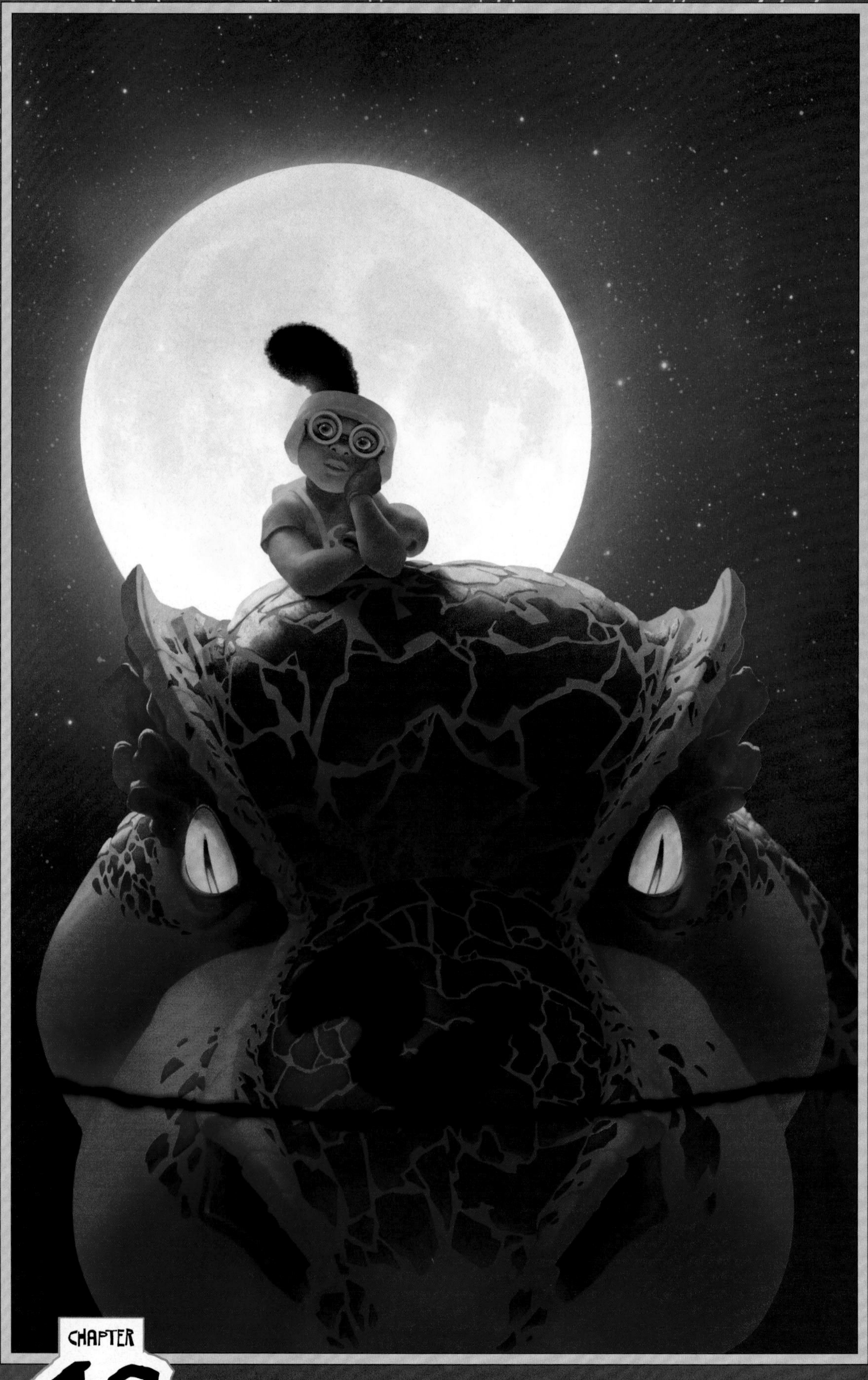

CHAPTER 46

"MS. FANTASTIC (PART ONE OF TWO)"

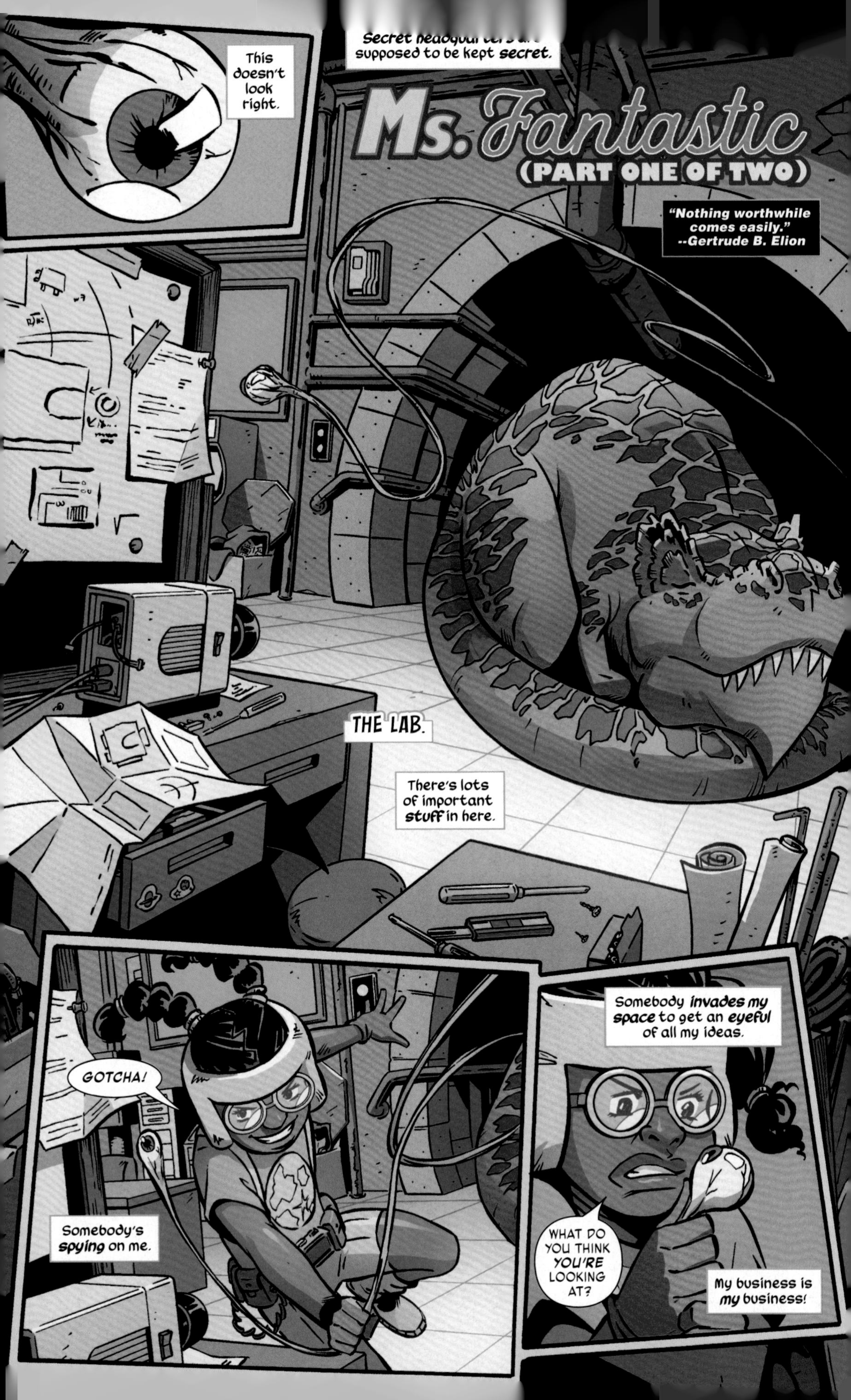
This doesn't look right.
Secret headquarters are supposed to be kept secret.
Ms. Fantastic
(PART ONE OF TWO)
"Nothing worthwhile comes easily." --Gertrude B. Elion
THE LAB.
There's lots of important stuff in here.
GOTCHA!
Somebody's spying on me.
Somebody invades my space to get an eyeful of all my ideas.
WHAT DO YOU THINK YOU'RE LOOKING AT?
My business is my business!

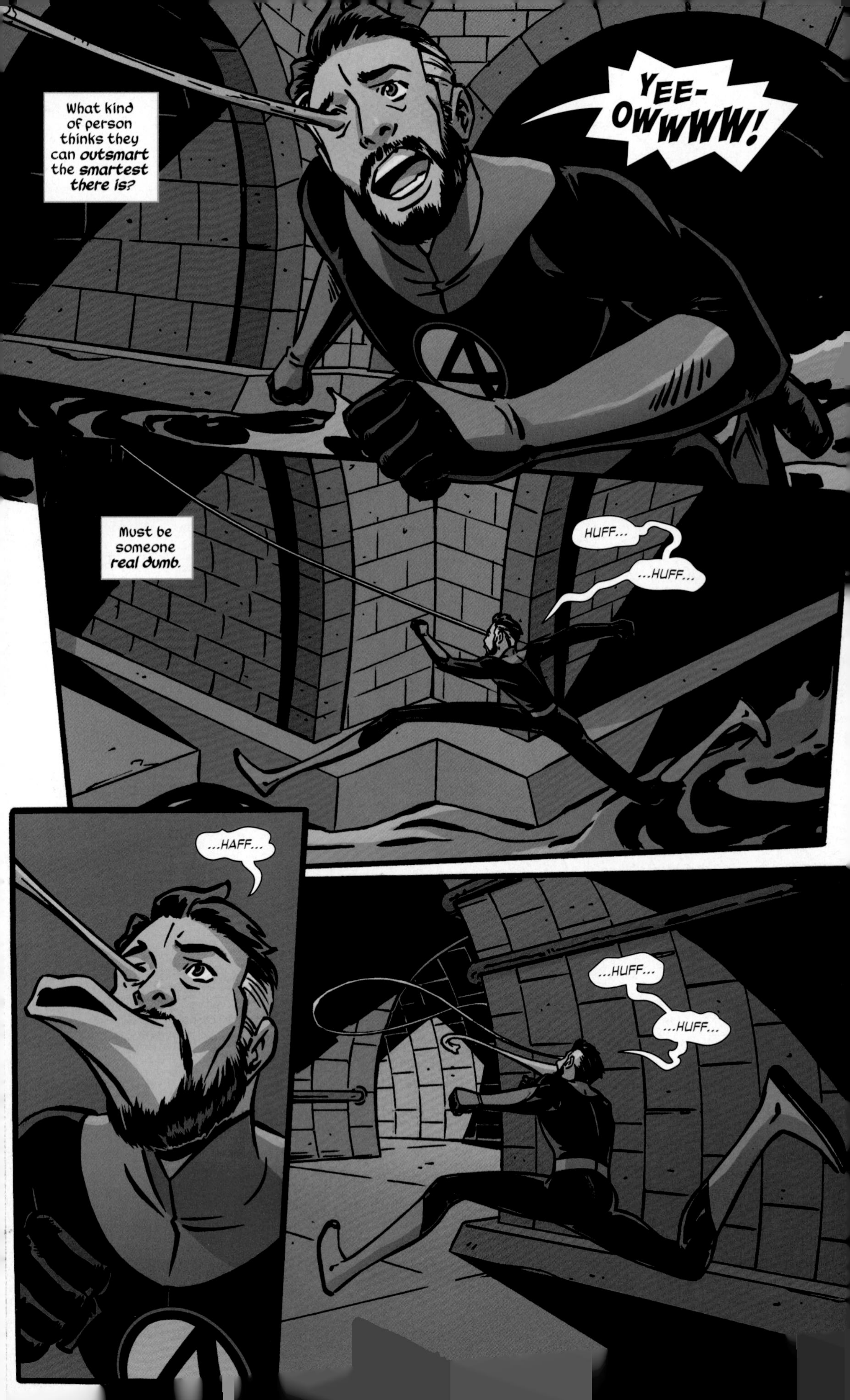
What kind of person thinks they can *outsmart* the *smartest there is?*
YEE-OWWWW!
Must be someone *real dumb.*
HUFF...
...HUFF...
...HAFF...
...HUFF...
...HUFF...

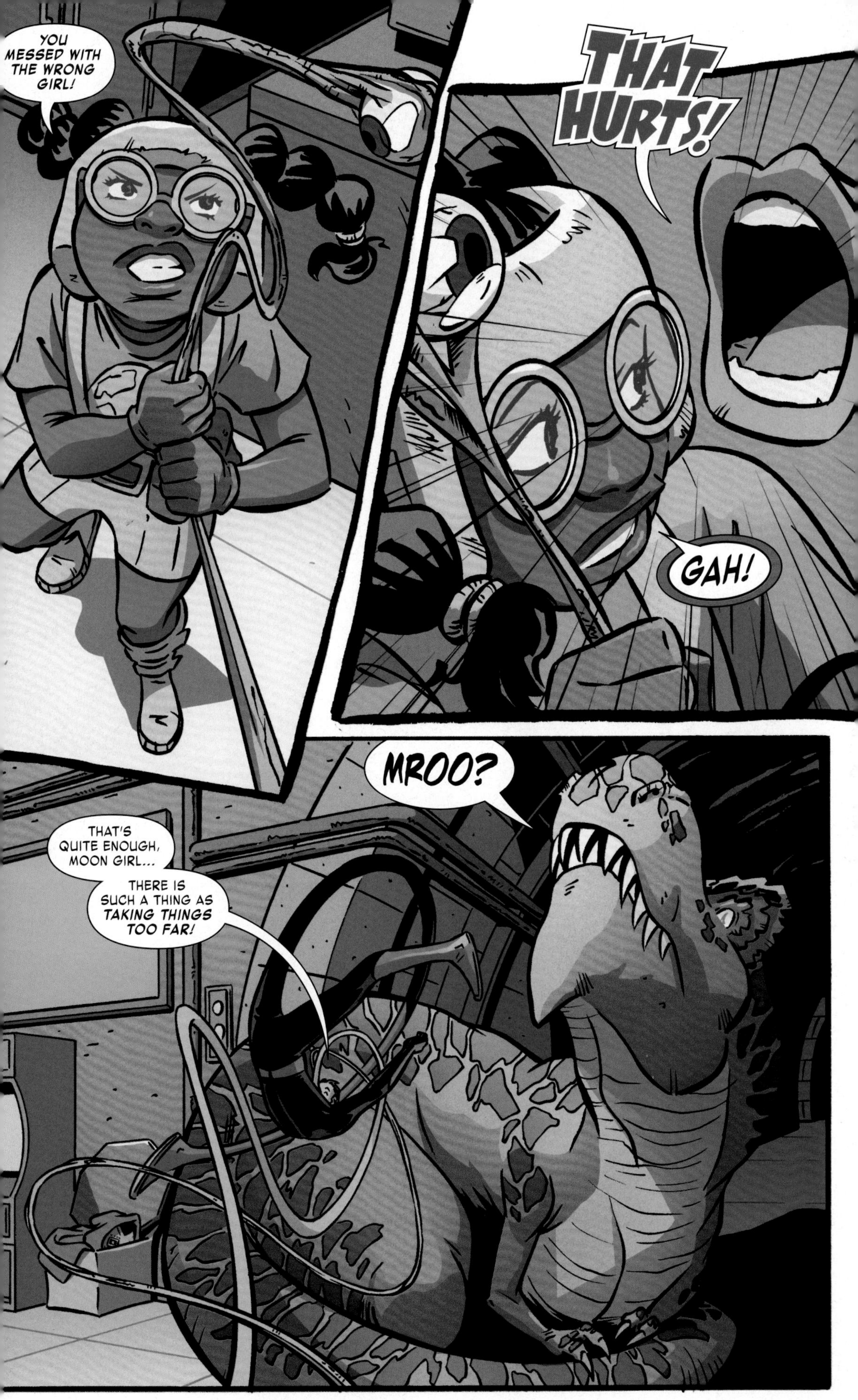
YOU MESSED WITH THE WRONG GIRL!
THAT HURTS!
GAH!
MROO?
THAT'S QUITE ENOUGH, MOON GIRL...
THERE IS SUCH A THING AS TAKING THINGS TOO FAR!

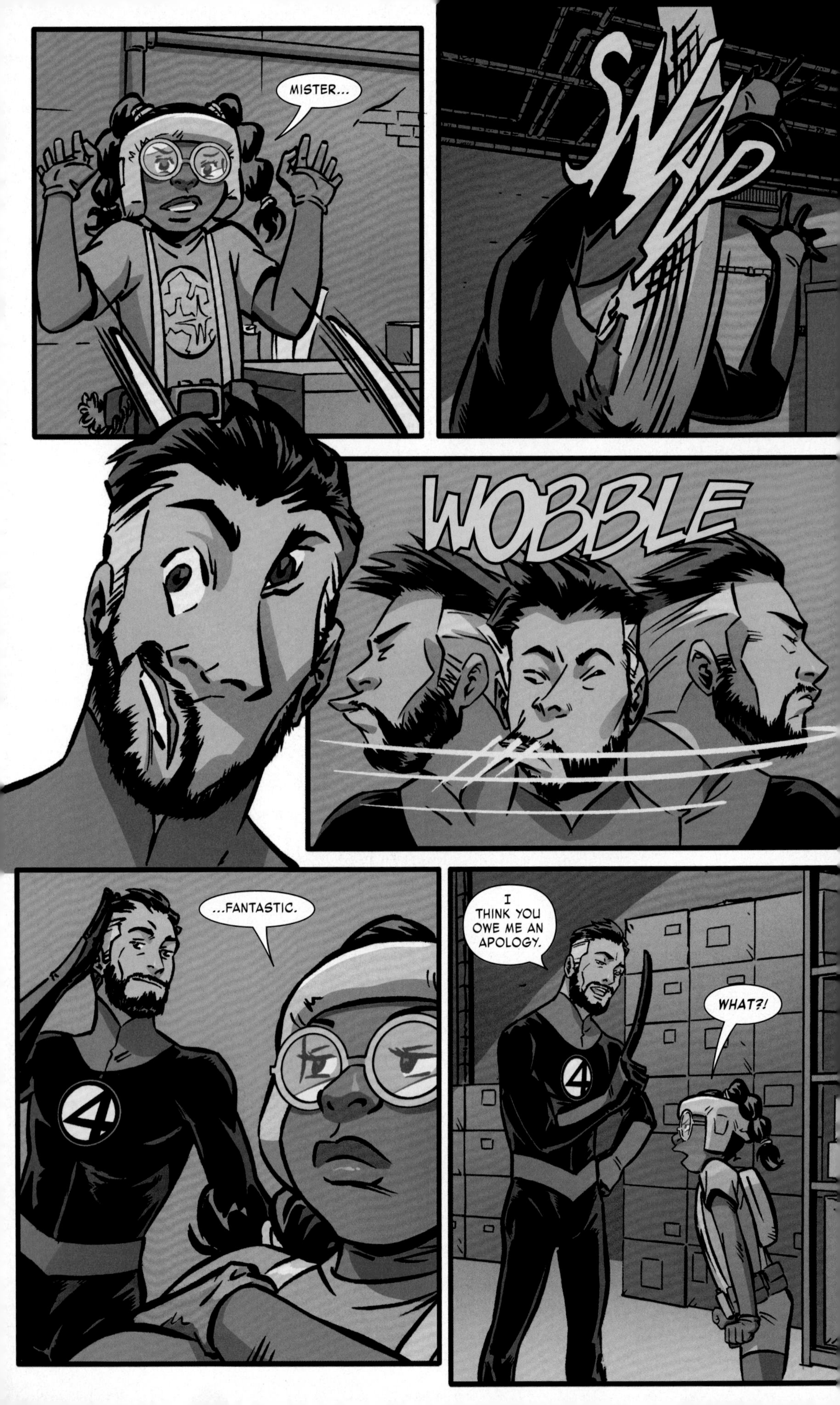
MISTER...
SNAP
WOBBLE
...FANTASTIC.
I THINK YOU OWE ME AN APOLOGY.
WHAT?!

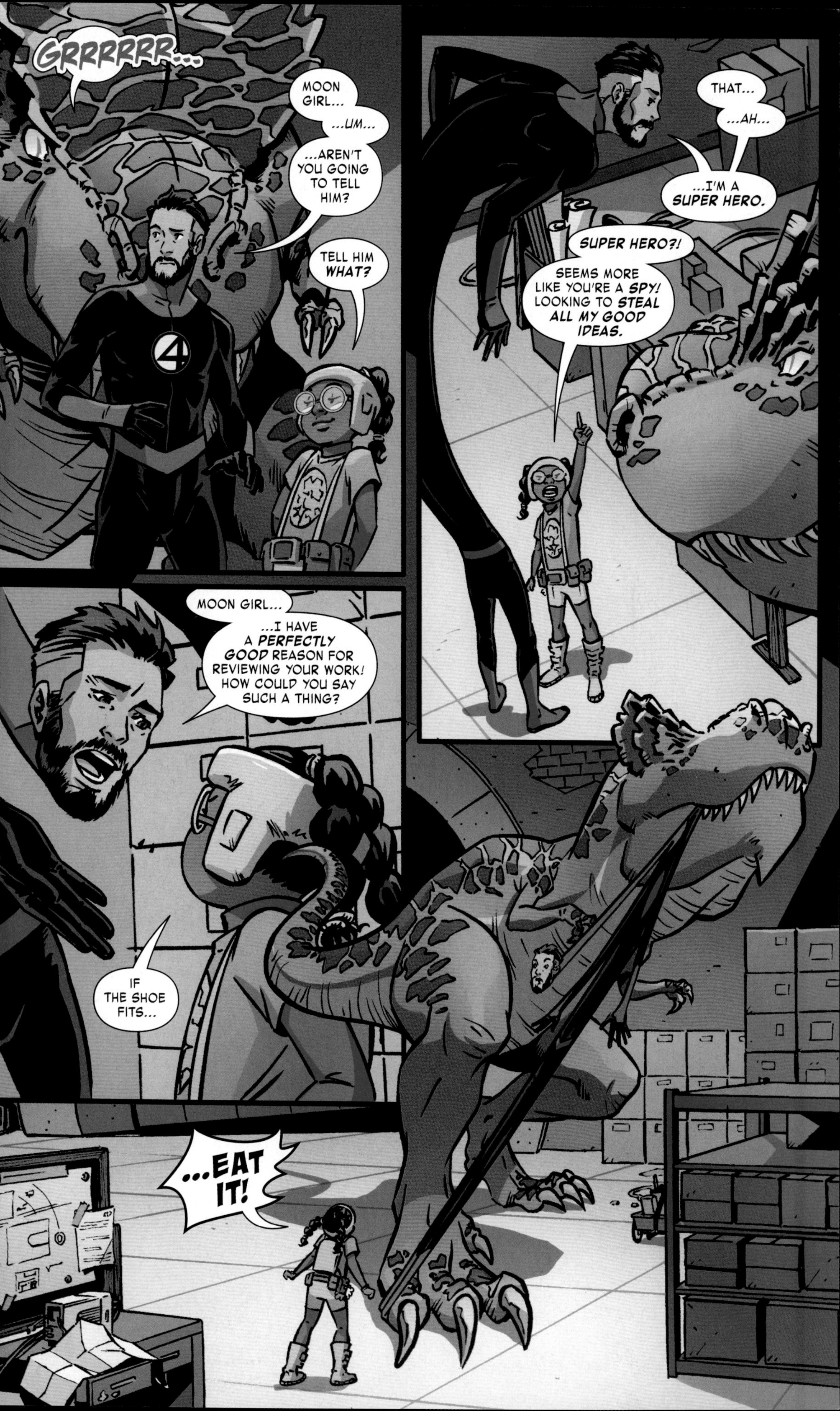
GRRRRRR...
MOON GIRL...
...UM...
...AREN'T YOU GOING TO TELL HIM?
TELL HIM WHAT?
THAT...
...AH...
...I'M A SUPER HERO.
SUPER HERO?!
SEEMS MORE LIKE YOU'RE A SPY! LOOKING TO STEAL ALL MY GOOD IDEAS.
MOON GIRL...
...I HAVE A PERFECTLY GOOD REASON FOR REVIEWING YOUR WORK! HOW COULD YOU SAY SUCH A THING?
IF THE SHOE FITS...
...EAT IT!

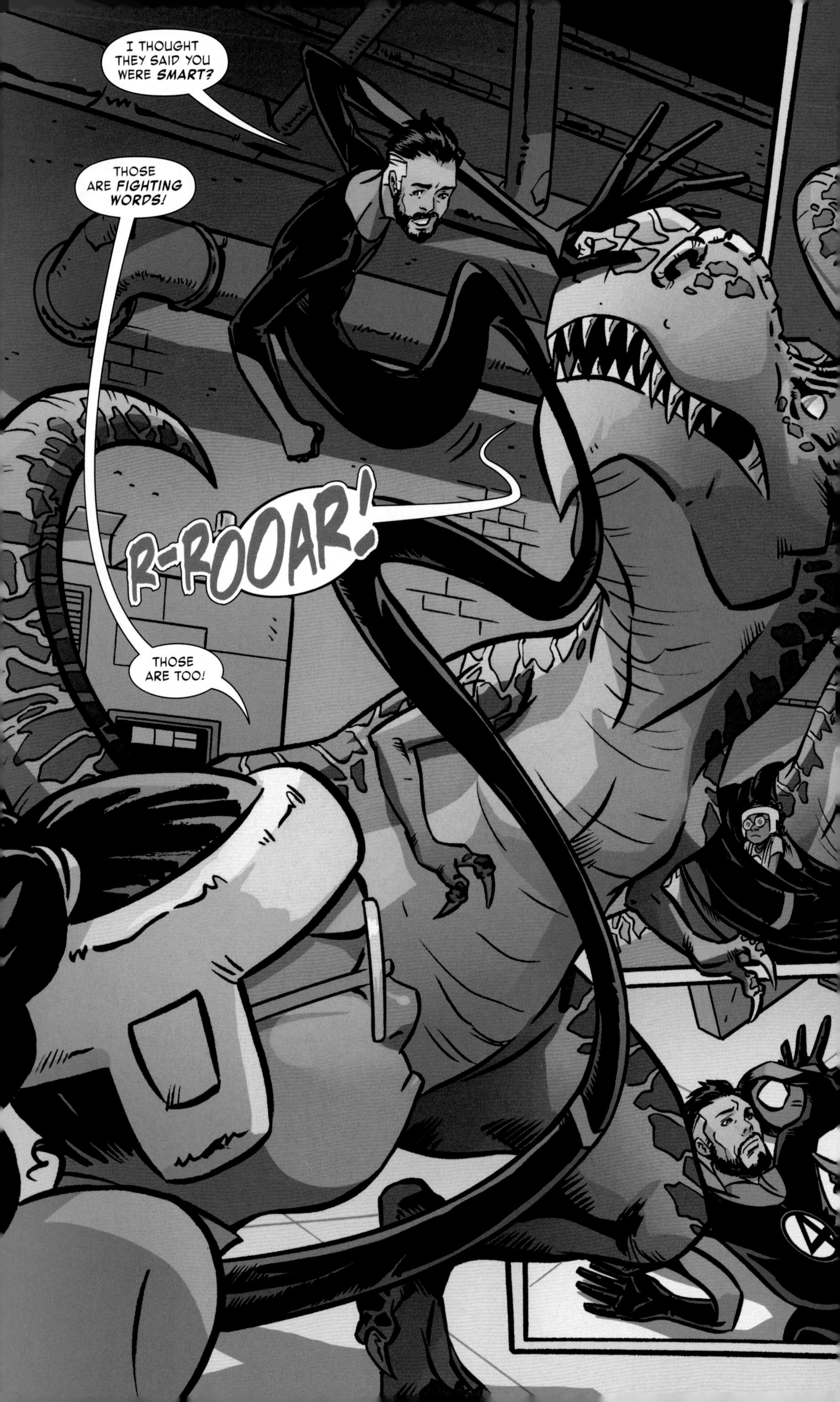
I THOUGHT THEY SAID YOU WERE SMART?
THOSE ARE FIGHTING WORDS!
R-ROOAR!
THOSE ARE TOO!

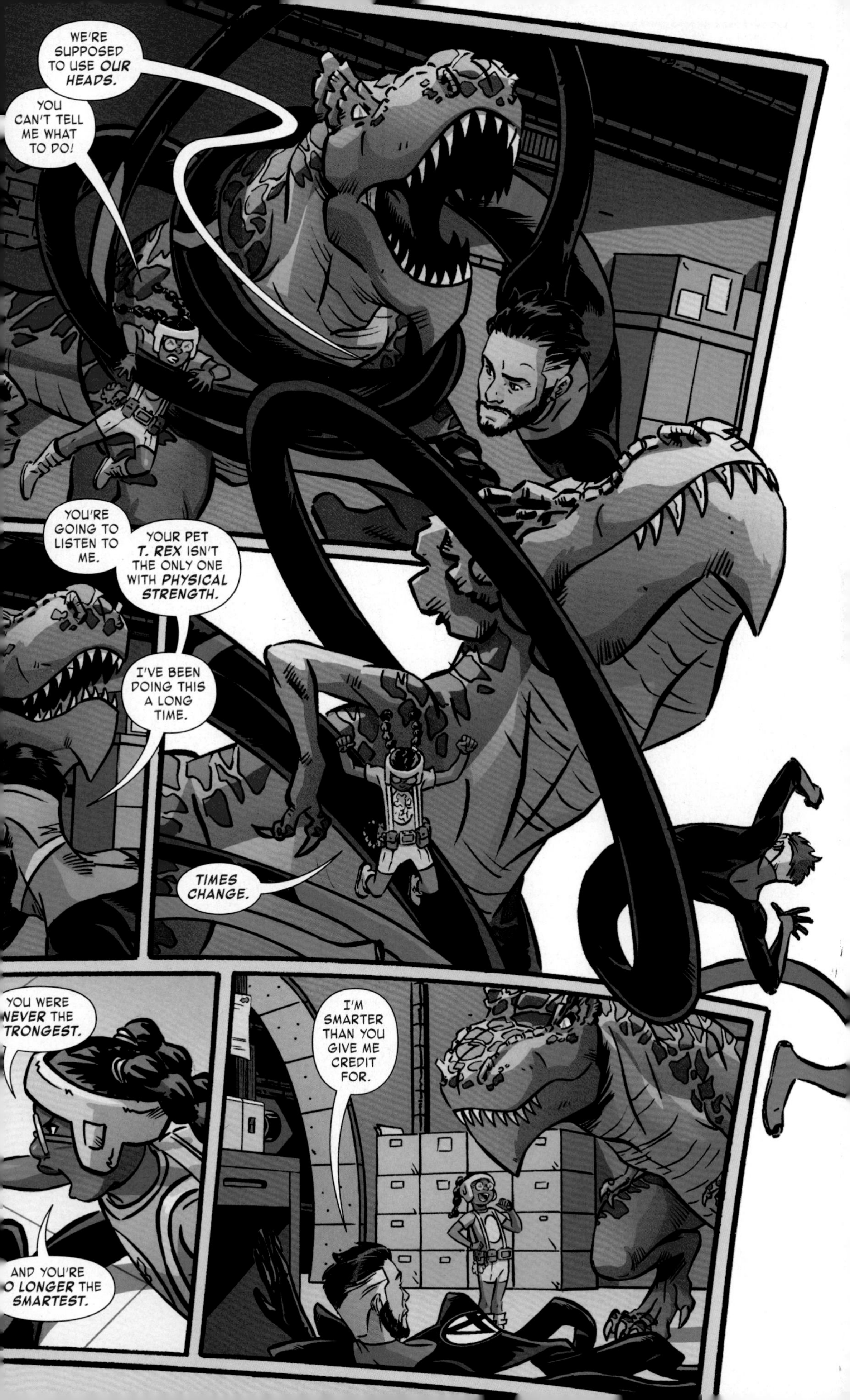

WE'RE SUPPOSED TO USE *OUR HEADS.*
YOU CAN'T TELL ME WHAT TO DO!
YOU'RE GOING TO LISTEN TO ME.
YOUR PET *T. REX* ISN'T THE ONLY ONE WITH *PHYSICAL STRENGTH.*
I'VE BEEN DOING THIS A LONG TIME.
TIMES CHANGE.
YOU WERE *NEVER* THE *TRONGEST.*
AND YOU'RE *O LONGER* THE *SMARTEST.*
I'M SMARTER THAN YOU GIVE ME CREDIT FOR.

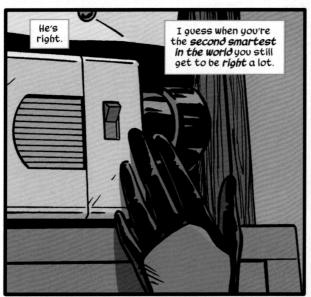
He's right.

I guess when you're the **second smartest in the world** you still get to be **right** a lot.

And that reminds me of something...

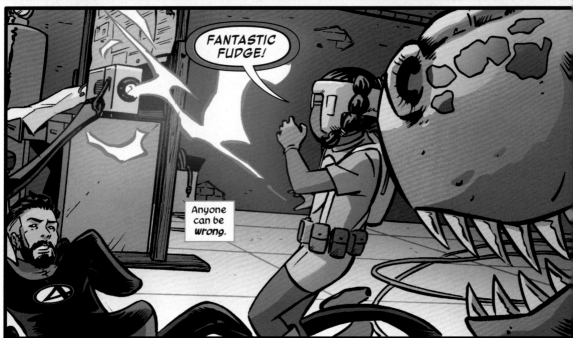
FANTASTIC FUDGE!

Anyone can be **wrong**.

KLAK

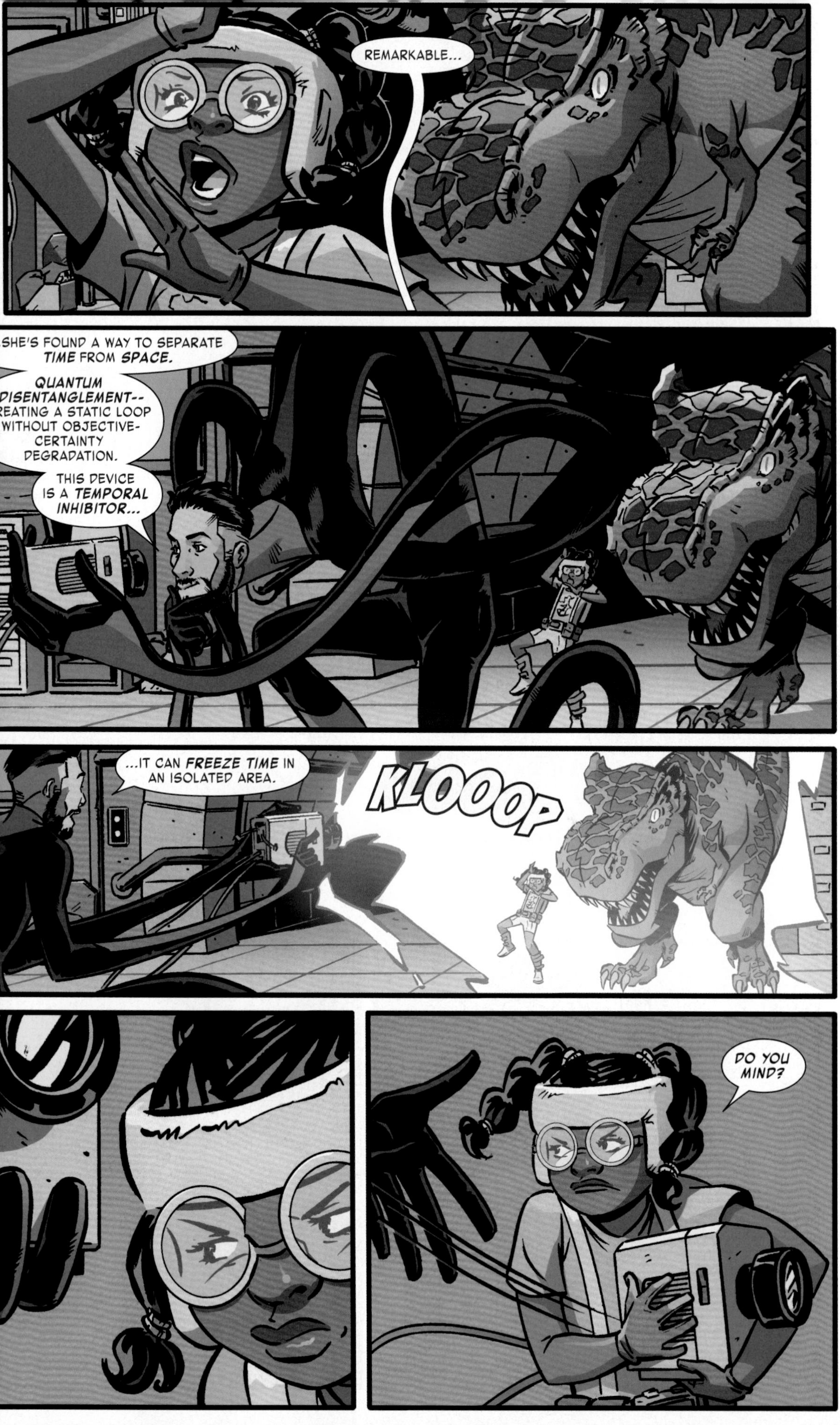
REMARKABLE...
.SHE'S FOUND A WAY TO SEPARATE *TIME* FROM *SPACE.*
QUANTUM DISENTANGLEMENT-- REATING A STATIC LOOP WITHOUT OBJECTIVE-CERTAINTY DEGRADATION.
THIS DEVICE IS A *TEMPORAL INHIBITOR...*
...IT CAN *FREEZE TIME* IN AN ISOLATED AREA.
KLOOOP
DO YOU MIND?

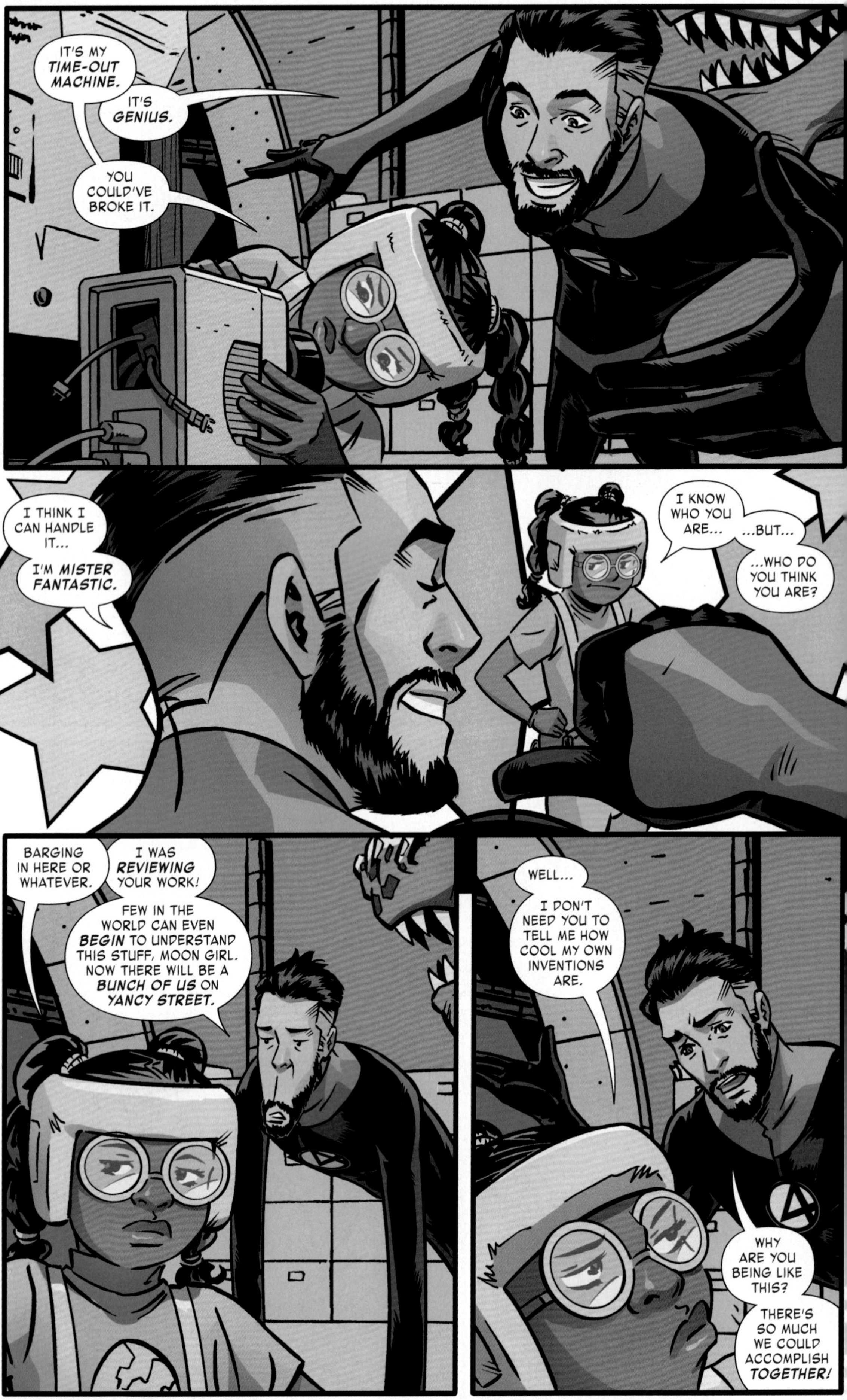
IT'S MY TIME-OUT MACHINE.
IT'S GENIUS.
YOU COULD'VE BROKE IT.
I THINK I CAN HANDLE IT...
I'M MISTER FANTASTIC.
I KNOW WHO YOU ARE...
...BUT...
...WHO DO YOU THINK YOU ARE?
BARGING IN HERE OR WHATEVER.
I WAS REVIEWING YOUR WORK!
FEW IN THE WORLD CAN EVEN BEGIN TO UNDERSTAND THIS STUFF, MOON GIRL. NOW THERE WILL BE A BUNCH OF US ON YANCY STREET.
WELL...
I DON'T NEED YOU TO TELL ME HOW COOL MY OWN INVENTIONS ARE.
WHY ARE YOU BEING LIKE THIS?
THERE'S SO MUCH WE COULD ACCOMPLISH TOGETHER!

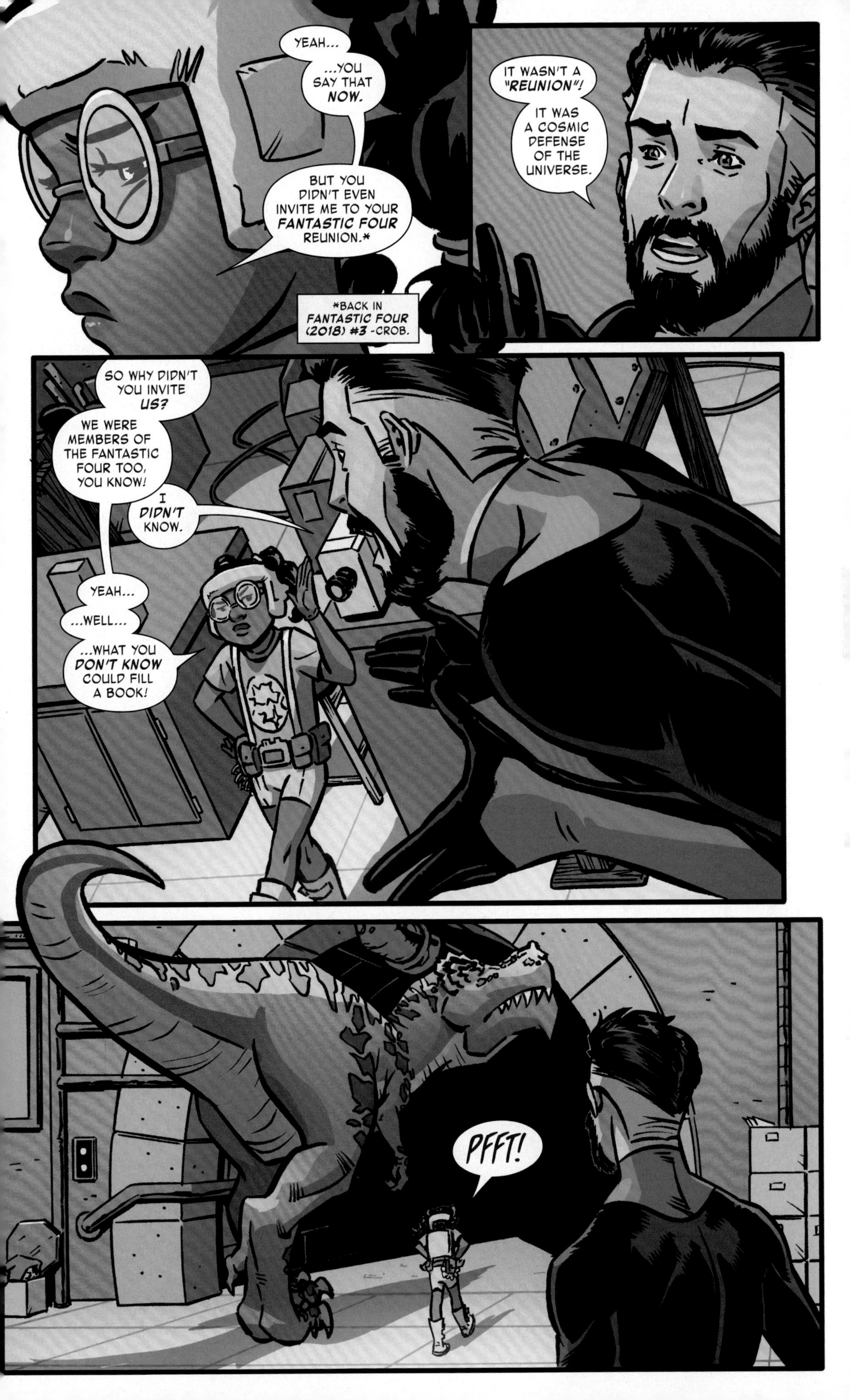
YEAH...
...YOU SAY THAT NOW.
BUT YOU DIDN'T EVEN INVITE ME TO YOUR FANTASTIC FOUR REUNION.*
*BACK IN FANTASTIC FOUR (2018) #3 -CROB.
IT WASN'T A "REUNION"!
IT WAS A COSMIC DEFENSE OF THE UNIVERSE.
SO WHY DIDN'T YOU INVITE US?
WE WERE MEMBERS OF THE FANTASTIC FOUR TOO, YOU KNOW!
I DIDN'T KNOW.
YEAH...
...WELL...
...WHAT YOU DON'T KNOW COULD FILL A BOOK!
PFFT!

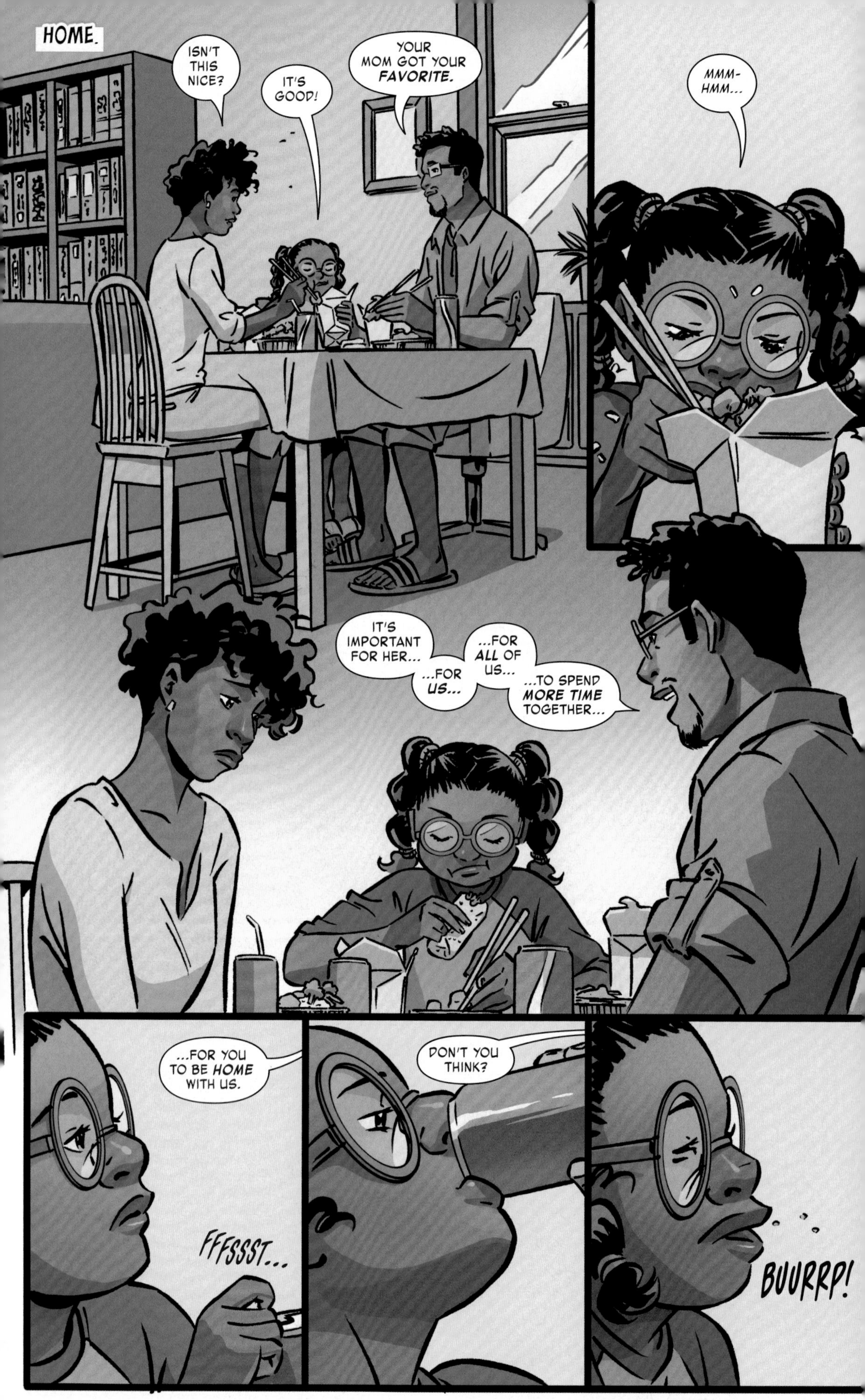
HOME.
ISN'T THIS NICE?
IT'S GOOD!
YOUR MOM GOT YOUR FAVORITE.
MMM-HMM...
IT'S IMPORTANT FOR HER...
...FOR US...
...FOR ALL OF US...
...TO SPEND MORE TIME TOGETHER...
...FOR YOU TO BE HOME WITH US.
FFFSSST...
DON'T YOU THINK?
BUURRP!

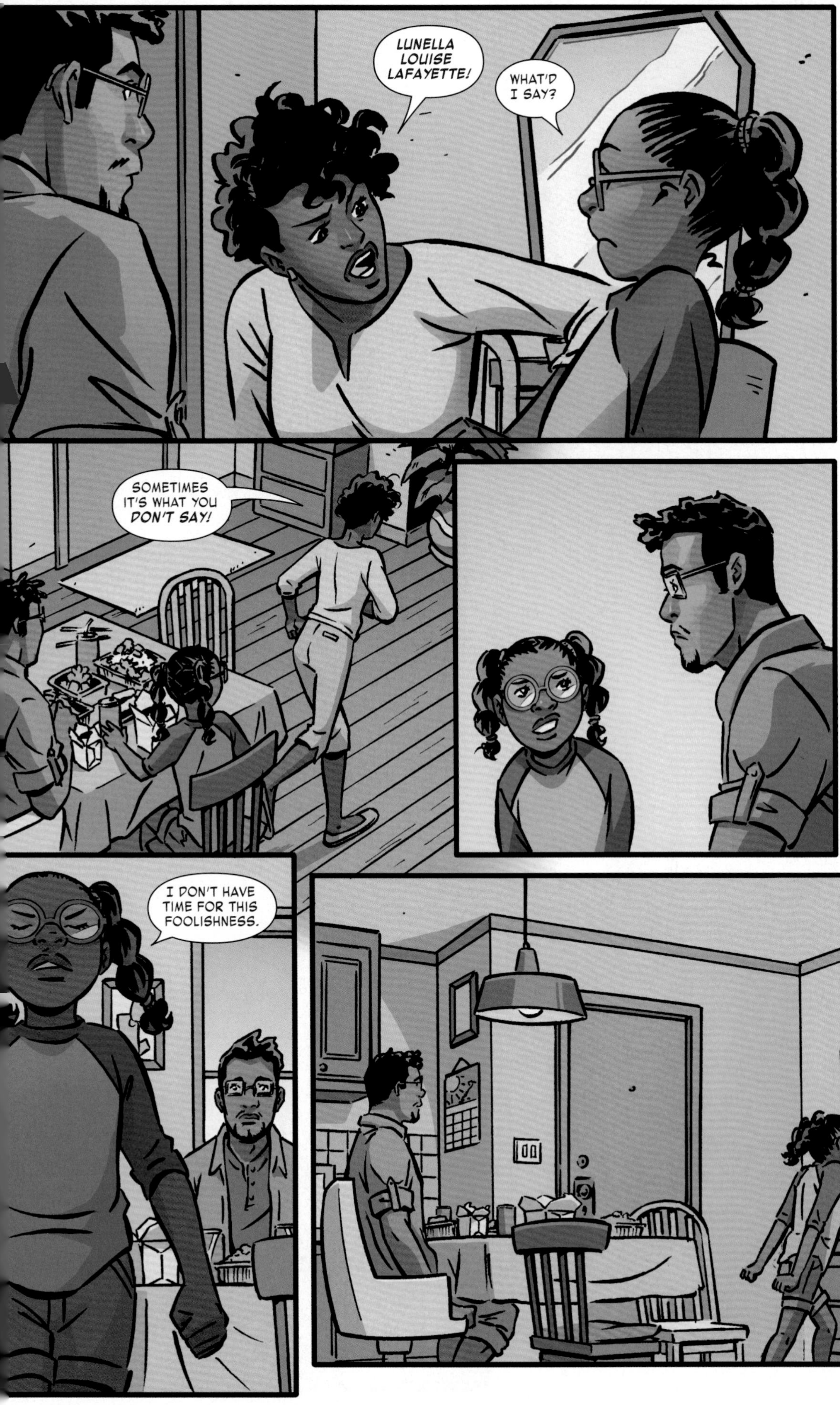
LUNELLA LOUISE LAFAYETTE!
WHAT'D I SAY?
SOMETIMES IT'S WHAT YOU *DON'T SAY!*
I DON'T HAVE TIME FOR THIS FOOLISHNESS.

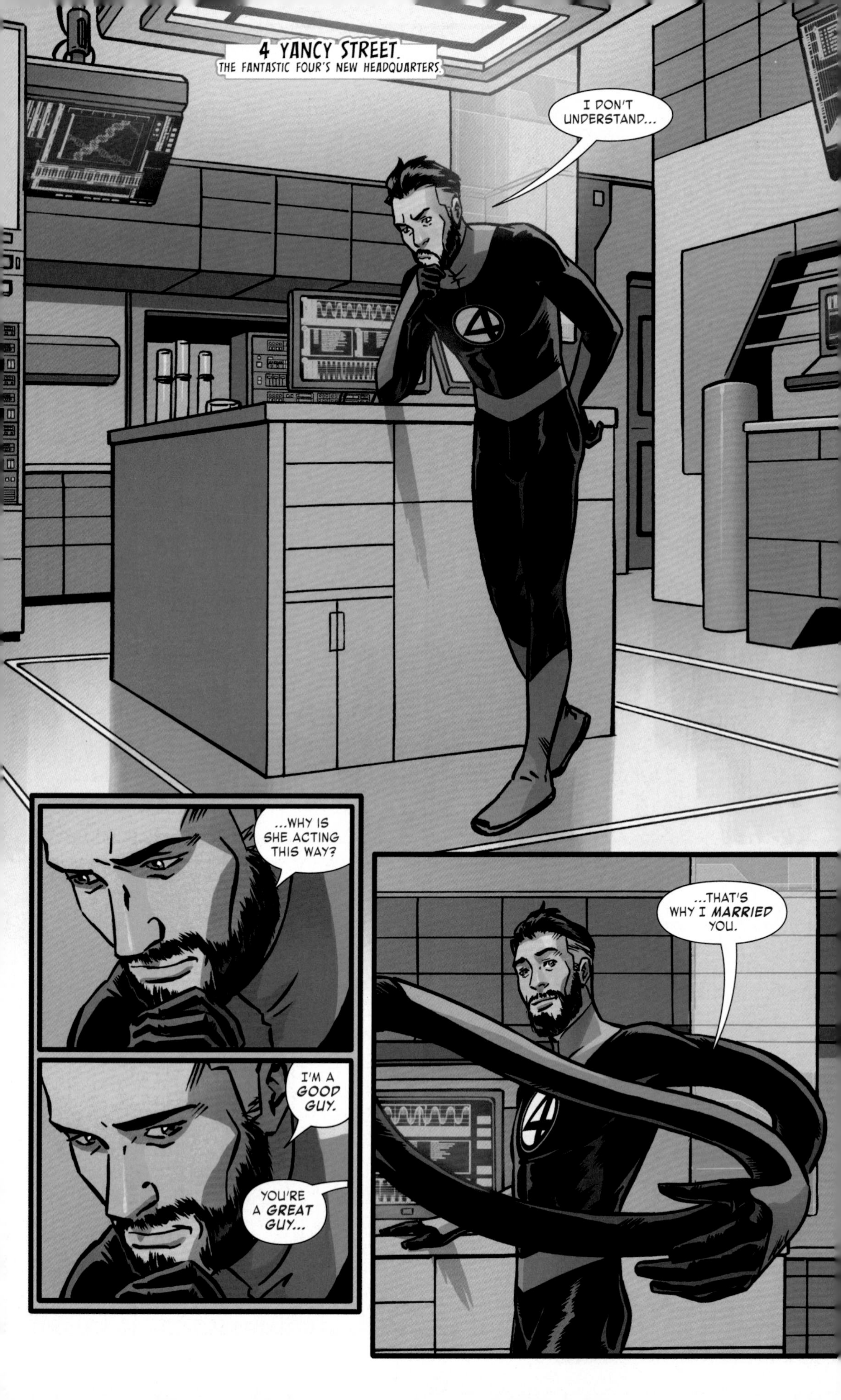
4 YANCY STREET.
THE FANTASTIC FOUR'S NEW HEADQUARTERS.
I DON'T UNDERSTAND...
...WHY IS SHE ACTING THIS WAY?
I'M A GOOD GUY.
YOU'RE A GREAT GUY...
...THAT'S WHY I MARRIED YOU.

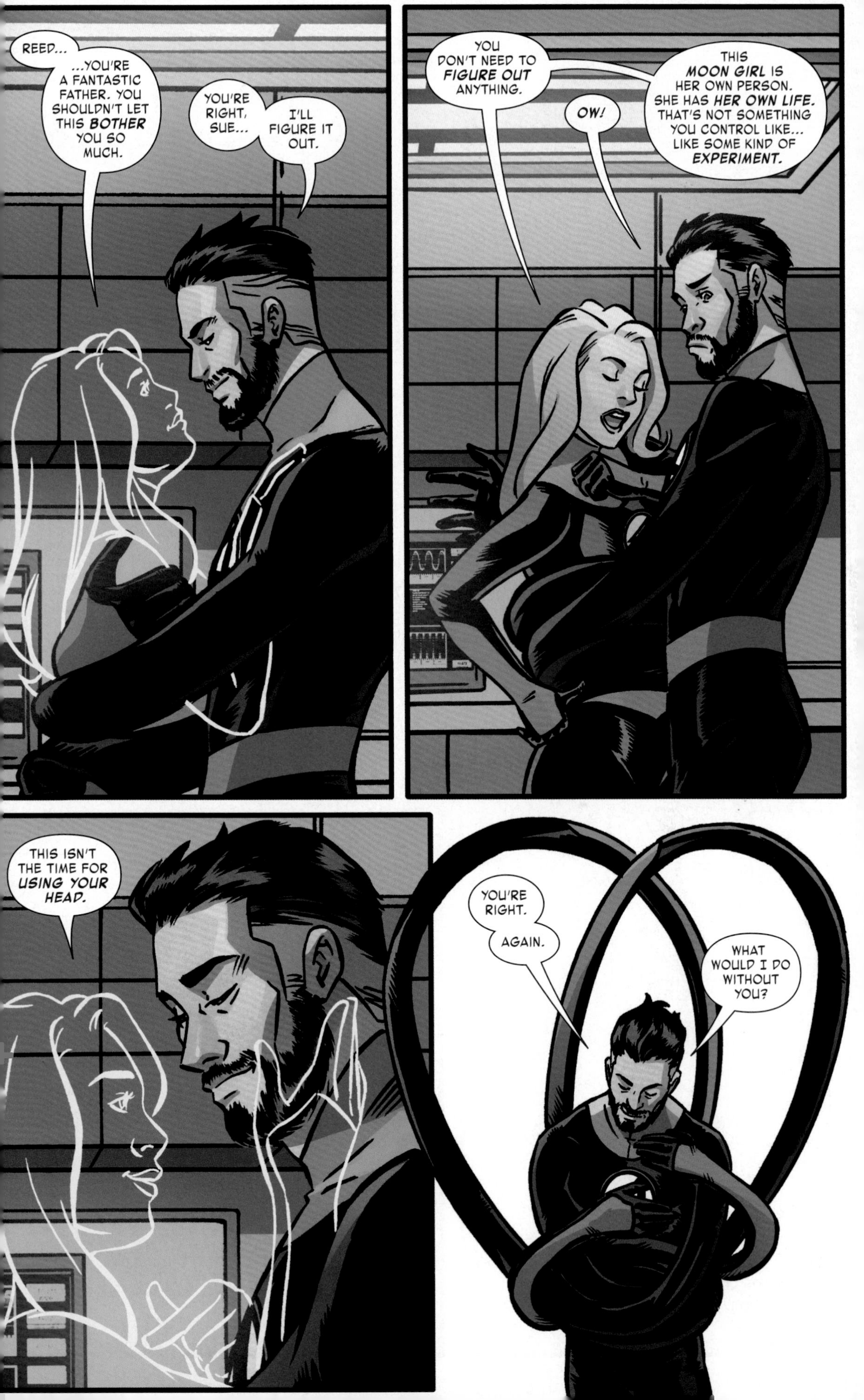
REED...
...YOU'RE A FANTASTIC FATHER. YOU SHOULDN'T LET THIS BOTHER YOU SO MUCH.
YOU'RE RIGHT, SUE...
I'LL FIGURE IT OUT.
YOU DON'T NEED TO FIGURE OUT ANYTHING.
OW!
THIS MOON GIRL IS HER OWN PERSON. SHE HAS HER OWN LIFE. THAT'S NOT SOMETHING YOU CONTROL LIKE... LIKE SOME KIND OF EXPERIMENT.
THIS ISN'T THE TIME FOR USING YOUR HEAD.
YOU'RE RIGHT.
AGAIN.
WHAT WOULD I DO WITHOUT YOU?

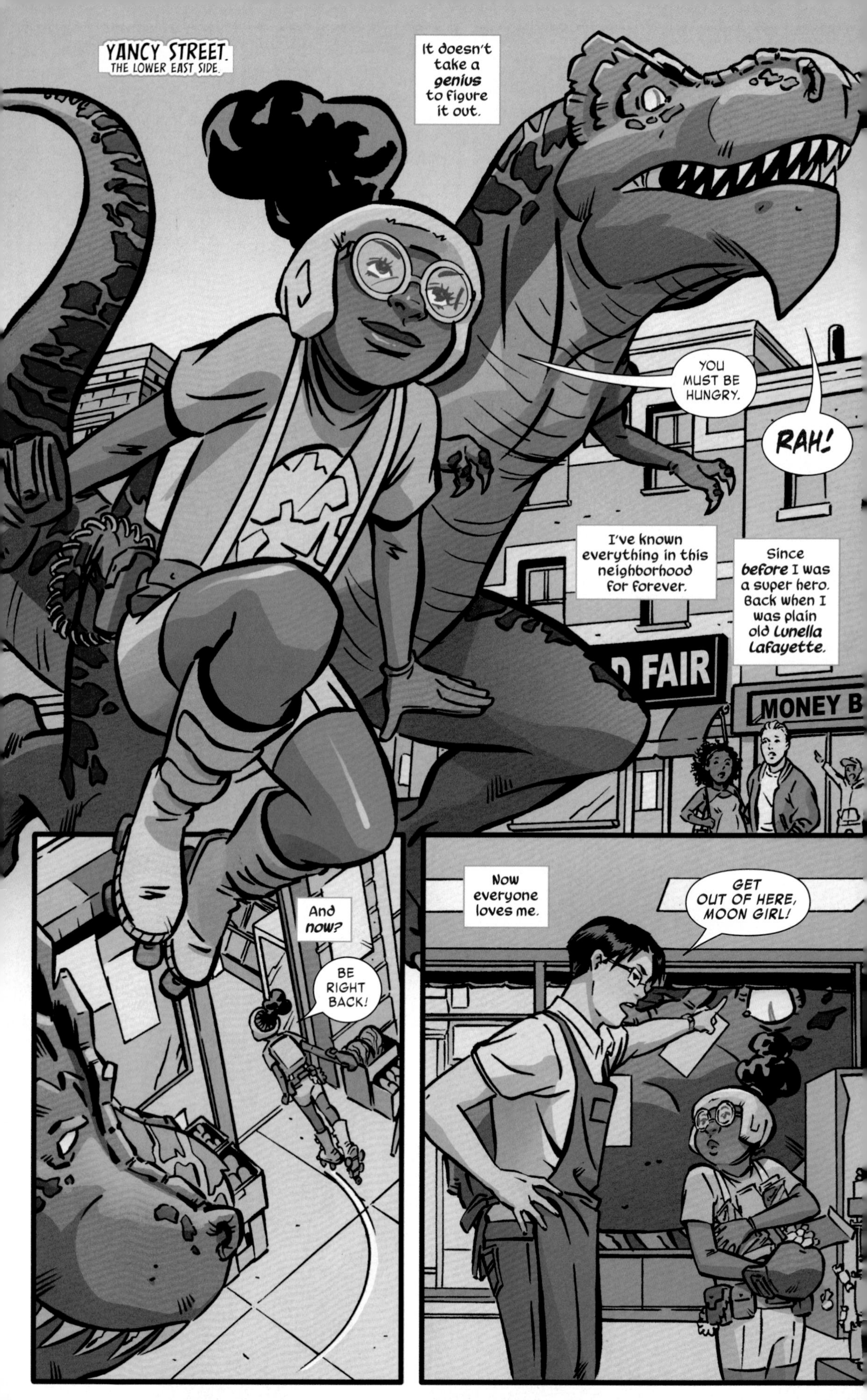

YANCY STREET. THE LOWER EAST SIDE.
It doesn't take a genius to figure it out.
YOU MUST BE HUNGRY.
RAH!
I've known everything in this neighborhood for forever.
Since before I was a super hero. Back when I was plain old Lunella Lafayette.
D FAIR
MONEY B
And now?
BE RIGHT BACK!
Now everyone loves me.
GET OUT OF HERE, MOON GIRL!

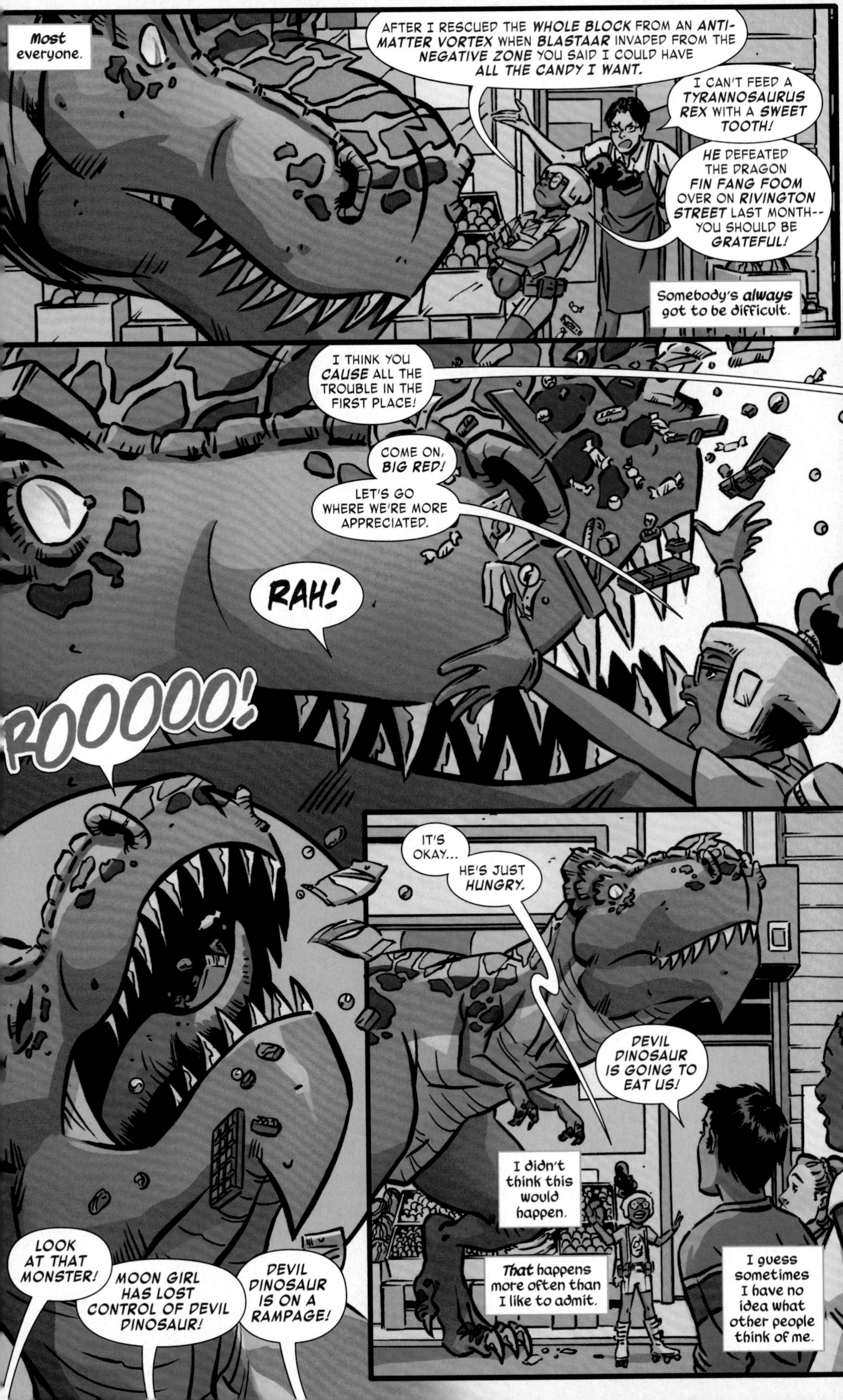

Most everyone.
AFTER I RESCUED THE WHOLE BLOCK FROM AN ANTI-MATTER VORTEX WHEN BLASTAAR INVADED FROM THE NEGATIVE ZONE YOU SAID I COULD HAVE ALL THE CANDY I WANT.
I CAN'T FEED A TYRANNOSAURUS REX WITH A SWEET TOOTH!
HE DEFEATED THE DRAGON FIN FANG FOOM OVER ON RIVINGTON STREET LAST MONTH-- YOU SHOULD BE GRATEFUL!
Somebody's always got to be difficult.
I THINK YOU CAUSE ALL THE TROUBLE IN THE FIRST PLACE!
COME ON, BIG RED!
LET'S GO WHERE WE'RE MORE APPRECIATED.
RAH!
ROOOOO!
LOOK AT THAT MONSTER!
MOON GIRL HAS LOST CONTROL OF DEVIL DINOSAUR!
DEVIL DINOSAUR IS ON A RAMPAGE!
IT'S OKAY...
HE'S JUST HUNGRY.
DEVIL DINOSAUR IS GOING TO EAT US!
I didn't think this would happen.
That happens more often than I like to admit.
I guess sometimes I have no idea what other people think of me.

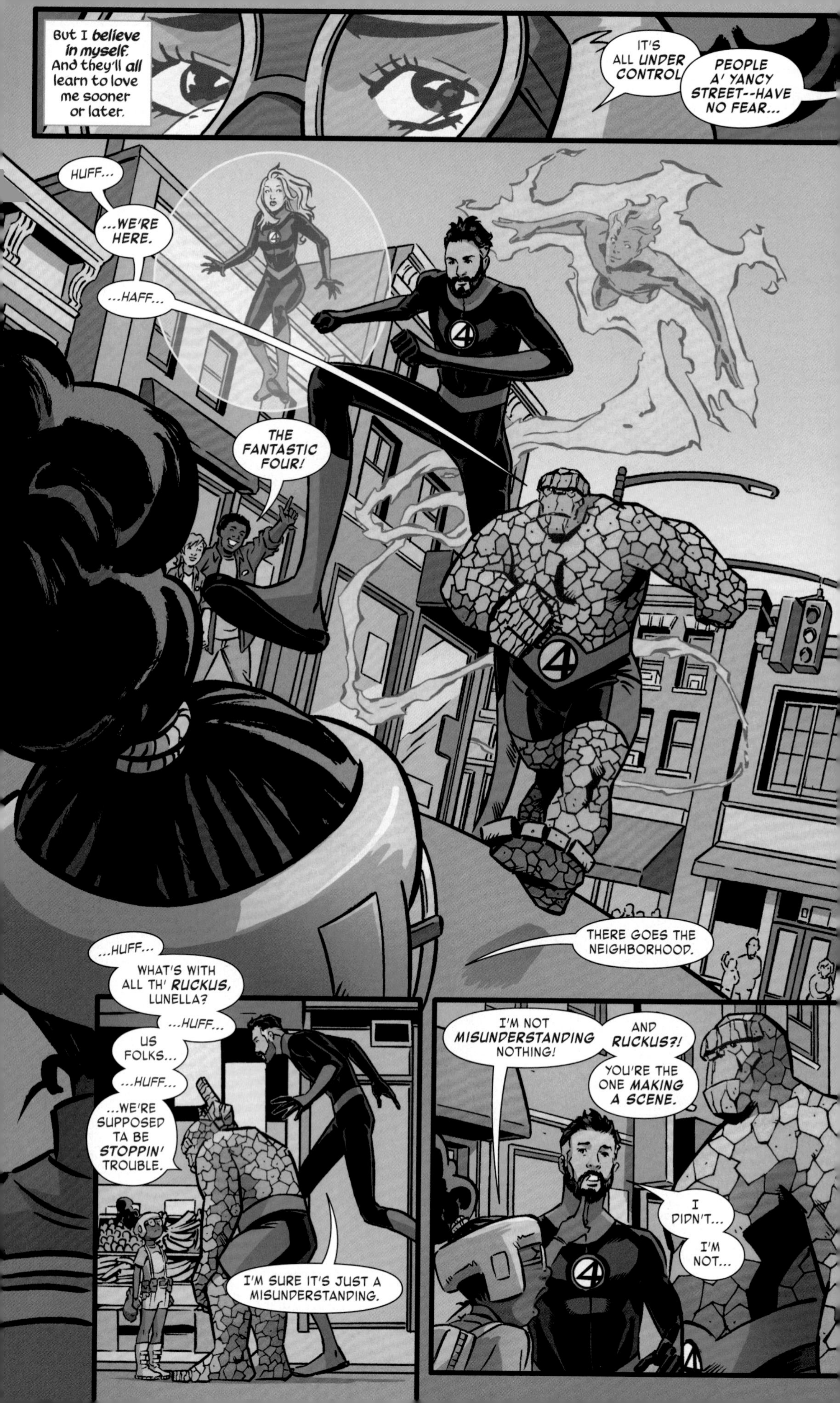
But I believe in myself. And they'll all learn to love me sooner or later.
IT'S ALL UNDER CONTROL
PEOPLE A' YANCY STREET--HAVE NO FEAR...
HUFF...
...WE'RE HERE.
...HAFF...
THE FANTASTIC FOUR!
THERE GOES THE NEIGHBORHOOD.
...HUFF...
WHAT'S WITH ALL TH' RUCKUS, LUNELLA?
...HUFF...
US FOLKS...
...HUFF...
...WE'RE SUPPOSED TA BE STOPPIN' TROUBLE.
I'M SURE IT'S JUST A MISUNDERSTANDING.
I'M NOT MISUNDERSTANDING NOTHING!
AND RUCKUS?!
YOU'RE THE ONE MAKING A SCENE.
I DIDN'T...
I'M NOT...

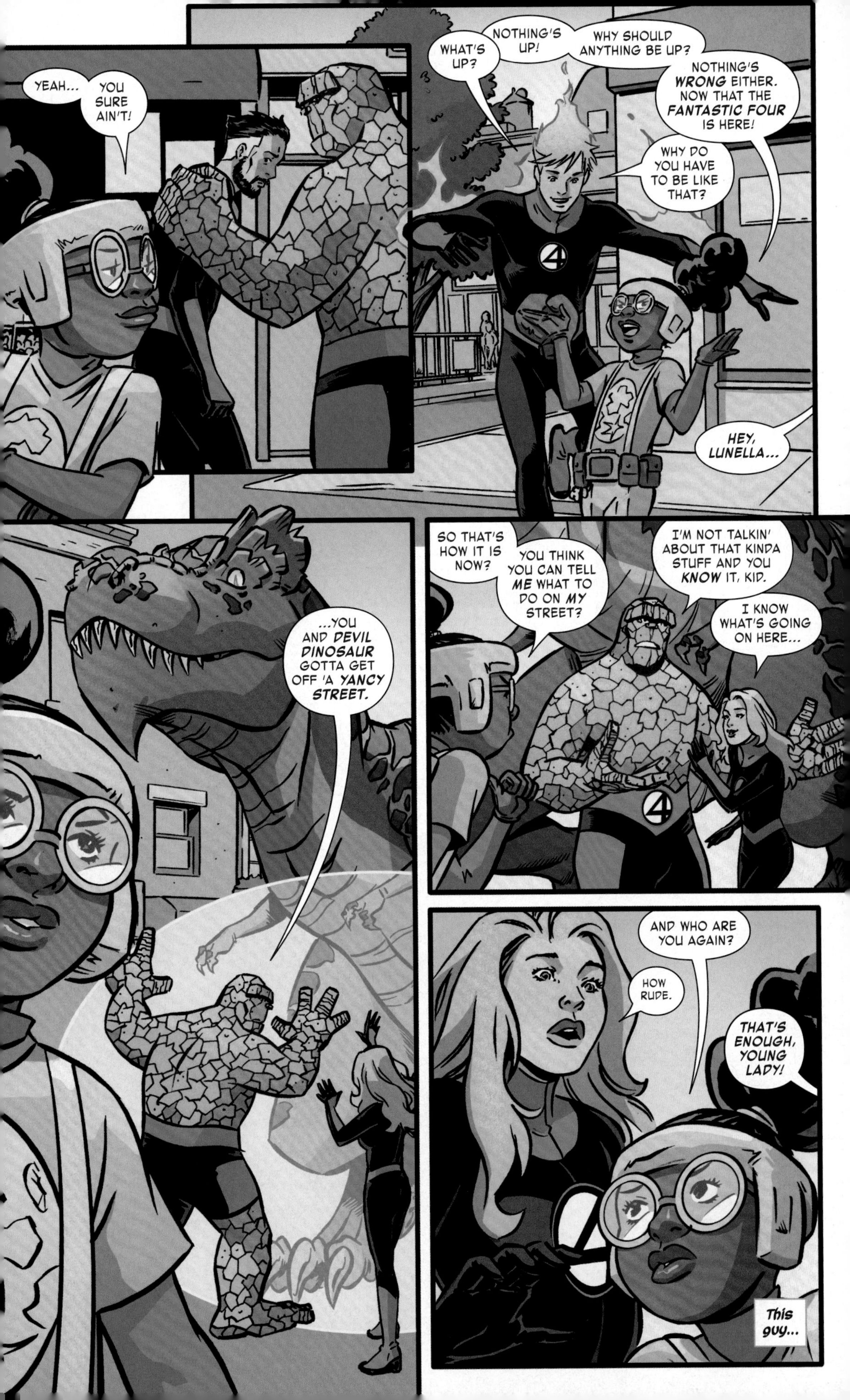
YEAH...
YOU SURE AIN'T!
WHAT'S UP?
NOTHING'S UP!
WHY SHOULD ANYTHING BE UP?
NOTHING'S WRONG EITHER. NOW THAT THE FANTASTIC FOUR IS HERE!
WHY DO YOU HAVE TO BE LIKE THAT?
HEY, LUNELLA...
...YOU AND DEVIL DINOSAUR GOTTA GET OFF 'A YANCY STREET.
SO THAT'S HOW IT IS NOW?
YOU THINK YOU CAN TELL ME WHAT TO DO ON MY STREET?
I'M NOT TALKIN' ABOUT THAT KINDA STUFF AND YOU KNOW IT, KID.
I KNOW WHAT'S GOING ON HERE...
AND WHO ARE YOU AGAIN?
HOW RUDE.
THAT'S ENOUGH, YOUNG LADY!
This guy...

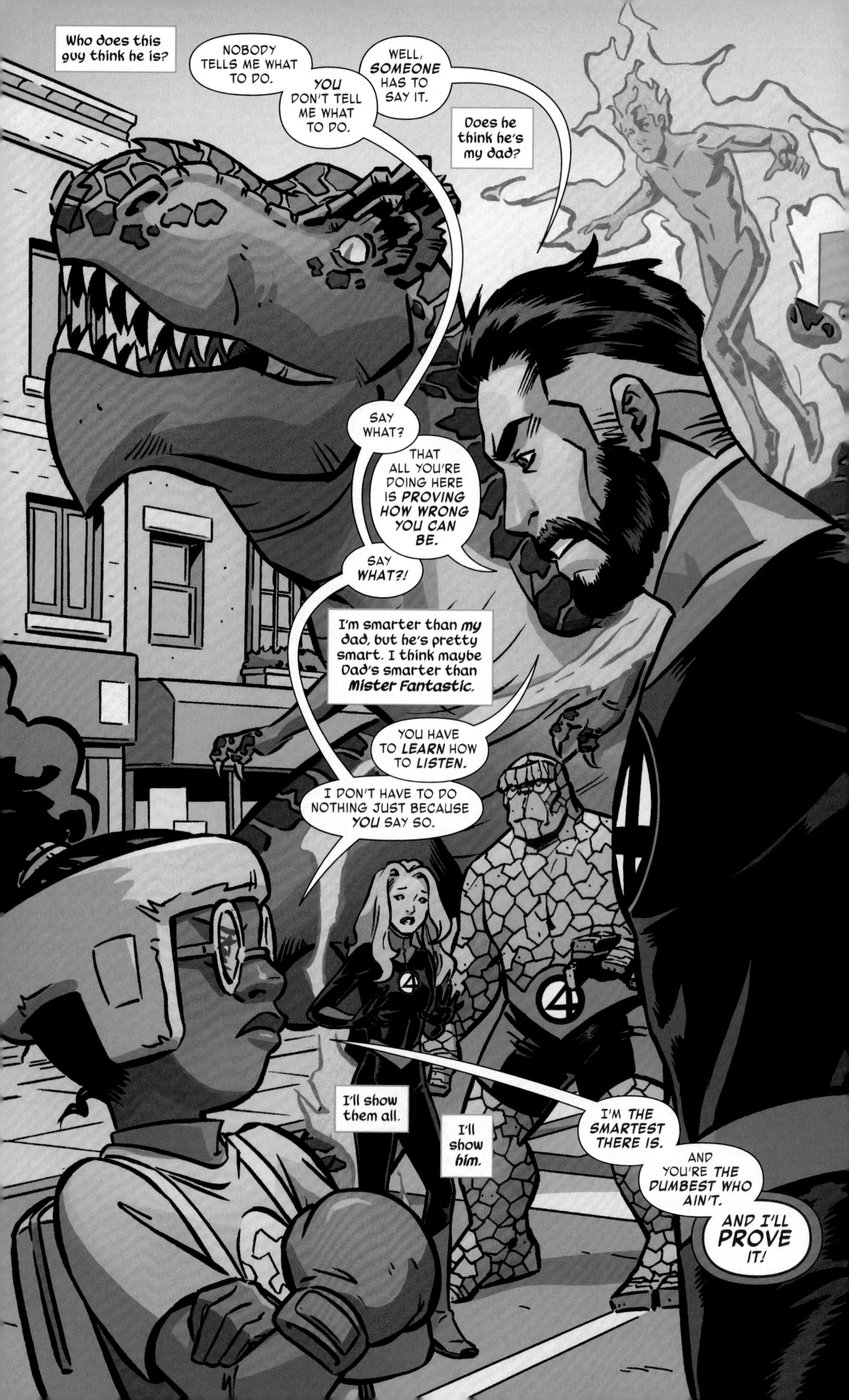
Who does this guy think he is?
NOBODY TELLS ME WHAT TO DO.
YOU DON'T TELL ME WHAT TO DO.
WELL, SOMEONE HAS TO SAY IT.
Does he think he's my dad?
SAY WHAT?
THAT ALL YOU'RE DOING HERE IS PROVING HOW WRONG YOU CAN BE.
SAY WHAT?!
I'm smarter than my dad, but he's pretty smart. I think maybe Dad's smarter than Mister Fantastic.
YOU HAVE TO LEARN HOW TO LISTEN.
I DON'T HAVE TO DO NOTHING JUST BECAUSE YOU SAY SO.
I'll show them all.
I'll show him.
I'M THE SMARTEST THERE IS.
AND YOU'RE THE DUMBEST WHO AIN'T.
AND I'LL PROVE IT!

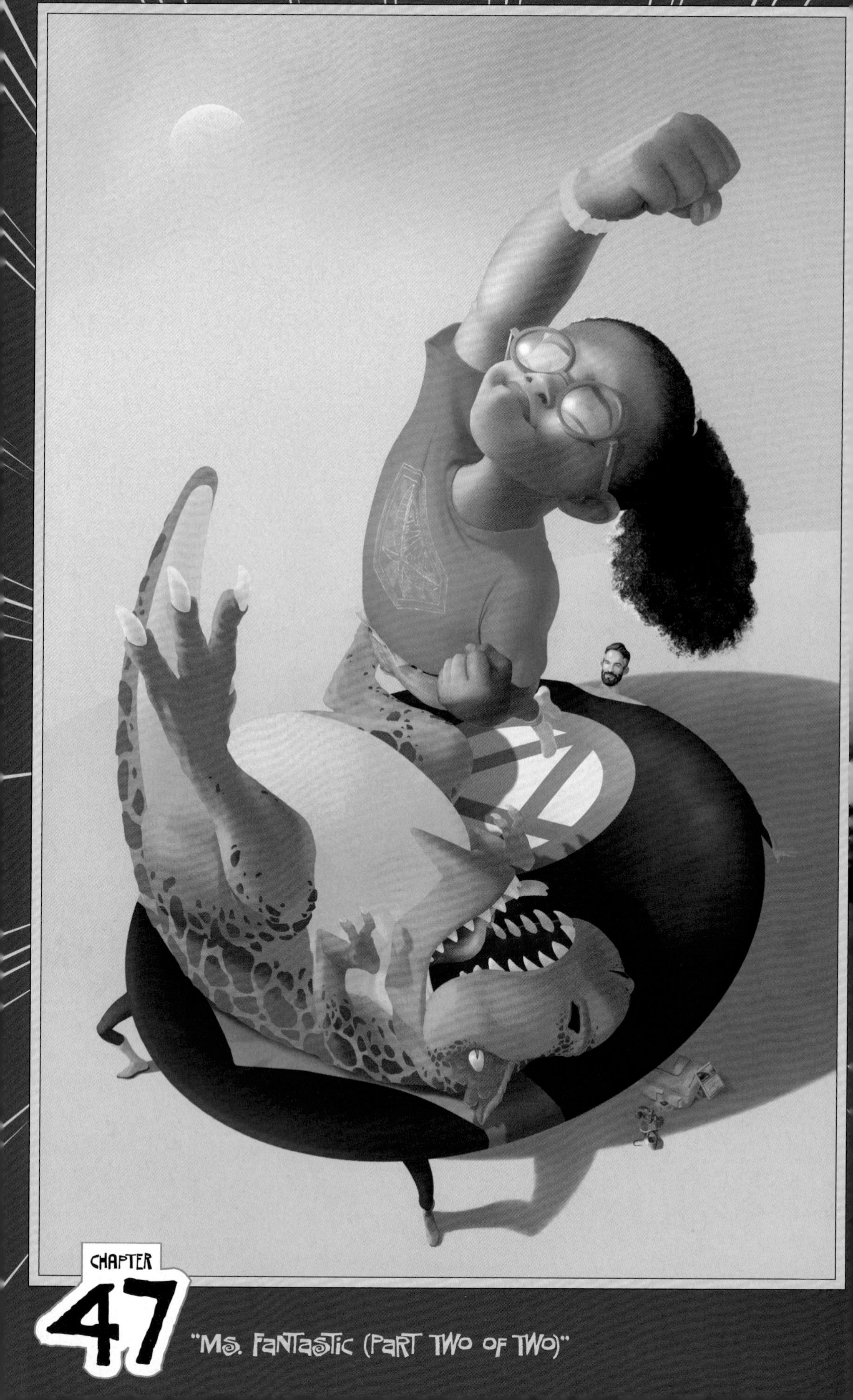

CHAPTER

47

"Ms. Fantastic (Part Two of Two)"

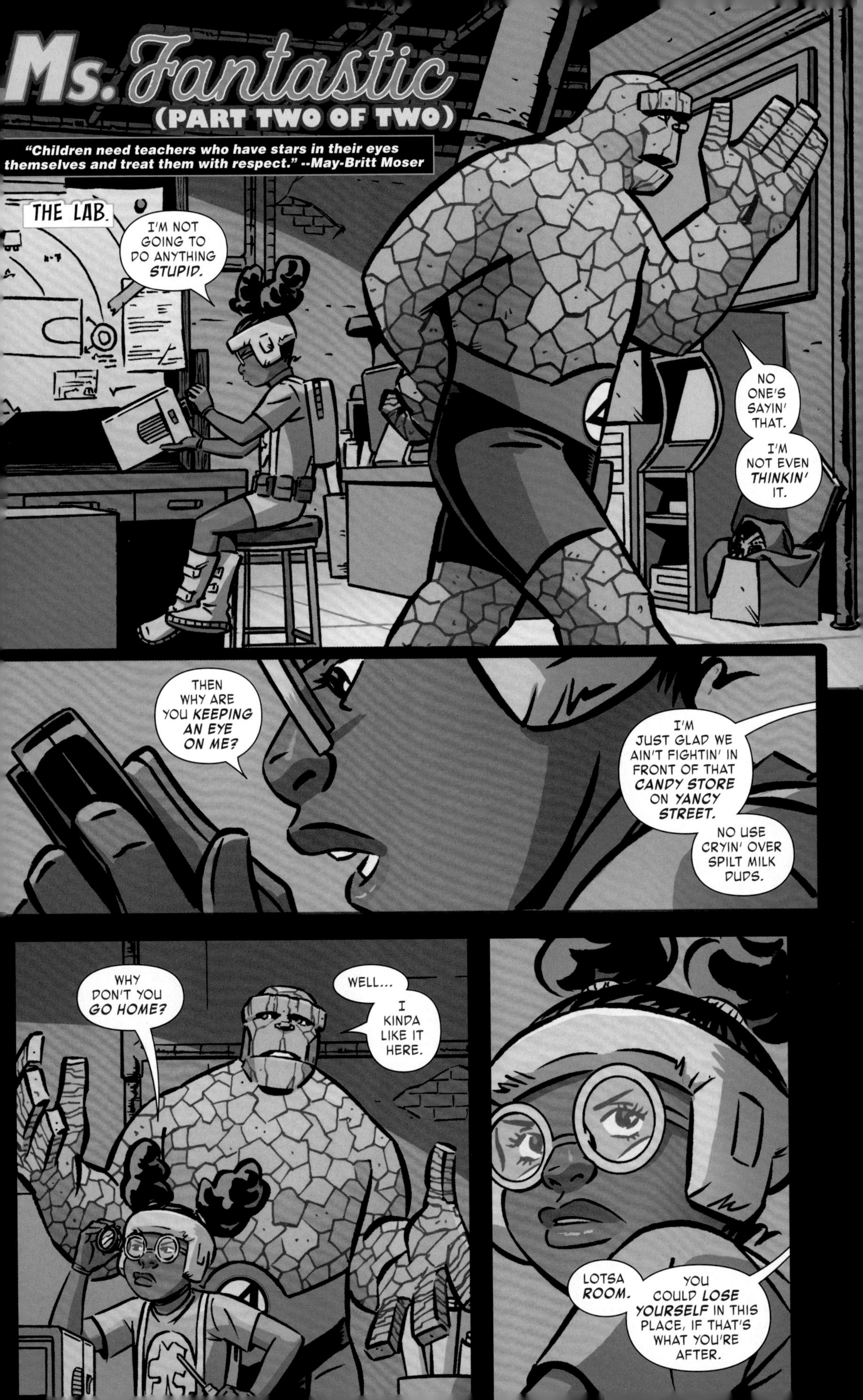
Ms. Fantastic
(PART TWO OF TWO)
"Children need teachers who have stars in their eyes themselves and treat them with respect." --May-Britt Moser
THE LAB.
I'M NOT GOING TO DO ANYTHING *STUPID.*
NO ONE'S SAYIN' THAT.
I'M NOT EVEN *THINKIN'* IT.
THEN WHY ARE YOU *KEEPING AN EYE ON ME?*
I'M JUST GLAD WE AIN'T FIGHTIN' IN FRONT OF THAT *CANDY STORE* ON *YANCY STREET.*
NO USE CRYIN' OVER SPILT MILK DUDS.
WHY DON'T YOU *GO HOME?*
WELL...
I KINDA LIKE IT HERE.
LOTSA *ROOM.*
YOU COULD *LOSE YOURSELF* IN THIS PLACE, IF THAT'S WHAT YOU'RE AFTER.

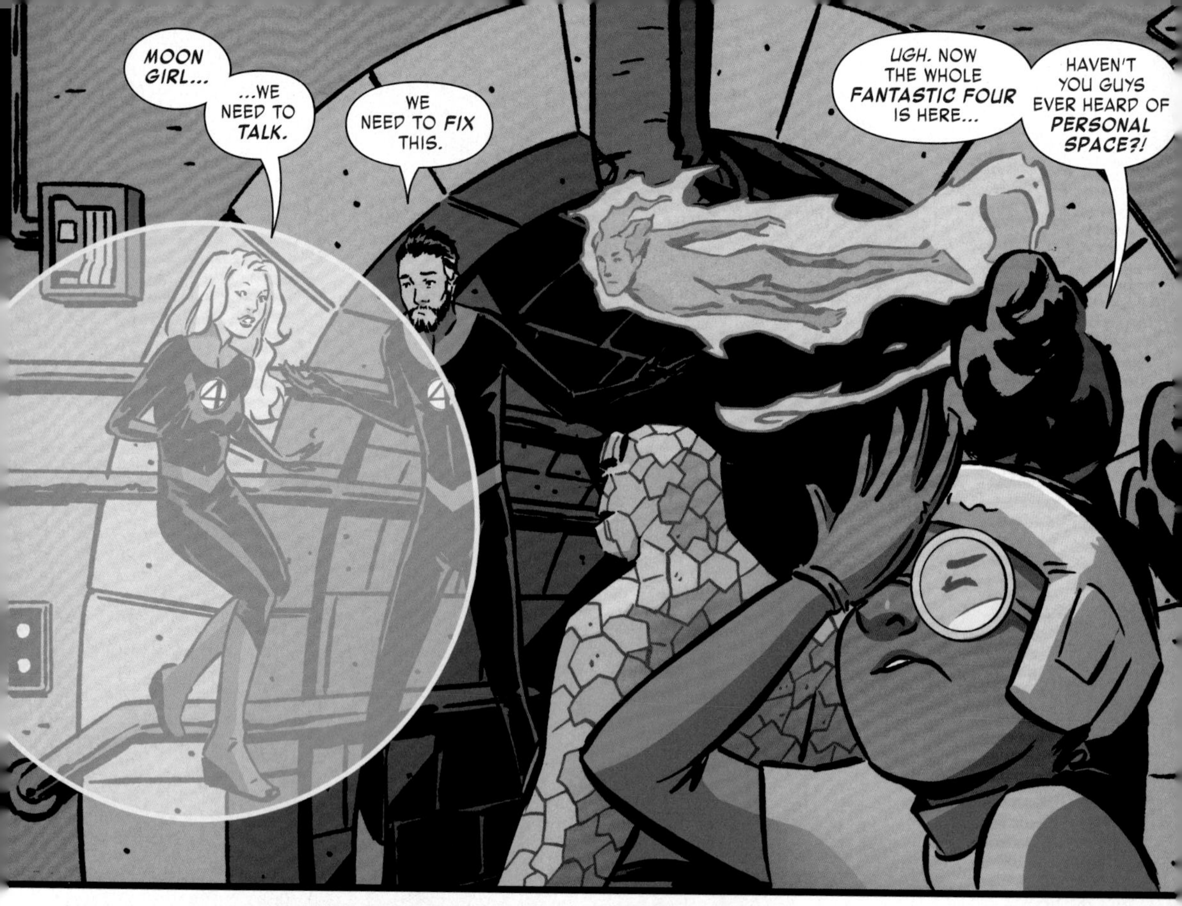
MOON GIRL...
...WE NEED TO TALK.
WE NEED TO FIX THIS.
UGH. NOW THE WHOLE FANTASTIC FOUR IS HERE...
HAVEN'T YOU GUYS EVER HEARD OF PERSONAL SPACE?!

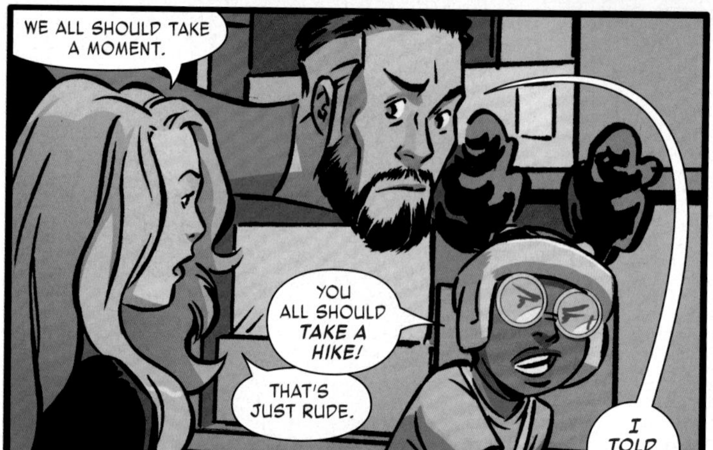
WE ALL SHOULD TAKE A MOMENT.
YOU ALL SHOULD TAKE A HIKE!
THAT'S JUST RUDE.
I TOLD YOU.

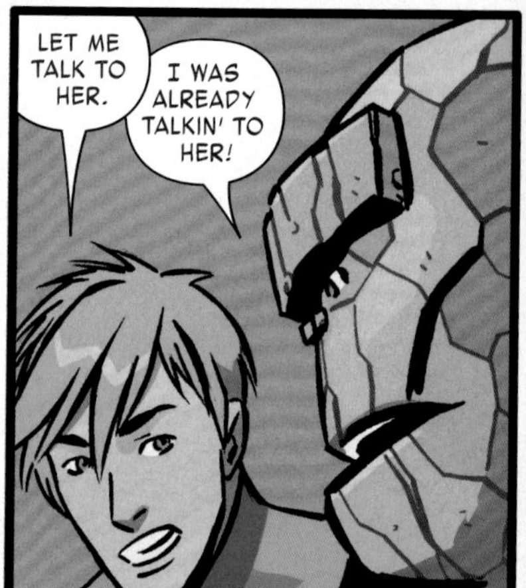
LET ME TALK TO HER.
I WAS ALREADY TALKIN' TO HER!

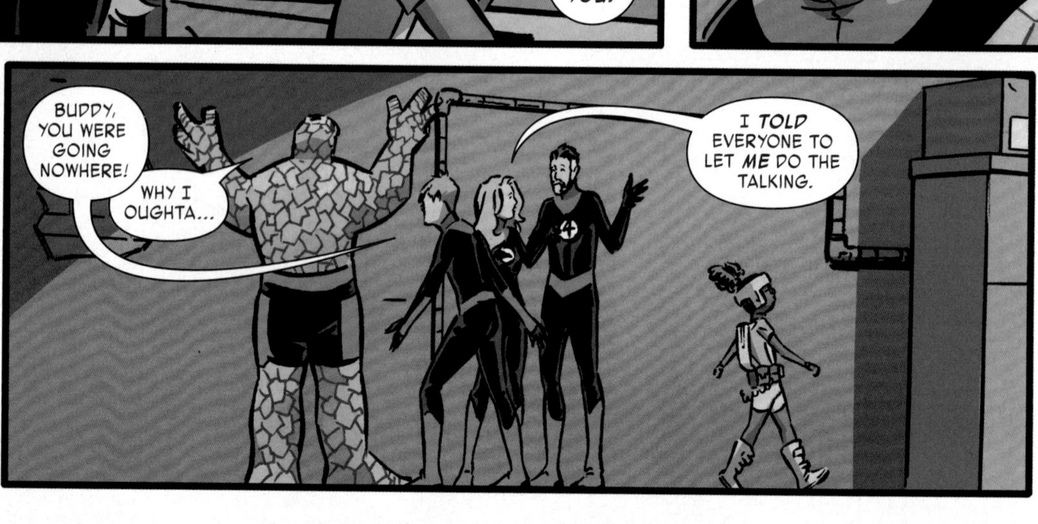
BUDDY, YOU WERE GOING NOWHERE!
WHY I OUGHTA...
I TOLD EVERYONE TO LET ME DO THE TALKING.

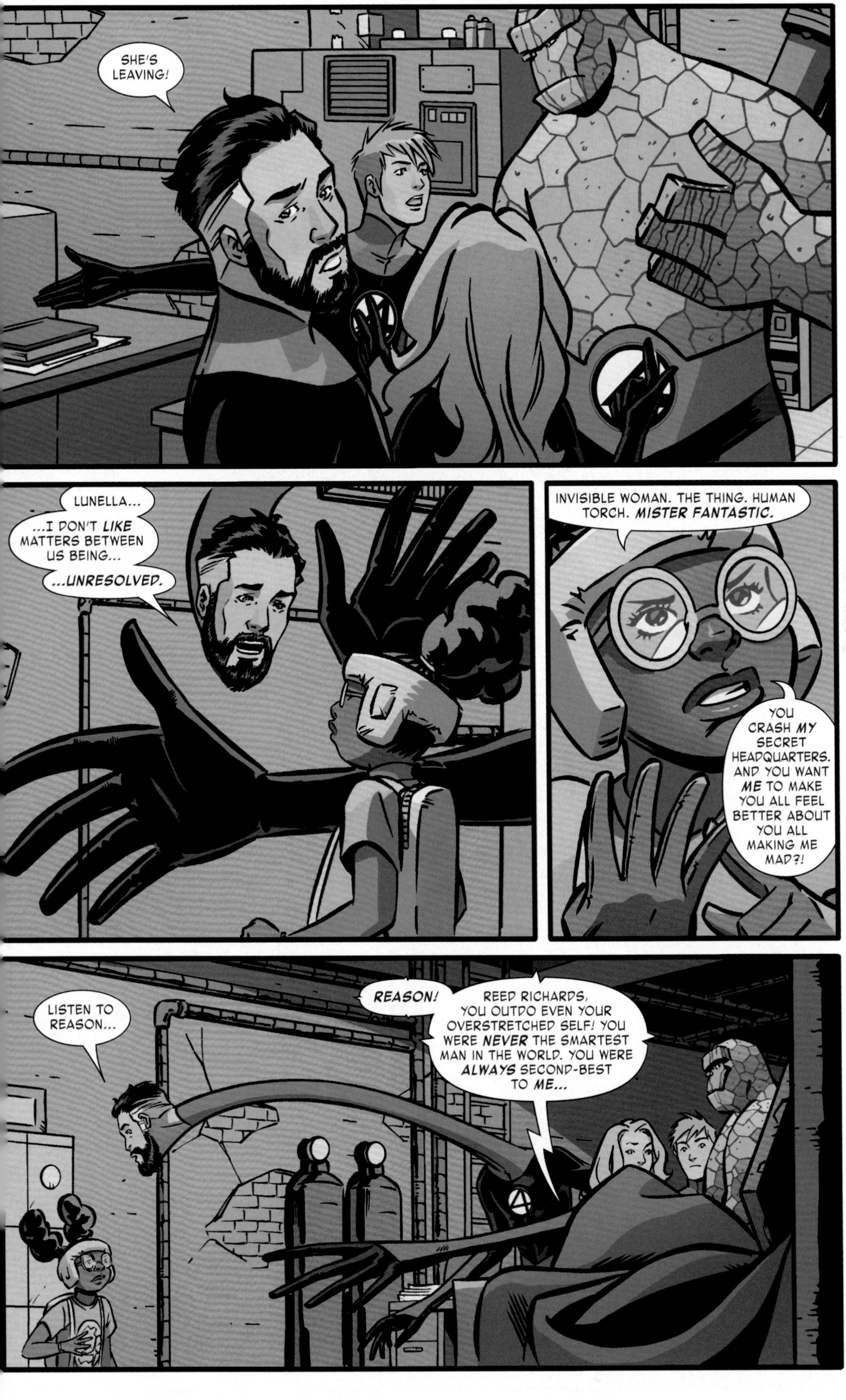
SHE'S LEAVING!
LUNELLA...
...I DON'T LIKE MATTERS BETWEEN US BEING...
...UNRESOLVED.
INVISIBLE WOMAN. THE THING. HUMAN TORCH. MISTER FANTASTIC.
YOU CRASH MY SECRET HEADQUARTERS. AND YOU WANT ME TO MAKE YOU ALL FEEL BETTER ABOUT YOU ALL MAKING ME MAD?!
LISTEN TO REASON...
REASON!
REED RICHARDS, YOU OUTDO EVEN YOUR OVERSTRETCHED SELF! YOU WERE NEVER THE SMARTEST MAN IN THE WORLD. YOU WERE ALWAYS SECOND-BEST TO ME...

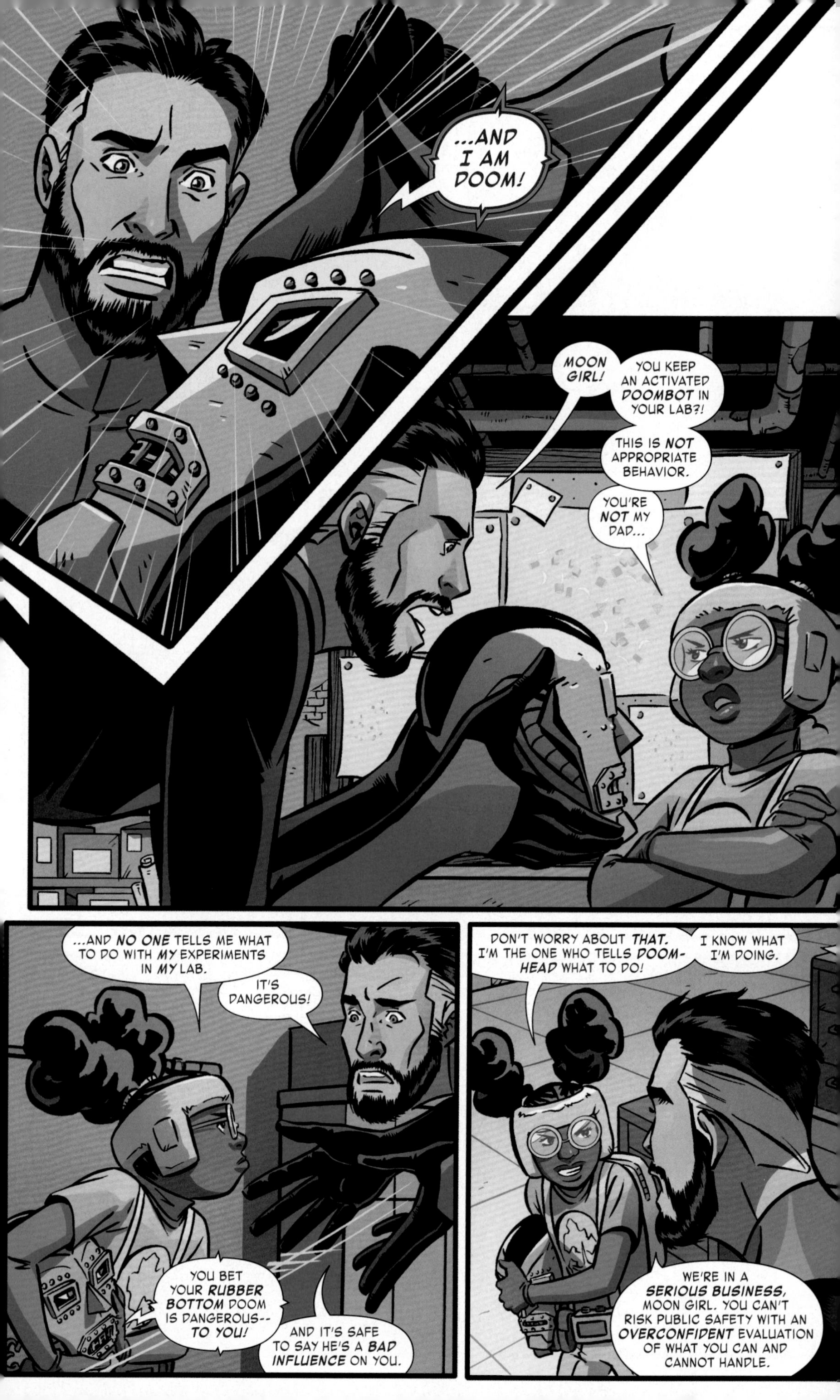
...AND I AM DOOM!
MOON GIRL!
YOU KEEP AN ACTIVATED DOOMBOT IN YOUR LAB?!
THIS IS NOT APPROPRIATE BEHAVIOR.
YOU'RE NOT MY DAD...
...AND NO ONE TELLS ME WHAT TO DO WITH MY EXPERIMENTS IN MY LAB.
IT'S DANGEROUS!
YOU BET YOUR RUBBER BOTTOM DOOM IS DANGEROUS-- TO YOU!
AND IT'S SAFE TO SAY HE'S A BAD INFLUENCE ON YOU.
DON'T WORRY ABOUT THAT. I'M THE ONE WHO TELLS DOOM-HEAD WHAT TO DO!
I KNOW WHAT I'M DOING.
WE'RE IN A SERIOUS BUSINESS, MOON GIRL. YOU CAN'T RISK PUBLIC SAFETY WITH AN OVERCONFIDENT EVALUATION OF WHAT YOU CAN AND CANNOT HANDLE.

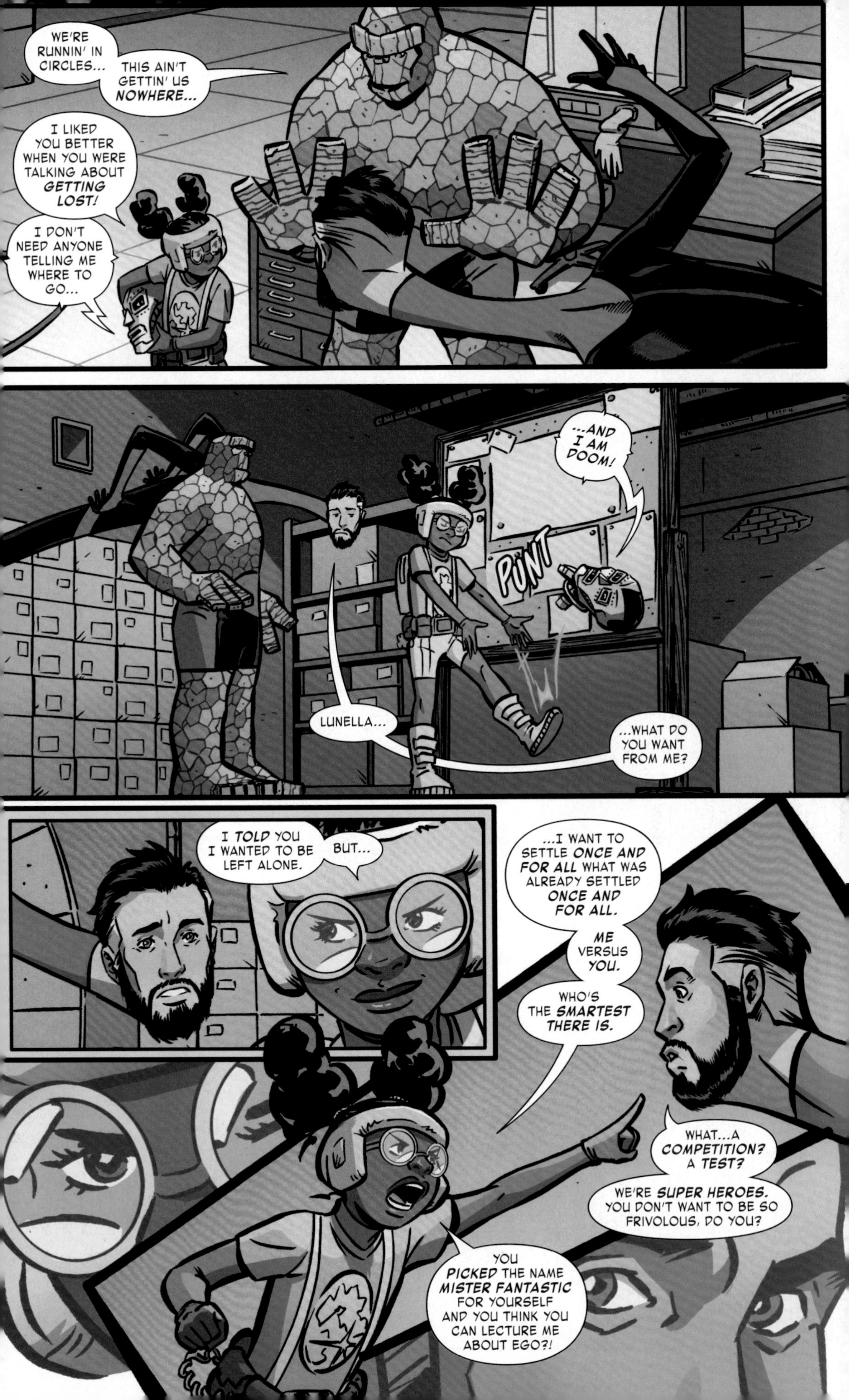

WE'RE RUNNIN' IN CIRCLES...
THIS AIN'T GETTIN' US NOWHERE...
I LIKED YOU BETTER WHEN YOU WERE TALKING ABOUT GETTING LOST!
I DON'T NEED ANYONE TELLING ME WHERE TO GO...
...AND I AM DOOM!
PUNT
LUNELLA...
...WHAT DO YOU WANT FROM ME?
I TOLD YOU I WANTED TO BE LEFT ALONE.
BUT...
...I WANT TO SETTLE ONCE AND FOR ALL WHAT WAS ALREADY SETTLED ONCE AND FOR ALL.
ME VERSUS YOU.
WHO'S THE SMARTEST THERE IS.
WHAT...A COMPETITION? A TEST?
WE'RE SUPER HEROES. YOU DON'T WANT TO BE SO FRIVOLOUS, DO YOU?
YOU PICKED THE NAME MISTER FANTASTIC FOR YOURSELF AND YOU THINK YOU CAN LECTURE ME ABOUT EGO?!

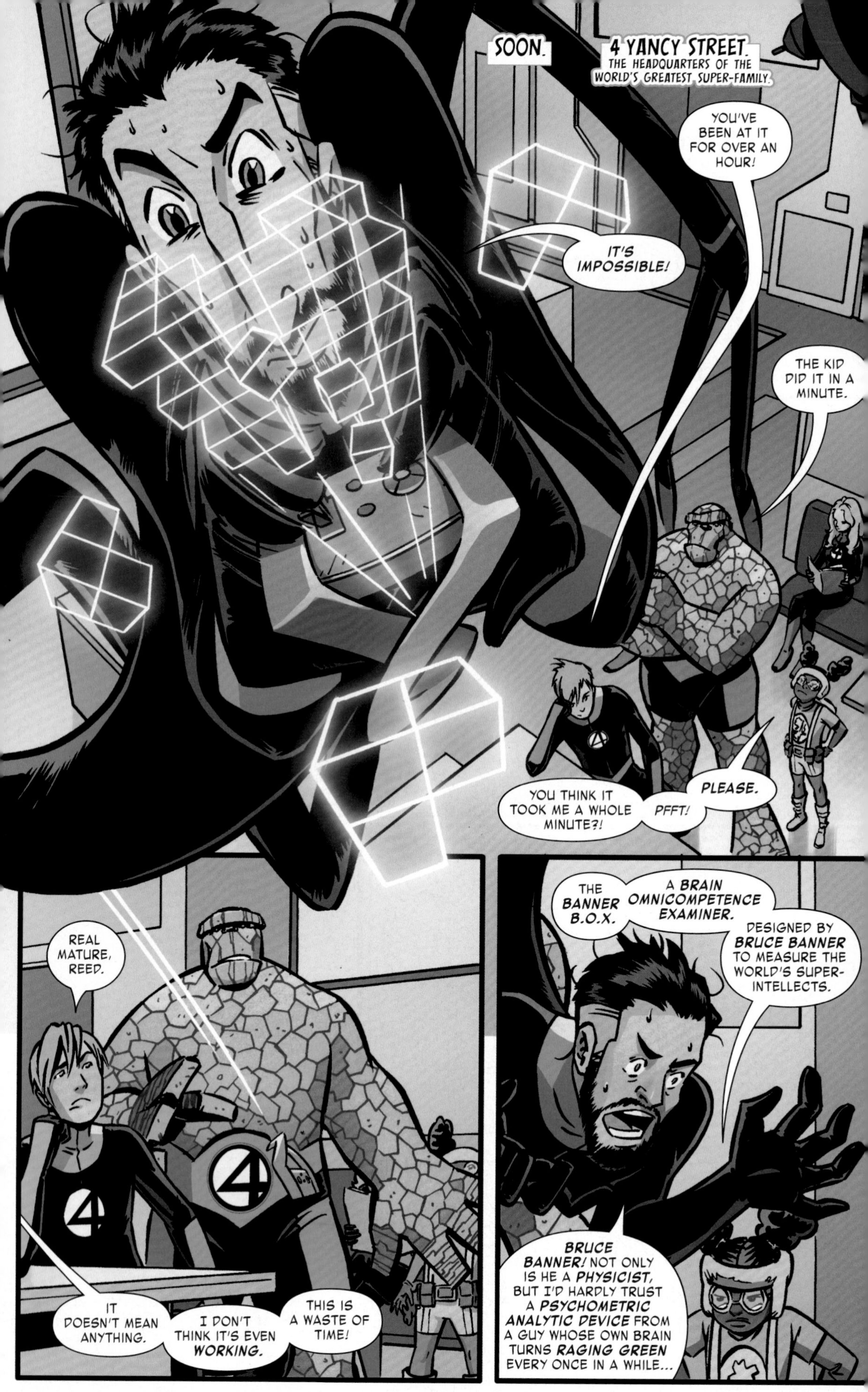
SOON.
4 YANCY STREET.
THE HEADQUARTERS OF THE WORLD'S GREATEST SUPER-FAMILY.
YOU'VE BEEN AT IT FOR OVER AN HOUR!
IT'S IMPOSSIBLE!
THE KID DID IT IN A MINUTE.
YOU THINK IT TOOK ME A WHOLE MINUTE?!
PFFT!
PLEASE.
REAL MATURE, REED.
IT DOESN'T MEAN ANYTHING.
I DON'T THINK IT'S EVEN WORKING.
THIS IS A WASTE OF TIME!
THE BANNER B.O.X.
A BRAIN OMNICOMPETENCE EXAMINER.
DESIGNED BY BRUCE BANNER TO MEASURE THE WORLD'S SUPER-INTELLECTS.
BRUCE BANNER! NOT ONLY IS HE A PHYSICIST, BUT I'D HARDLY TRUST A PSYCHOMETRIC ANALYTIC DEVICE FROM A GUY WHOSE OWN BRAIN TURNS RAGING GREEN EVERY ONCE IN A WHILE...

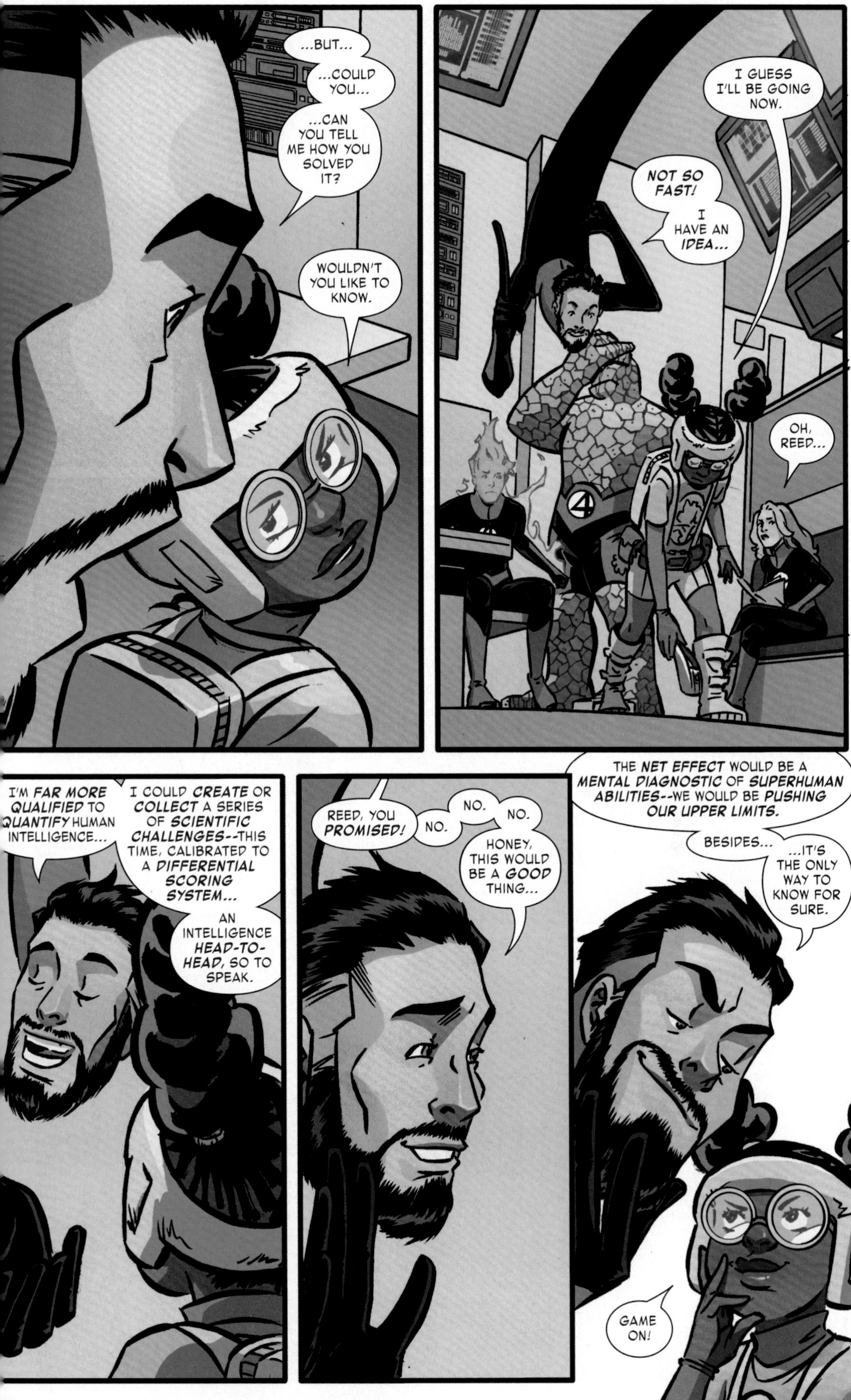
...BUT...
...COULD YOU...
...CAN YOU TELL ME HOW YOU SOLVED IT?
WOULDN'T YOU LIKE TO KNOW.
I GUESS I'LL BE GOING NOW.
NOT SO FAST!
I HAVE AN IDEA...
OH, REED...
I'M FAR MORE QUALIFIED TO QUANTIFY HUMAN INTELLIGENCE...
I COULD CREATE OR COLLECT A SERIES OF SCIENTIFIC CHALLENGES--THIS TIME, CALIBRATED TO A DIFFERENTIAL SCORING SYSTEM...
AN INTELLIGENCE HEAD-TO-HEAD, SO TO SPEAK.
REED, YOU PROMISED!
NO.
NO.
NO.
HONEY, THIS WOULD BE A GOOD THING...
THE NET EFFECT WOULD BE A MENTAL DIAGNOSTIC OF SUPERHUMAN ABILITIES--WE WOULD BE PUSHING OUR UPPER LIMITS.
BESIDES...
...IT'S THE ONLY WAY TO KNOW FOR SURE.
GAME ON!

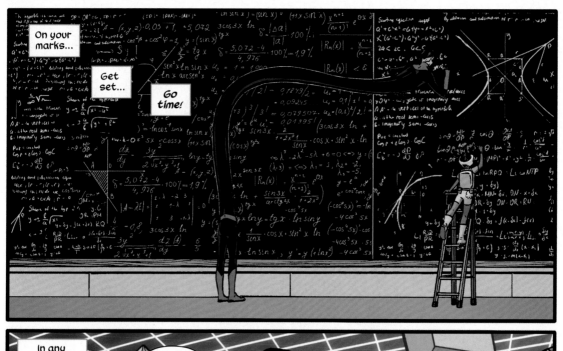

On your marks...

Get set...

Go time!

In any competition there's *the mind game.*

ANYTHING YOU CAN DO I CAN DO BETTER.

QUIET! I'M THINKING!

ANYTHING YOU CAN THINK I CAN THINK *SMARTER.*

If I can *get inside his head,* maybe I can throw Mister Fantastic off.

He's the smartest I've ever seen.

Not counting the *million times* I've eyeballed a mirror!

But am I making the world a better place?

Not as much as him...

That's for sure.

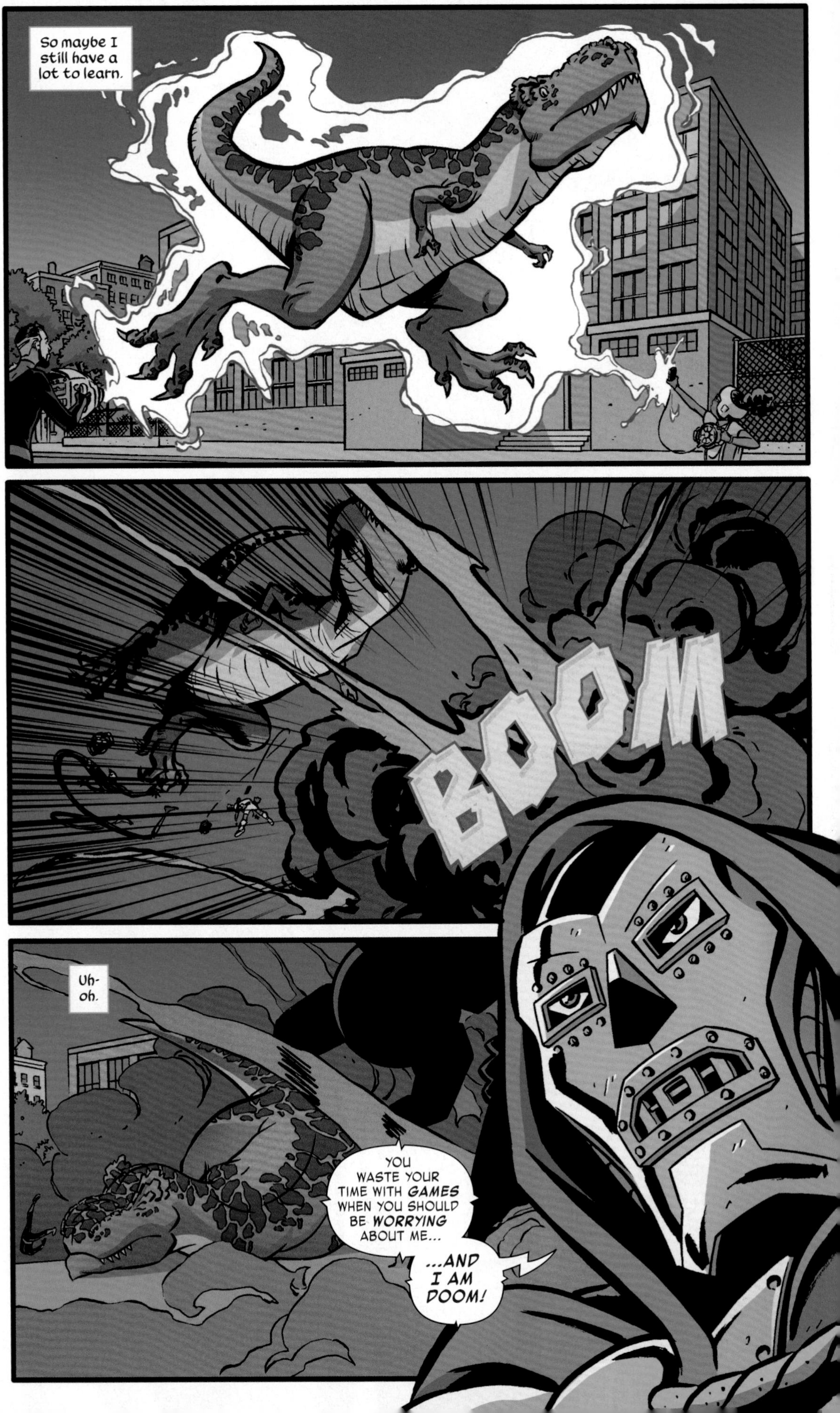
So maybe I still have a lot to learn.
BOOM
Uh-oh.
YOU WASTE YOUR TIME WITH GAMES WHEN YOU SHOULD BE WORRYING ABOUT ME...
...AND I AM DOOM!

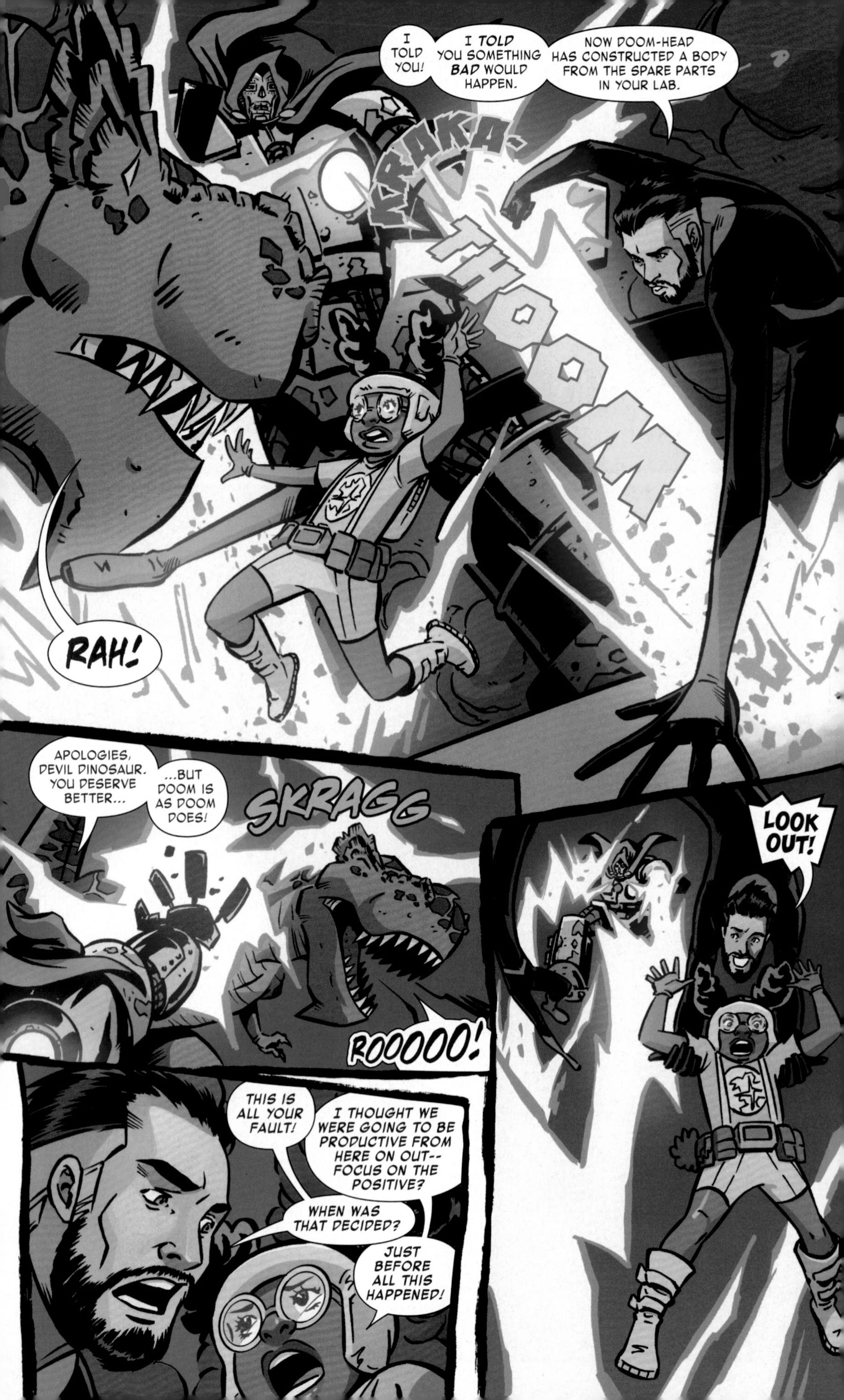
I TOLD YOU!
I TOLD YOU SOMETHING BAD WOULD HAPPEN.
NOW DOOM-HEAD HAS CONSTRUCTED A BODY FROM THE SPARE PARTS IN YOUR LAB.
KRAKA-
THOOOM
RAH!
APOLOGIES, DEVIL DINOSAUR. YOU DESERVE BETTER...
...BUT DOOM IS AS DOOM DOES!
SKRAGG
ROOOOO!
LOOK OUT!
THIS IS ALL YOUR FAULT!
I THOUGHT WE WERE GOING TO BE PRODUCTIVE FROM HERE ON OUT-- FOCUS ON THE POSITIVE?
WHEN WAS THAT DECIDED?
JUST BEFORE ALL THIS HAPPENED!

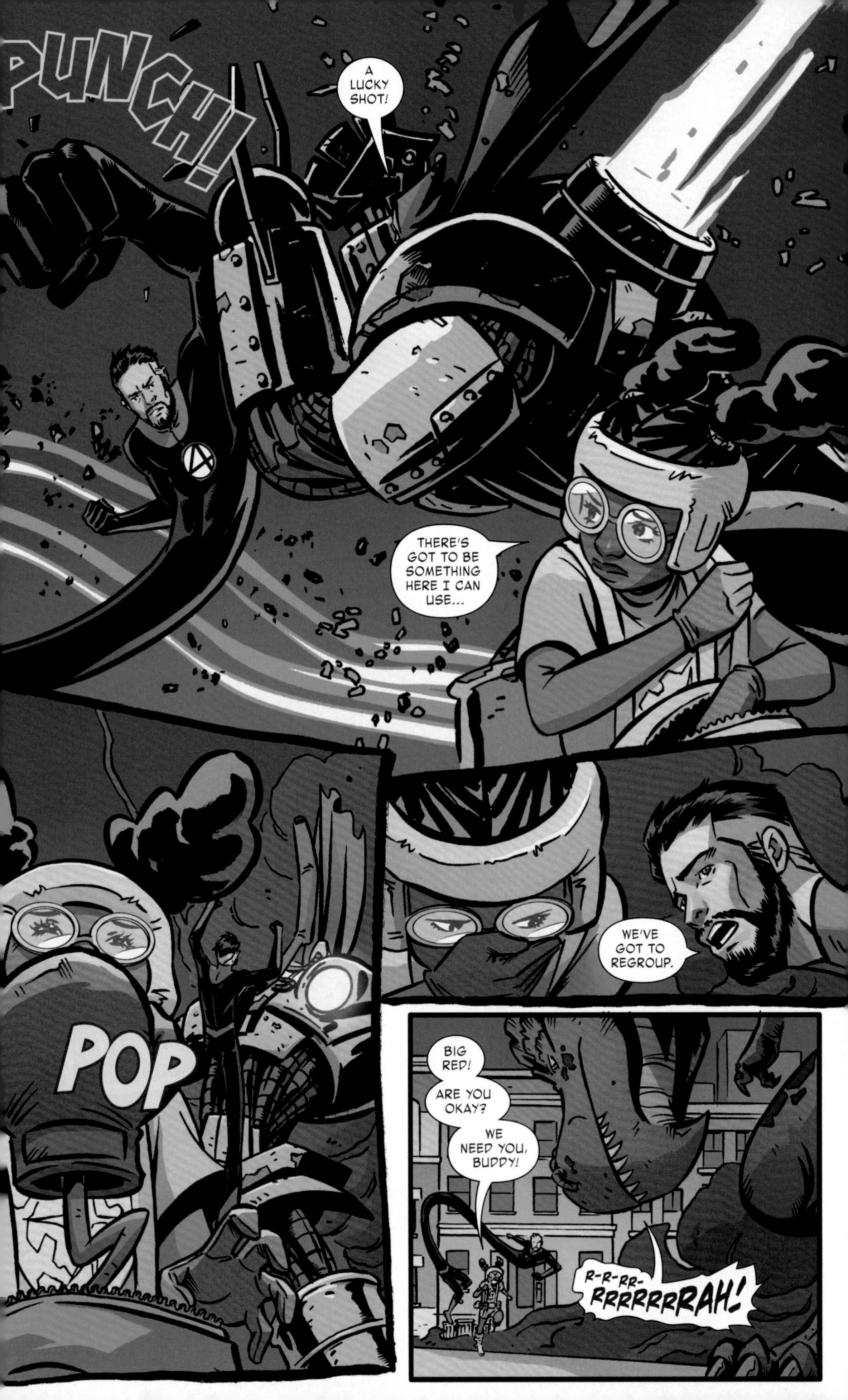

PUNCH!
A LUCKY SHOT!
THERE'S GOT TO BE SOMETHING HERE I CAN USE...
POP
WE'VE GOT TO REGROUP.
BIG RED!
ARE YOU OKAY?
WE NEED YOU, BUDDY!
R-R-RR-RRRRRRRAH!

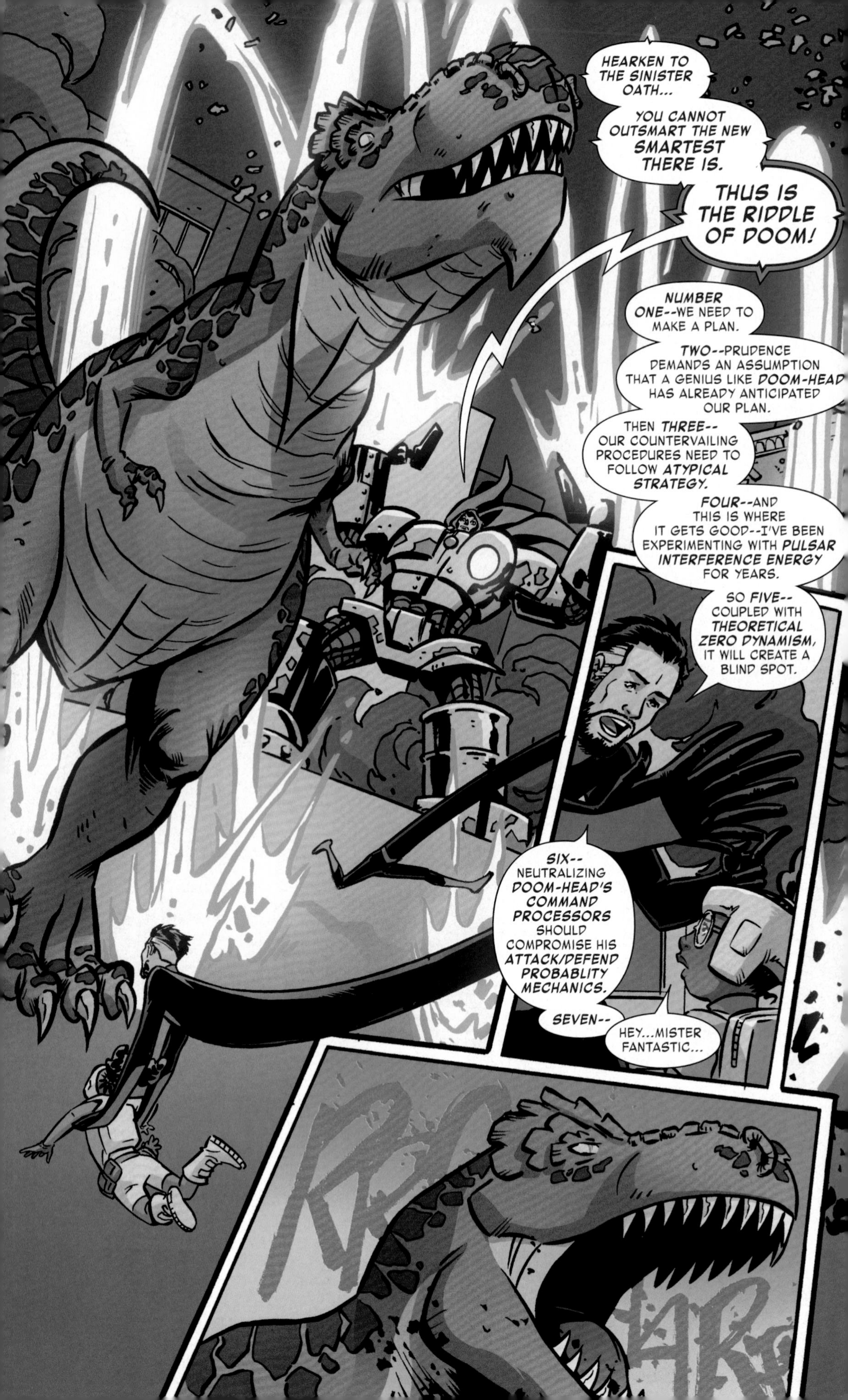

HEARKEN TO THE SINISTER OATH...
YOU CANNOT OUTSMART THE NEW SMARTEST THERE IS.
THUS IS THE RIDDLE OF DOOM!
NUMBER ONE--WE NEED TO MAKE A PLAN.
TWO--PRUDENCE DEMANDS AN ASSUMPTION THAT A GENIUS LIKE DOOM-HEAD HAS ALREADY ANTICIPATED OUR PLAN.
THEN THREE--OUR COUNTERVAILING PROCEDURES NEED TO FOLLOW ATYPICAL STRATEGY.
FOUR--AND THIS IS WHERE IT GETS GOOD--I'VE BEEN EXPERIMENTING WITH PULSAR INTERFERENCE ENERGY FOR YEARS.
SO FIVE--COUPLED WITH THEORETICAL ZERO DYNAMISM, IT WILL CREATE A BLIND SPOT.
SIX--NEUTRALIZING DOOM-HEAD'S COMMAND PROCESSORS SHOULD COMPROMISE HIS ATTACK/DEFEND PROBABLITY MECHANICS.
SEVEN--
HEY...MISTER FANTASTIC...

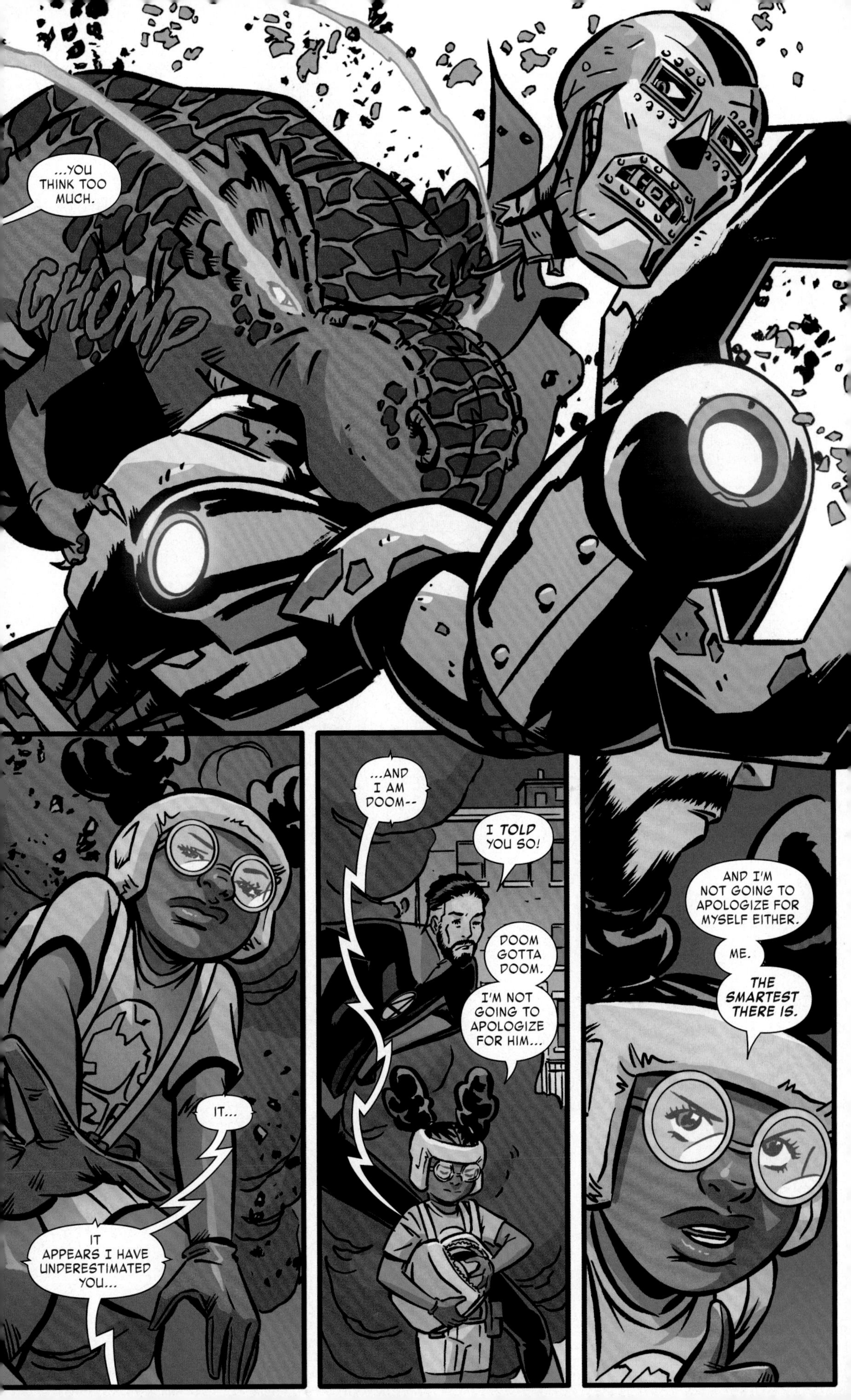
...YOU THINK TOO MUCH.
CHOMP
IT...
IT APPEARS I HAVE UNDERESTIMATED YOU...
...AND I AM DOOM--
I *TOLD* YOU SO!
DOOM GOTTA DOOM.
I'M NOT GOING TO APOLOGIZE FOR HIM...
AND I'M NOT GOING TO APOLOGIZE FOR MYSELF EITHER.
ME.
THE SMARTEST THERE IS.

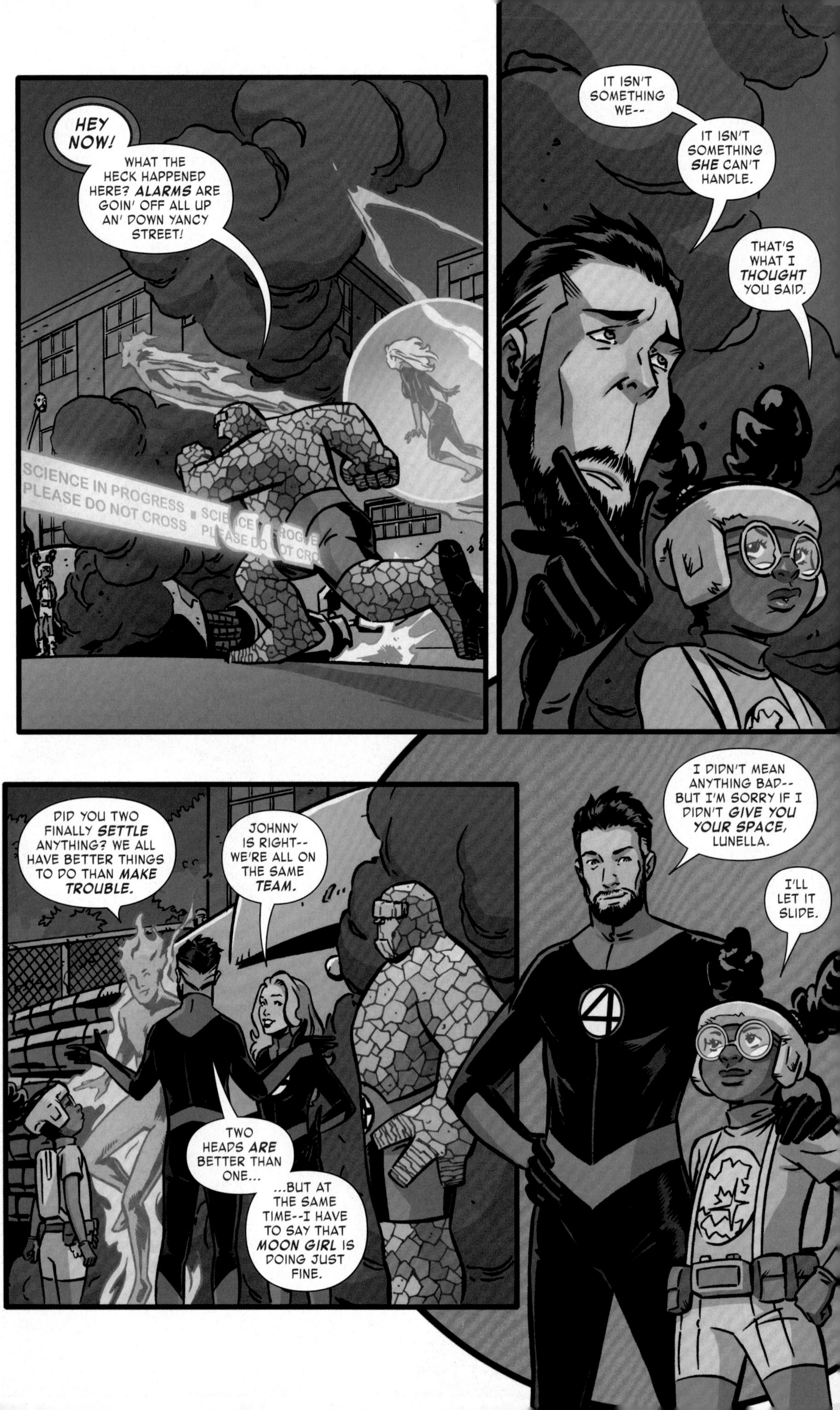
HEY NOW!
WHAT THE HECK HAPPENED HERE? ALARMS ARE GOIN' OFF ALL UP AN' DOWN YANCY STREET!
SCIENCE IN PROGRESS PLEASE DO NOT CROSS
IT ISN'T SOMETHING WE--
IT ISN'T SOMETHING SHE CAN'T HANDLE.
THAT'S WHAT I THOUGHT YOU SAID.
DID YOU TWO FINALLY SETTLE ANYTHING? WE ALL HAVE BETTER THINGS TO DO THAN MAKE TROUBLE.
JOHNNY IS RIGHT-- WE'RE ALL ON THE SAME TEAM.
TWO HEADS ARE BETTER THAN ONE...
...BUT AT THE SAME TIME--I HAVE TO SAY THAT MOON GIRL IS DOING JUST FINE.
I DIDN'T MEAN ANYTHING BAD-- BUT I'M SORRY IF I DIDN'T GIVE YOU YOUR SPACE, LUNELLA.
I'LL LET IT SLIDE.

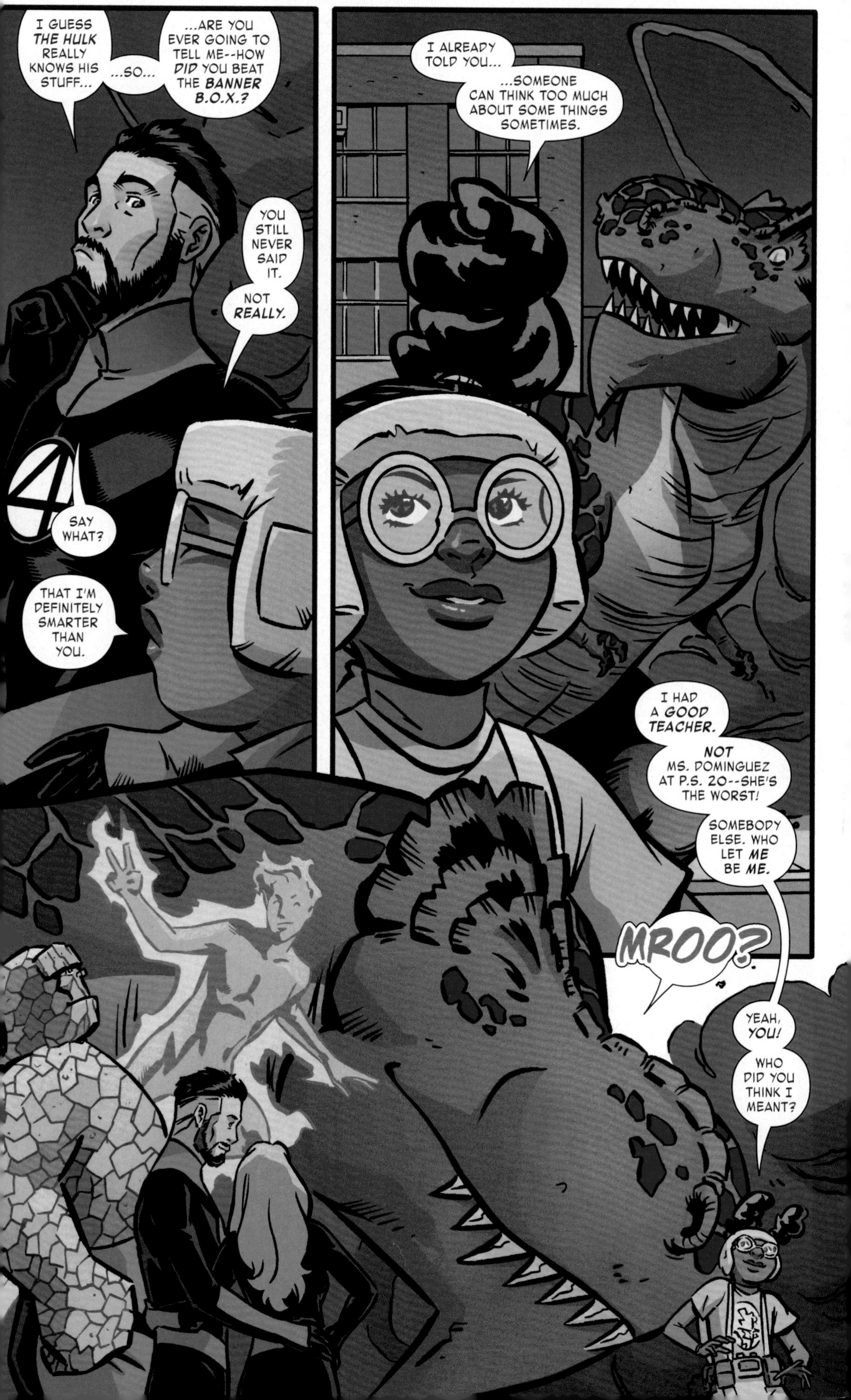
I GUESS THE HULK REALLY KNOWS HIS STUFF...
...SO...
...ARE YOU EVER GOING TO TELL ME--HOW DID YOU BEAT THE BANNER B.O.X.?
YOU STILL NEVER SAID IT.
NOT REALLY.
SAY WHAT?
THAT I'M DEFINITELY SMARTER THAN YOU.
I ALREADY TOLD YOU...
...SOMEONE CAN THINK TOO MUCH ABOUT SOME THINGS SOMETIMES.
I HAD A GOOD TEACHER.
NOT MS. DOMINGUEZ AT P.S. 20--SHE'S THE WORST!
SOMEBODY ELSE. WHO LET ME BE ME.
MROO?
YEAH, YOU!
WHO DID YOU THINK I MEANT?

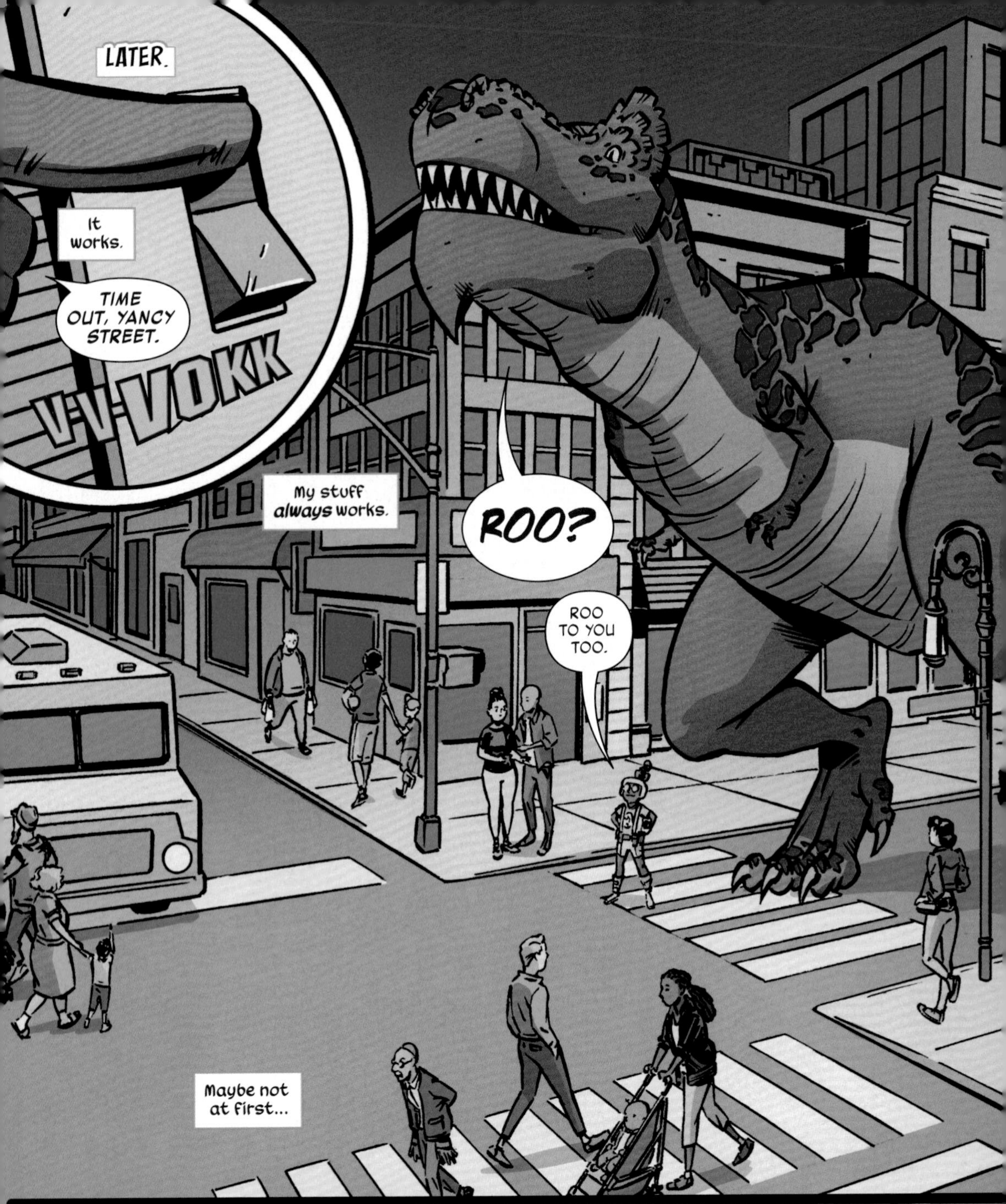
LATER.
It works.
TIME OUT, YANCY STREET.
V-V-VOKK
My stuff *always* works.
ROO?
ROO TO YOU TOO.
Maybe not at first...

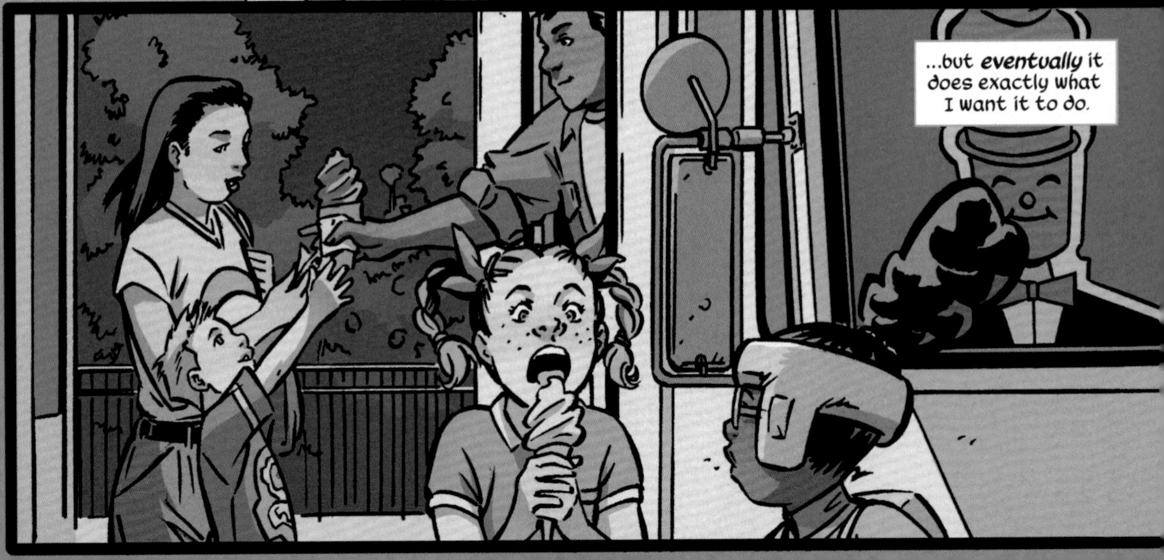
...but *eventually* it does exactly what I want it to do.

THERE! NOW I'VE GOT THE WHOLE PLACE TO MYSELF!

MROO?

OH... ...RIGHT... I MEANT OURSELVES.

I'm thinking this is great.

I used to think of everything.

WITH NOBODY TO TELL US WHAT WE CAN OR CAN'T DO!

RAH!

Believe me.

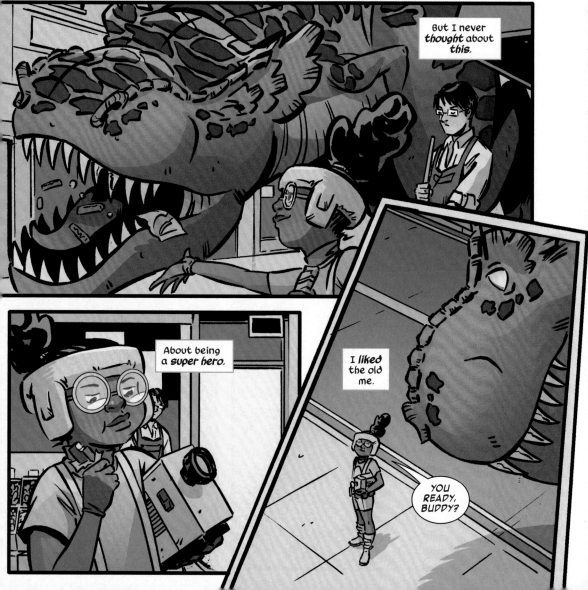

But I never thought about this.

About being a super hero.

I liked the old me.

YOU READY, BUDDY?

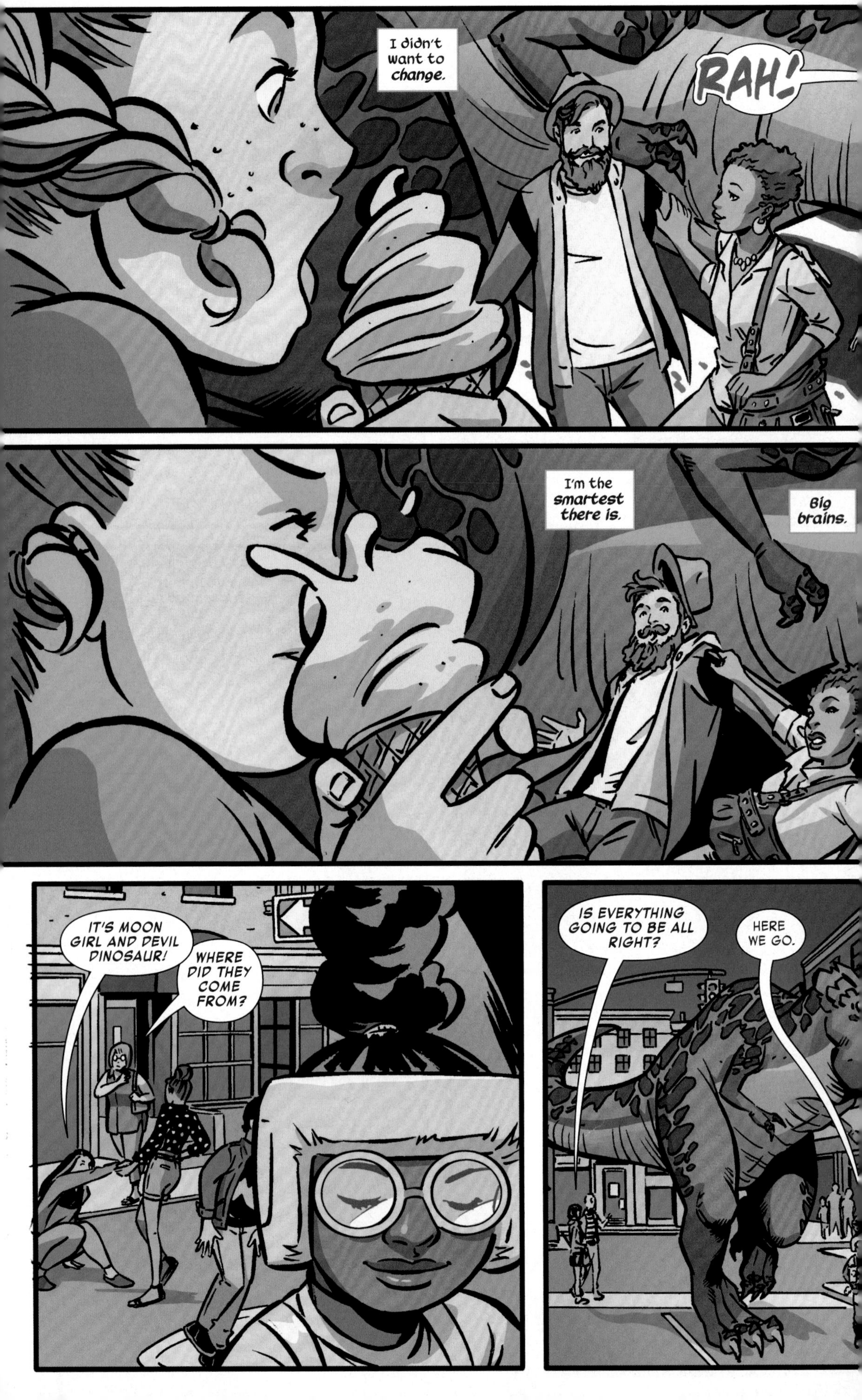
I didn't want to change.
RAH!
I'm the smartest there is.
Big brains.
IT'S MOON GIRL AND DEVIL DINOSAUR!
WHERE DID THEY COME FROM?
IS EVERYTHING GOING TO BE ALL RIGHT?
HERE WE GO.

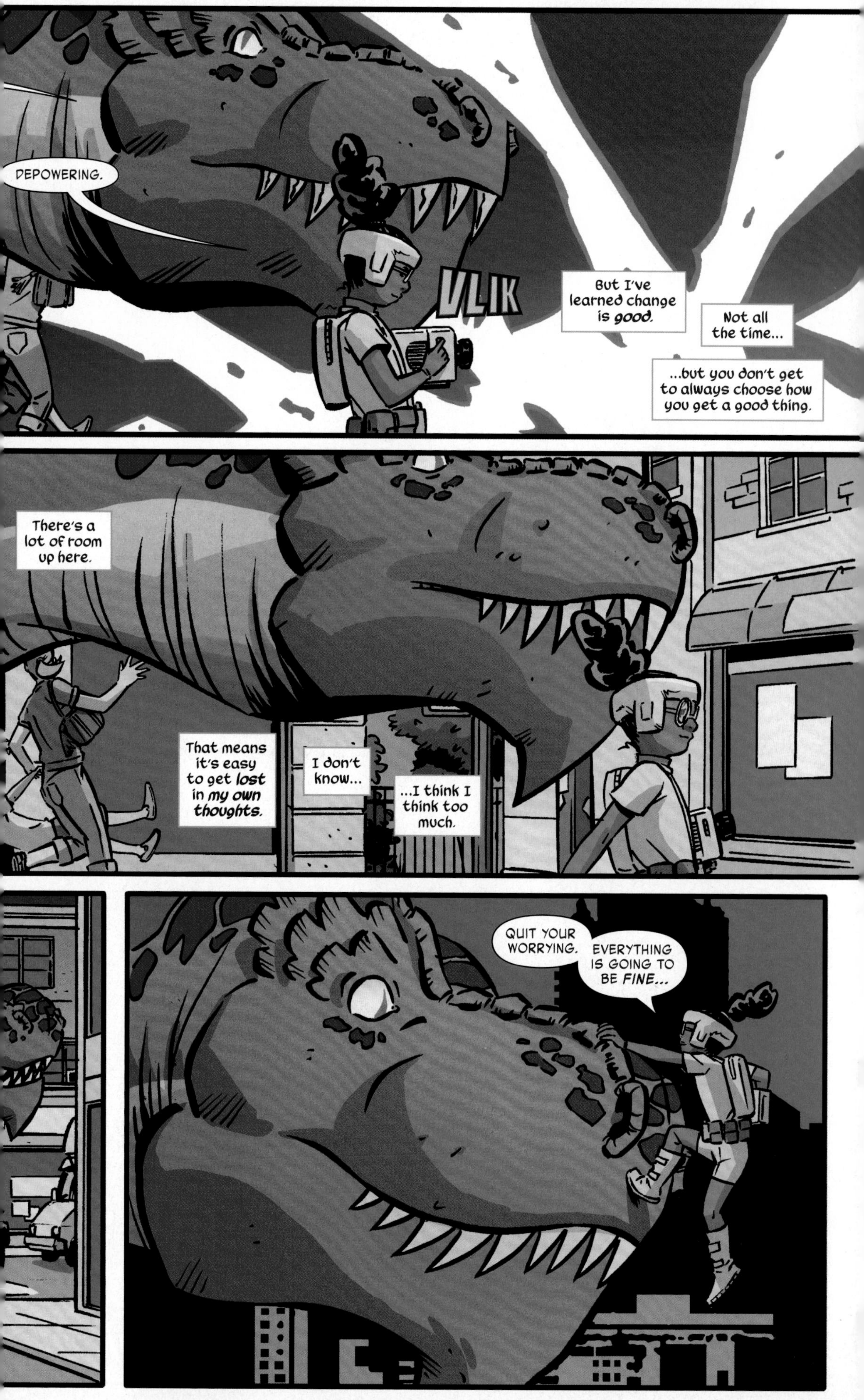

DEPOWERING.
VLIK
But I've learned change is *good*.
Not all the time...
...but you don't get to always choose how you get a good thing.
There's a lot of room up here.
That means it's easy to get *lost* in *my own thoughts*.
I don't know...
...I think I think too much.
QUIT YOUR WORRYING.
EVERYTHING IS GOING TO BE *FINE*...

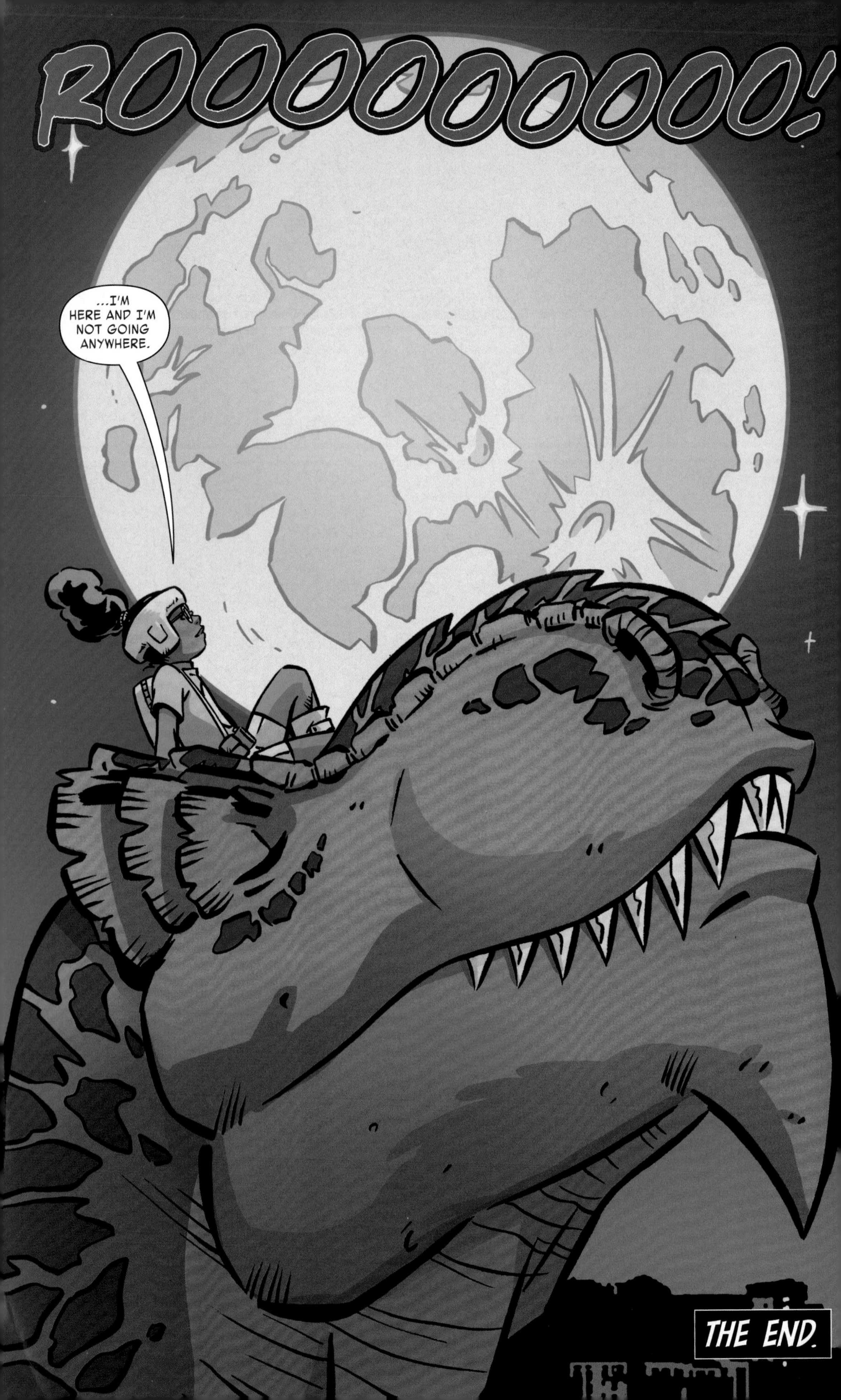
ROOOOOOOOO!
...I'M HERE AND I'M NOT GOING ANYWHERE.
THE END.

MAIL BAG AND DEVIL DINOSAUR

nd there you have it! The big finale to the first-ever MOON GIRL AND DEVIL DINOSAUR ongoing eries. You can tell future generations that you were there for all of it. That's a special thing. But for the rst time in my professional career, I'm finding myself short on words! Luckily, I can rely on some folks ho are way talented and super thoughtful to articulate the drama of the moment--just like every issue!

--Chris Robinson

've had such an amazing time working on MOON GIRL AND DEVIL DINOSAUR with Brandon, Amy, latacha, Alitha, Travis, Chris, Jordan and everyone else who's contributed over the course of the book. appreciate all the fans' support and love for the book, and it's been cool to see a book connect with o many young readers. I'm sad to see it come to an end, but it had a good run! Forty-seven issues is ne longest continuous run I've done on any book, and I'm not likely to break that record anytime soon."

--Tamra Bonvillain

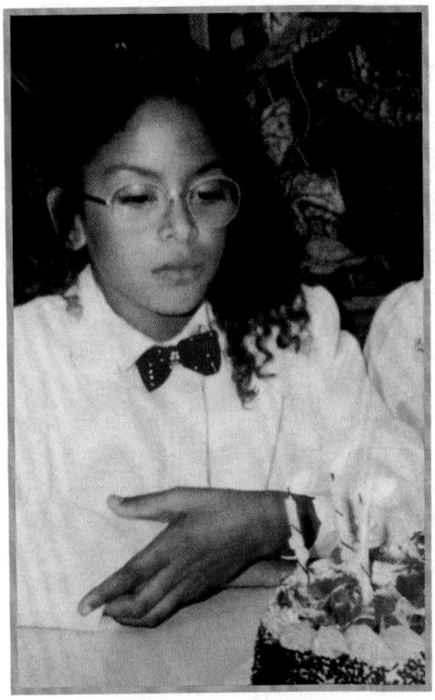

'You are Moon Girl!' That's what people have said to me all these years, o which I reply: 'She's nothing like me--I'm not that smart!' I'd have loved o read MOON GIRL AND DEVIL DINOSAUR when I was 9--it would ave been so awesome! But physically? Yeah, we're a lot alike. By contrast, I've had the good fortune to draw her over all nese years for Marvel, the House of Ideas. My younger self vould be jumping with joy if she had known that one day omeone like me would be the star of a comic like this one. t's cool to think that so many of you, the fans, have grown up with ner and that her adventures will be part of you forever, particularly for he youngest among you. It's always super exciting to receive your etters, see the cosplayers and feel all that love that you've sent our vay. Over all these years, MOON GIRL AND DEVIL DINOSAUR nas been such an important part of my life and of the team around me, people I've absolutely loved working with. So I'd like to hank Amy, Brandon, Tamra and Travis, all the editors involved, Emily, Chris, Mark and all of you lot, the fans, for the wonderful years we've had together. Moon Girl forever!"

--Natacha Bustos

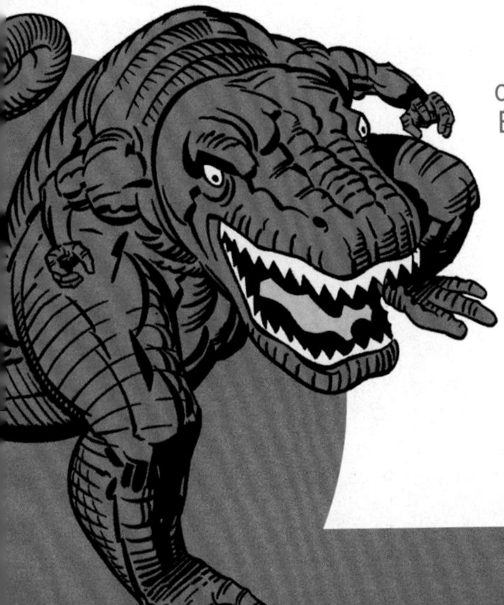

"I hope it was as much fun for you as it was for us. A thousand pages of MOON GIRL AND DEVIL DINOSAUR adventures! There will always be Spider-Man and Avengers and X-Men comics. Moon Knight and Hawkeye will make their comebacks. Even Devil Dinosaur gets trotted out every so often with a new series. But a brand-new character headlining 47 issues only happens for one reason: the fans. Thanks for reading and responding and sharing your love for Lunella Lafayette. She wouldn't have come this far without you. Be on the lookout for more Moon Girl being the Smartest There Is throughout the Marvel Universe of comics. You can also find her cosplaying at conventions, already in a handful of video games, at school book fairs and soon starring in her new cartoon."

--Brandon Montclare

MOON GIRL AND DEVIL DINOSAUR

#42 COVER SKETCH BY NATACHA BUSTOS

MOON GIRL AND DEVIL DINOSAUR
MOON GIRL AND DEVIL DINOSAUR

MOON GIRL AND DEVIL DINOSAUR
MOON GIRL AND DEVIL DINOSAUR
MOON GIRL AND DEVIL DINOSAUR
HALL MONITO

A
B

MOON GIRL AND DEVIL DINOSAUR

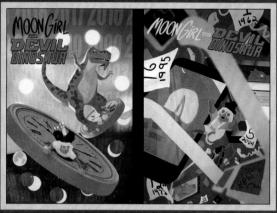

#44-47 COVER SKETCHES BY RAHZZAH